# STEALING HOME

# STEALING HOME

*Los Angeles, the Dodgers,
and the Lives Caught in Between*

# ERIC NUSBAUM

**PUBLIC**AFFAIRS

*New York*

PublicAffairs
Hachette Book Group
1290 Avenue of the Americas, New York, NY 10104
www.publicaffairsbooks.com
@Public_Affairs

First Edition: March 2020

Published by PublicAffairs, an imprint of Perseus Books, LLC, a subsidiary of Hachette Book Group, Inc. The PublicAffairs name and logo is a trademark of the Hachette Book Group.

The Hachette Speakers Bureau provides a wide range of authors for speaking events. To find out more, go to www.hachettespeakersbureau.com or call (866) 376-6591.

The publisher is not responsible for websites (or their content) that are not owned by the publisher.

Print book interior design by Jeff Williams.

Library of Congress Cataloging-in-Publication Data
Names: Nusbaum, Eric, author.
Title: Stealing home : Los Angeles, the Dodgers, and the lives caught in
  between / Eric Nusbaum.
Description: First edition. | New York : PublicAffairs, 2020. | Includes
  bibliographical references and index.
Identifiers: LCCN 2019041742 (print) | LCCN 2019041743 (ebook) | ISBN
  9781541742215 (hardcover) | ISBN 9781541742192 (epub)
Subjects: LCSH: Los Angeles Dodgers (Baseball team)—History—20th century.
  Dodger Stadium (Los Angeles)—History—20th century. | Chávez Ravine
  (Los Angeles, Calif.)—History—20th century. | Mexican-Americans—Housing—
California—Los Angeles—History—20th century.
Classification: LCC GV875.L6 N87 2020  (print) | LCC GV875.L6  (ebook) |
  DDC 796.357/640979494—dc23
LC record available at https://lccn.loc.gov/2019041742
LC ebook record available at https://lccn.loc.gov/2019041743

ISBNs: 978-1-5417-4221-5 (hardcover), 978-1-5417-4219-2 (ebook)

*For Janelle, Clay, and Marco—*
*my home, wherever we are.*

*Illustrations by Adam Villacin*

# CONTENTS

This town is full of echoes. It seems like they are caught in the cracks of the walls, or under the stones. When you are walking, it seems like they follow your steps. You hear crackling, and laughter. Some laughs are quite old, as though they are tired of laughing. And voices that are worn out from being used so long. You hear all this. Someday the time will come when these sounds fade away.

JUAN RULFO, from *Pedro Paramo*

# TWO NOTES

## I.

There used to be a place in Los Angeles called the Stone Quarry Hills. The hills are still there, but the place is gone. The Stone Quarry Hills were located just north of what is now downtown LA. They were split by five ravines:

Sulphur Ravine
Cemetery Ravine
Reservoir Ravine
Solano Canyon
Chavez Ravine

Chavez Ravine was named for one of the most powerful men in the city. Julian Chavez had come to Los Angeles from New Mexico in the 1830s, when the city was still a small and distant outpost. In the ensuing decades he became an elected official and a landowner with vast holdings. But Julian Chavez did not own the Chavez Ravine. Rather, he owned property nearby along the banks of the Los Angeles River. The Chavez Ravine got its name because of a trail that happened to run through and over it and that ultimately ended at the Chavez property.

Long before Julian Chavez arrived, before Los Angeles was even an idea, the hills were a resource and refuge for the Tongva people. By the end of the twentieth century, the Tongva had been enslaved for generations, and Julian Chavez was dead. But his name would live on in the form of a road that wound through the ravine that he never actually owned. In the years to come, Chavez Ravine Road would become the site of a respiratory hospital, a brickyard, and a naval armory. Then, somewhere a little further along the line, the name Chavez Ravine outgrew the road and outgrew the actual ravine.

Chavez Ravine consumed Sulphur Ravine and Cemetery Ravine and Reservoir Ravine. Solano Canyon would be spared, but the Stone Quarry Hills were erased.

The action of this book is largely centered around the three communities that once sat nestled in these hills. Their names were Palo Verde, La Loma, and Bishop. They were erased. First, they were physically erased by powerful forces beyond the control of their residents. Then they lost their names: they became part of Chavez Ravine.

The contemporary Chavez Ravine has no geographic border and does not appear on any maps of Los Angeles. It is a place, but it isn't. It is really a code word for the mysteries and pleasures of baseball. It is the metaphysical plane upon which Dodger Stadium exists, slightly outside the realm of daily life in the city. It is a state of mind. It is a vibe.

One thing Chavez Ravine isn't, and never was, is a singular community. The communities whose prior destruction made the construction of Dodger Stadium possible had their own personalities, their own magic, and their own names. In the course of reporting, researching, and finally writing this book, I have come to believe that those names matter, both for reasons of historical accuracy and reasons of emotional truth: Palo Verde, La Loma, and Bishop.

## II.

This book has been written from a combination of first-person interviews, primary sources, and secondary sources. It is nonfiction—as accurate and as true of a book as I could write. But many of its central characters lived in a time and place that saw them under-documented, under-recorded, and undervalued by society. I have tried to be clear about any resulting mysteries and incongruities in the historical record. This is not an academic book; it's a story, whose impact I believe would have been lessened with the inclusion of copious in-text citations and notes. At the back of the book, you'll find an explanation and a list of sources. Before you read, I would also like to offer a preemptive thanks to the people who sat with me for interviews, to the librarians who guided me, and to the journalists, historians, storytellers, and artists whose research and work made mine possible.

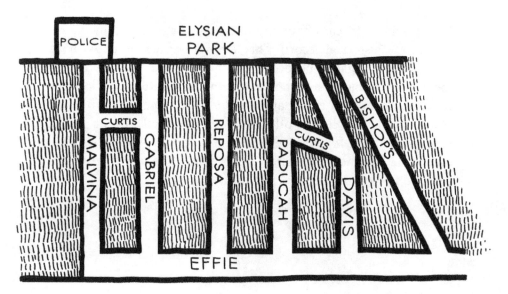

*Palo Verde*

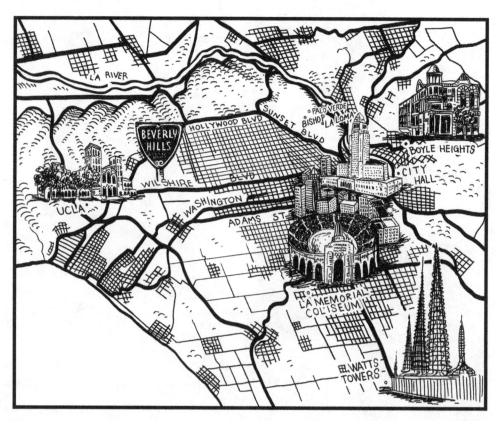

*Los Angeles*

# PREFACE

On May 8, 1959, Abrana Aréchiga stood in the entryway of her home as Los Angeles County Sheriff's deputies broke down her door. This was the end. She watched as strange, silent men loaded her furniture onto waiting trucks. She wailed as deputies carried her adult daughter by the wrists and ankles down the front stairs. Outside, she bent and picked up a rock, feeling the weight of it in her hand. Finally, she sat, helpless, as a bulldozer plowed into her living room.

She wore a simple dress and a black sweater. Her hair was flecked with gray. Members of the local press crowded around her, capturing everything, squeezing the moment for all it was worth so that the images of her anguish could run on front pages and lead the evening news and live on for decades in libraries and archives. The reporters nearly swallowed her up in the madness. They climbed up onto parked cars and lampposts to get the best possible angles.

Afterward, as night fell, Abrana was surrounded by the people she loved. Her husband, Manuel, her children and grandchildren. There were cousins and family friends from the Palo Verde neighborhood. They came up over the hill by the carload, the same way the sheriff's deputies had come earlier that afternoon, single file. These people who were her neighbors once. These people with whom she had built a life.

They sat around a campfire and mourned for what was gone and sang sad songs and remembered the good old days. If you look at the photos, they could have been anywhere. But this was the middle of Los Angeles. There were scrubby plants and a few trees. There was dirt. Behind them were a makeshift tent, a clothesline strung between two trees, and the empty lots where houses used to be. In the distance was the humming of the freeway. They ate and drank and tried to ignore the photographers creeping around and the blinding, wheezing flashbulbs.

It was a beautiful, clear Southern California night. The high in downtown that day was 76 degrees, and the low was 58. The heavy summer winds were still gathering themselves over the ocean. Across the city, the jacarandas were beginning to bloom: purple flowers sprouting on unassuming branches.

Abrana Aréchiga was in her sixties, but she seemed older. She was thin and wiry, and her face had a severe aspect. She was not known to be a sentimental person, but she must have been tired. Or if she wasn't tired, she was seething. Or if she wasn't seething, she was mourning. She had lived a life underlined by tragedy: she had lost a husband and a child before she turned forty. She had lived hand to mouth for many years and built a home for herself far away from the place she was born. Right before she died, she would tell a reporter that this eviction was the lowest point in her life, the greatest injustice that she ever faced.

I can picture her looking out into the darkness beyond the campfire at the empty space where her home had been, picture her looking for the shape of it: the familiar silhouette of the big wood-frame house against the dark sky. The house had grown over the years, room by room, as her family grew. It had taken on a life of its own in the hills overlooking the city. There had been goats and chickens out back and venetian blinds on the windows. Abrana had insisted on venetian blinds. Or maybe she wasn't thinking any of that. Maybe she kept herself busy playing host, feeding her grandchildren, fending off reporters and visiting politicians. Maybe she was already worrying about what might come next.

Abrana and Manuel Aréchiga came to this place, Palo Verde, in 1922. They bought an empty parcel of land on Malvina Avenue and pitched a tent. They built their home one two-by-four, one shingle, one nail at a time. With other families, mostly like theirs, mostly immigrants from Mexico, they built a community out of nothing right in the middle of Los Angeles. And now it was gone.

===

THE REMAINS OF Abrana Aréchiga's home at 1771 Malvina Avenue are buried somewhere underneath the distant parking lots of what is now Dodger Stadium. It wasn't supposed to be this way. But it is.

Today we call this area Chavez Ravine. If, like me, you grew up in Los Angeles, you can probably hear longtime Dodger announcer Vin Scully saying the words in a sort of sweet, folksy way, almost singing them:

*Chavez Ravine.*
*Chavez Ravine.*
*Chavez Ravine.*

When Vin Scully says something, it is like God speaking. His voice is ambient in the Southern California air. It is the voice inside your head.

In my experience, Chavez Ravine is beautiful and idyllic. It isn't even a place. It's more than that. It's a state of mind, a heightened sense of being that you achieve when you visit. There are palm trees. There are magnificent sunsets and vistas that open up on the downtown skyline and the San Gabriel Mountains. The shadows crawl across the field at Dodger Stadium like cars edging forward in freeway traffic. The parking lots sprawl out for acres beyond the terraced decks and the low-slung outfield pavilions.

When I think about growing up in Los Angeles, I don't think about going to the beach, the mall, or the movies. I think about making that rush-hour drive to a Dodger game. I think about getting there late and catching the first inning on the radio: Vin Scully in simulcast. I think about buying a scalper ticket or a six-dollar bleacher seat. I think about how I never felt more at home in my city than I did there, among tens of thousands of perfect strangers. I think about how silly it is that for millions of us, civic identity is tied up in something as tenuous as a baseball team; then I think that it's not silly at all, that baseball does have magical powers, or at least it can, and that our caring is what gives it those powers. I think about the long walk back to the car and the slow crawl out of the parking lot and the stadium lights receding into the darkness.

=

A DECADE BEFORE Abrana watched her house reduced to a pile of bones, President Harry Truman signed the Federal Housing Act of 1949. The bill would make way for the construction of huge new public-housing projects in cities across the country. This was before the term *housing project* became a loaded one. To the people who believed in it, public housing really was a project for the betterment of humanity: a key to unlocking the great potential of hardworking Americans and a way to maximize the brilliant notions of architects and planners who calculated that they could design communities in optimal ways and thereby enhance human happiness. It was utopian, and in the wake of World War II, utopia seemed worth striving for. "This legislation permits us to take a long step toward increasing the well-being and happiness of millions of our fellow citizens," Truman wrote upon signing the bill into law. "Let us not delay in fulfilling that high purpose."

He could not have known it at the time, but in fulfilling that purpose, Truman would also be unleashing one of the great civic dramas in the history of the United States, a story with everything: corruption, Communism, racism, misguided idealism, displacement, grand visions, evil schemes, and the mystical power of baseball; a story about manifest destiny as it played out in Mexico and the West, and then continued unabated even after the frontier was tamed; a story about the human costs of ambition, both public and private; a story about families.

When I was a junior in high school in Culver City, California, not terribly far from Dodger Stadium, a man named Frank Wilkinson came to speak to our history class about the horror that was the McCarthy era or, as he would have put it, the J. Edgar Hoover era. Wilkinson had been a victim of the Red Scare. In fact, it had nearly ruined him, had sent him to prison, and had almost killed his entire family, but we'll get to that. He appeared before us in the school auditorium, stooped, white-haired, and grandfatherly. He spoke with the sort of conviction that gets you in trouble, even when you are on the side of righteousness, which Wilkinson believed himself to be.

Wilkinson had been a public-housing official in Los Angeles. His demise began when Truman signed that bill into law. It began, more or less, the moment that he knocked on Abrana Aréchiga's door with an eviction notice in his hand.

I don't remember exactly what Wilkinson told us that day about McCarthy, Hoover, and the House Un-American Activities Committee. But I remember how he began his presentation. He asked us to raise our hands if we were fans of the Los Angeles Dodgers. I was sixteen. Baseball was my life. I played on the high school team. I occasionally called into the Dodgers postgame radio show to answer trivia questions. My hand, of course, shot up.

"Well," said Wilkinson. "Dodger Stadium should not exist."

Dodger Stadium should not exist.

Yet no building more perfectly captures the history of Los Angeles or more perfectly captures the history of baseball in America up to the point of its opening in 1962. Dodger Stadium should not exist. There are a million reasons why, yet all those reasons are precisely what give the stadium its power.

This book tells three stories that ultimately coalesce into one bigger story about Los Angeles as it sped toward its destiny as a major-league city. There is the story of Abrana Aréchiga and her family as they journeyed north from Mexico, ultimately settled into the community of Palo Verde, and then fought like hell for their homes. There is the story of Frank Wilkinson, who sought to make a better world but then became the means by which his enemies obliterated any possibility that the world he envisioned would come to fruition. Then there is the story of baseball itself.

I hope that this book provides both an intimate look at the journeys and motivations of its principal characters and a sweeping impression of a city and two countries to which it has belonged. The book includes familiar faces such as Jackie Robinson, Duke Snider, and the Mexican general Antonio López de Santa Anna, as well as less familiar ones such as Clifford Clinton, a crusading downtown LA cafeteria owner, and Fritz B. Burns, a visionary real-estate developer and showman who helped turn Los Angeles into the city that it is today.

I come at this book as a person who has spent many hours watching, writing about, and thinking about baseball. I come at it as a reporter who has worked in the United States and Mexico. I come at it as a native Angeleno who believes the story of my city has too often been told from the perspective of writers perched firmly on the East Coast and peering west as if through a pair of binoculars. On some level, I think I have wanted to write this book since the day I saw Frank Wilkinson in high school. The story broke my heart. I struggled to reconcile that Dodger Stadium, a place that I loved so much, was also the source of pain to so many people. I have never had to pick up the pieces of a broken life like Frank Wilkinson or build a life from scratch like Abrana Aréchiga. I have never been displaced like the residents of Palo Verde, La Loma, and Bishop. But all four of my grandparents were, and I grew up hearing their stories. My father's parents were Jews in Poland during World War II. They both lost their homes and eventually their entire families in the Holocaust. My mother and her family lived in Havana until 1961. After the Cuban Revolution, they had to leave their apartment and their belongings behind because although my grandmother was Cuban, my grandfather was from the United States.

One of the recurring themes of this book is how we rewrite history to suit our own present aims. This was especially true in the early days of baseball and especially true in the early days of Los Angeles. It has also been true when it comes to the story of baseball *in* Los Angeles. The story of Dodger Stadium has been condensed and mythologized. It has become—with good reason—a fable. The real history is less like a fable and more like the story of a crime that Los Angeles perpetuated on itself.

For all its magic, Frank Wilkinson was right: Dodger Stadium should not exist. This book is my attempt to tell the story of why it does.

## Part I

---

# AMONG THE ROCKS

# 1.

Monte Escobedo, Zacatecas, sits high up in Mexico's Sierra Madre mountain range. This is where, in March 1897, at seven thousand feet above sea level, a baby girl named Abrana Cabral was born. The exact date and circumstances of her birth are lost to history. We don't know whether she was born on a bed, or a sofa, or a kitchen table. We don't know what her mother felt like for the nine months she carried Abrana or at the moment her daughter entered the world. We don't know what kind of parents Abrana had. But we do know their names. They were Vacilla Bañuelos and Juan Cabral. We know that they were rural people. They lived on a remote ranch nestled between green valleys and lakes.

Decades later, when she was living in the United States, Abrana would name her first son Juan, after her father. Decades after that, in the early 1950s, this younger Juan would journey to the ranch where his mother was born. He went with his wife, Nellie; their daughter, Helen; and two friends, Camilo and Feliz Arévalo. They drove south from Los Angeles, where Abrana ultimately settled and raised her family in the community of Palo Verde, all the way to Zacatecas. It was a sort of pilgrimage. It was like driving back in time.

When they reached Fresnillo, an industrial city at the base of the Sierra Madres, they had to leave their car behind and hire a man with a truck. The truck carried them up the rough, steep roads to Monte Escobedo. There were no bathrooms, no rest stops. There were trees and lakes and grassy fields. The little girl bounced along on their laps.

"It was mountains. Hills. You don't see no neighbors, no nothing. Just a house there," Feliz recalled. Juan and Nellie were gone. Abrana was many years gone. But Feliz remembered: "You'd go in the truck, and all you'd see is rocks on the roadsides. They used to make fences out of rocks, rocks, rocks all the way up."

=

ALL WE CAN do is guess about what Abrana's childhood was like up there among the rocks. But somehow, in the thin air, she grew up hard and stubborn like the rocks themselves.

The simplest way to trace the outlines of Abrana's journey is through official government documents, but documents alone paint an incomplete picture. In Abrana's case they are riddled with errors and inconsistencies. The truth is that Abrana was born into a world that was not particularly concerned with details like her birthday or even the proper spelling of her name. That didn't change when she set out for America.

Abrana Cabral crossed into the United States at Laredo, Texas, on October 10, 1916. She was nineteen years old and pregnant when she traversed the narrow wooden bridge spanning the Rio Grande. She would have been walking among businessmen and fellow immigrants. In making her way to the border, she would have been traveling through the wreckage of the ongoing Mexican Revolution. She would have been carrying the baby, her memories of home, and probably very little in the way of money or belongings. In a practical sense she would have been thoroughly unprepared for her new life. But she was willing to risk the journey, so in another sense she was exactly as prepared as she needed to be.

Abrana was probably traveling with her husband, Nicolas Ybarra, the father of the little girl growing inside her. Nicolas was also from Monte Escobedo. Together, they were part of an entire generation fleeing north, drawn by the promise of stability and economic opportunity at a time when Mexico offered neither. US companies were luring cheap labor across the border. They called it the *enganche*, the hook. The hook was steady wages and relative safety from violence. The hook is what caused entire towns to empty out, often with all the residents going to the same place. In the case of Abrana and Nicolas and the people of Monte Escobedo, that place was Morenci, Arizona, where the Phelps Dodge company needed strong men willing to do hard labor in hard conditions. The work of mining copper was hot and dark and miserable, but it paid out for every single shift, and there were shifts to be had.

Abrana would have taken a train up to the border. Mexico had industrialized swiftly in the early years of the twentieth century. With the advent of a national railroad, people and goods were moving around the country like never before, and small, isolated towns like Monte Escobedo suddenly didn't feel so small or isolated. Her last stop on the threshold of America was Nuevo Laredo. Nuevo Laredo had been a source of contention during the revolution. In 1914, just two years before Abrana passed through, much of the city had been burned to the ground. Crossing the bridge into Texas would have seemed like the end of a long journey for her: leaving a smoldering Mexico for the promise of the United States. But it was really just the beginning.

# 2.

IN MARCH 1847 THE US ARMY, UNDER WINFIELD SCOTT, LANDED IN Veracruz and took the city following a bloody siege. Old stone walls crumbled. Women and children starved and crumbled beside them. Scott had 13,500 men in his command: officers, enlisted soldiers, volunteers, slaves. He had President James K. Polk and the wind of manifest destiny at his back. Winfield Scott thought that invading Mexico was both reckless and immoral. Unlike Polk, Scott did not believe that the US had a God-given mandate to conquer the entire continent. But Scott was also America's most decorated and respected general: if his country was going to fight a war, he was going to goddamn lead it. Scott's idea was to land in the port city of Veracruz and march his troops across the humid, soft countryside, up over the rocky volcanoes, and finally into the Valley of Mexico, nestled seven thousand feet above sea level.

Scott was an ornery commander. He was big and vain and brilliant. Ulysses S. Grant once called him "the finest specimen of manhood my eyes had ever beheld." He had no formal military education and was largely self-taught as a tactician, but he had always been a keen student of history. Three centuries earlier, another conquering army had landed in Mexico, marched through the same countryside, and traversed the same mountains. It was from them that Scott took his inspiration.

Scott's adversary, the Mexican general Antonio López de Santa Anna, must have felt the weight of this history. He must have known that what began with Hernán Cortés would certainly not end with Winfield Scott. Santa Anna was a proud and mercurial person, and he had recently declared himself president of Mexico (not for the first or last time). Santa Anna called himself the Napoleon of the West. But for all that, his countrymen were unsure how to feel about him. His career had been as jagged as the terrain in

11

his country, filled with soaring peaks and desolate valleys. When he lost his leg in battle almost a decade earlier, Santa Anna ordered it buried with full military honors.

Determined not to let Mexico fall to another conqueror, Santa Anna met the US Army in the hills just outside of Xalapa. His troops appeared to have the invaders overmatched. They equaled the Americans in size and firepower and held a superior defensive position on familiar terrain: Xalapa was Santa Anna's hometown. But an American captain discovered a mountain trail that allowed Scott's troops to outflank Santa Anna and catch him by surprise from above. The battle was devastating and short. It ended with Santa Anna escaping on horseback, in such a desperate hurry that he left his wooden leg behind on the battlefield.

The path to Mexico City was now clear for the Americans. They pushed the Mexican Army deeper and deeper into their country, into themselves. In Puebla the Americans rested and gathered their strength for the final phase of the conquest. All that remained was for the Mexican troops to make their last stand and for Scott's army to drive all the way to the Mexican heart, barely beating, the city that was once called Tenochtitlan. On September 12, 1847, the Americans finally turned their attention to Chapultepec Castle.

The castle looms on a hill high over Mexico City. This hill has been a sacred place since pre-Columbian times. Aztec priests used to climb it in rituals. Emperors vacationed there. The castle, constructed by lackeys to the Spanish crown in an exercise of colonial vanity, had been abandoned in the decades following Mexican independence. Eventually it was converted into a military college. Scott's troops launched their cannonballs and bullets at dawn and sustained the barrage until nightfall. Holding the castle as their countrymen escaped to a nearby fort was a motley group of just four hundred men and boys. They were Mexican soldiers, and they were unrelenting military cadets who refused to surrender. Teenagers dying alongside wary veterans.

The story goes that after every other Mexican soldier was run down or run off by the invaders, only six cadets remained. They were children, really. As young as thirteen years old. Their names were Juan de la Barrera, Agustín Melgar, Juan Escutia, Vicente Suárez, Francisco Márquez, and Fernando Montes de Oca. Eventually they would come to be known collectively as los Niños Héroes.

They held out in their castle, on their tall hill, against the conquering US Army. They held out, even as Santa Anna watched from a distant perch through his field glasses as the bulk of his troops retreated. Legend has it that as the Americans entered the castle proper, one of the cadets, Juan Escutia, wrapped himself in the Mexican flag and leaped from the side of the building so that the flag would not fall into enemy hands. He died—in the fall, or by bullet or by bayonet. They all died.

# 3.

MORENCI, ARIZONA, WAS A SMALL TOWN, BUT IT WAS CROWDED. IT probably came to seem like all of Monte Escobedo was there, stuffed into little houses with cousins and friends and old neighbors from back home. To live there, you had to pay a dollar a year to the mining company for what was really just the rough outline of a house. After that, it was up to you. Scrap wood and rubber and whatever else you could find to make a livable home. No running water. No electricity. The landscape was orange and red. It was a beautiful place sometimes. The sky wide and bright. The washes and ravines seemed to roll on forever, like waves coming out from the Earth. The San Francisco River wound its way across the countryside like a garter snake, the streak of green vegetation along its banks cutting through the rocks.

There were smelters in Morenci and nearby Clifton, and under the mountains were the deep mine shafts, lit up by candles and filled with the voices of the miners and the sounds of pickaxes against rock. The mines ran four thousand feet below the surface. There were hundreds of miles of tunnels, held up by wooden beams. There were new people coming into town every day. There was a train station nearby, there were horses, and there was a little Catholic church and, higher up the hill, a Catholic cemetery. The roads were dirt, and the men were rough. Above it all hung a cloud of smoke from the smelters that was so poisonous it could kill flowers.

It was like living under a magnifying glass. The sun coming down hot in the summers and the company watching everything all the time. Life was mostly work: the work of mining copper ore, the work of moving rocks from one place to another, the hot and dangerous work of smelting, the work of maintaining a home with almost nothing, when a day's wages would buy just a dozen eggs.

*Abrana Aréchiga*

The work of maintaining your dignity as Phelps Dodge and the other big companies tried to keep those wages down. The work of organizing so that if you were Mexican, or Italian, or Yugoslavian, you might one day be paid the same as a "white" American. The work of learning a new language and a new culture. The work of holding on to your place in a city that was growing by the minute. In just a few years the conjoined towns of Clifton and Morenci would grow from a pocket of two hundred people to a region with a population of ten thousand. In 1912 Arizona became the forty-eighth state.

Clifton was the whiter, more developed town. It's still there: frozen in time in the bare, undulating hills. The main commercial drag, Chase Creek Street, once rowdy with saloons and player pianos and men marching to and from their mining jobs, is now quiet and untouched. There's an empty union hall with a mural celebrating one hundred years of organized labor in town. There's a historical museum displaying the high chair that Supreme Court Justice Sandra Day O'Connor sat in when she was a baby. (She grew up shooting jackrabbits on a nearby ranch.) There are big black scars on the cliffs where the smelters once operated.

Old Morenci is gone now. Before it was demolished, Morenci was a steep little village built vertically on a series of hillsides. To give you a sense of just how quickly Morenci grew, the copper companies that built and maintained it didn't even bother to give the hillsides names. It was just Hill A, Hill B, and so on. The migrants from Monte Escobedo wound up on Hill AC. That was where the Mexicans lived. Everyone called it Chihuahuita—Little Chihuahua, which is what every Mexican neighborhood in every small town in the Southwest seemed to be called. Abrana and Nicolas lived on Hill AC. That's where, on March 21, 1917, just five months after Abrana crossed, she gave birth to her first daughter, Delphina.

———

TWO WEEKS AFTER Delphina was born, on April 5, 1917, the United States declared war on Germany. Two months after that, on June 5, her father registered for the draft. On his draft card, Nicolas Ybarra was listed as a "smelter laborer" for the Phelps Dodge Corporation, Morenci Branch. His immigration status was "alien." He was listed as having no military experience and as being tall, with a medium build, brown eyes, and black hair. He was listed as having two dependents: a wife and a daughter.

Nicolas Ybarra was not the only immigrant from Monte Escobedo to fill out a draft card in Morenci. By the time the war came, Manuel Aréchiga had been living in America for more than six years. He had arrived in Morenci back in 1910, before Arizona had even achieved statehood. He had seen Morenci grow as copper prices rose with the war breaking out in Europe. He had experienced the double standard faced by Mexican laborers in and around the mines. He lived on Hill AC, not too far from Abrana and Nicolas.

In late 1915, Clifton-Morenci was one of the worst-paying mining districts in Arizona. Mexican miners made $2.39 per shift compared to $2.89 for Anglos. In other towns, miners made as much as $3.50 per shift. This imbalance resulted in one of the largest strikes in the state's history: one that would culminate in equal wages for Mexican workers and in a violent antiunion backlash throughout Arizona's copper country.

Manuel Aréchiga's draft card says that he was born on March 22, 1888. It says that he had black hair and brown eyes, medium height and a medium build. He had no obvious physical disabilities. But despite the years in America, on the fourth line of the card, filled out in thick black cursive, his naturalization status, like Ybarra's, is listed as "alien."

Manuel's selective service registration put him in a strange position. A few months prior to the passage of the Selective Service Act of 1917, Congress overrode the veto of President Woodrow Wilson to enact a set of highly restrictive and blatantly racist immigration laws. The Immigration Act of 1917 created a literacy test for new immigrants, created an immigrant head tax, and specifically blocked entry of immigrants from Asia. The bill also banned an absurdly long list of undesirables, including "idiots, imbeciles, and feeble-minded persons," epileptics, alcoholics, paupers, anarchists, polygamists, the "mentally or physically defective," and contract laborers.

The bill was a disaster for the agricultural, mining, and railroad businesses in the Southwest that relied on immigrant labor from Mexico. So in 1918 the Wilson administration used a loophole to grant a series of waivers to those industries. That meant immigrants from Mexico such as Manuel Aréchiga could now legally work in the United States as long as they were sponsored by a company. This is how in September 1918, Manuel Aréchiga, who was already registered for the draft in the United States, a country he had been living in for nearly a decade, came to have his picture taken at the border in El Paso for what was called an alien laborer's identification card.

Manuel's sponsoring employer was the Chicago Burlington and Quincy Railroad's Alliance Division, located in Alliance, Nebraska. On this particular piece of paper he is listed as five feet, eight-and-a-half inches tall, with a mole near his left eye. The picture of him, in black and white, shows a somber-looking man of about thirty with deep sunken eyes and thick eyebrows. His hair is thick, almost like a bowl cut, and parted on the left. He has a thin mustache. His gaze is aimed downward, which makes it hard to see his mouth. But he is wearing a vest, a collared shirt, and a tie. He looks like a man out of place.

# 4.

AFTER SANTA ANNA'S ARMY WAS ROUTED BY THE AMERICANS OUT-side of Xalapa, the general fled without his wooden leg, which fell into the hands of the Fourth Regiment of Illinois Volunteers. The Illinois men would gain acclaim during the war for their drunkenness and their willingness to murder civilians. They kept the leg and brought it home with them as a souvenir. It still sits in a glass case in a museum in Springfield.

This much is true, factually. But there is another story about the Illinois soldiers and Santa Anna's leg. It's a myth. It did not happen. But for many years, people told it like it did.

According to the story, at Xalapa the Illinois men met a US officer by the name of Abner Doubleday. Doubleday was an enterprising West Point graduate who, like many of the soldiers in Scott's army, would go on to great fame in the Civil War. He would, in fact, fire the first shot by a Union soldier at Fort Sumter. But in Doubleday's case, soldiering would only be a small part of his legacy. Doubleday would gain greater fame as the anointed inventor of baseball, America's national pastime. The Baseball Hall of Fame would eventually be constructed in his hometown of Cooperstown, New York.

Once the wounded had been cleared off the battlefield at Xalapa and the dead had been buried, Doubleday suggested that the leg found by the Illinois regiment was the perfect size and shape to put to use in playing the sport he had recently conjured up. He gathered the Illinois men into a huddle and explained the rules, charting out the positions and lecturing on the most effective techniques. He marked off foul lines and bases in the marshy long grass of Xalapa's Parque Los Berros and divided the troops into two sides. And thus, according to mythology, the first baseball game on Mexican soil was played on a sunny April afternoon in 1847. For a ball, the players improvised, wrapping a small rock in leather. For a bat, they used the wooden leg of General Antonio López de Santa Anna.

# 5.

IN 1920 COYOTES DESCENDED ON DOUGLAS, ARIZONA. THEY CAME down from the Chiricahua Mountains, out of the desert and into town. They loped down the wide paved streets in front of pharmacies and clothing shops and restaurants. They trotted past the Gadsden Hotel, where mining executives and visiting politicians stayed and where a Tiffany stained-glass window showing the desert landscape in beautiful bright colors overlooked the lobby. At night, as Douglas slept, the coyotes ate dogs and cats. They were big and lithe, and their coats were flecked with yellow.

Dr. Alan M. Wilkinson was an ear, nose, and throat specialist in Douglas. But before that—before he was a doctor or a father, before he was anything—he was a Methodist. He had come to Douglas from northern Michigan as part of his service during World War I and settled into a Craftsman house with his wife, Ada, and their four children. He was for helping the poor and for clean living. He was against dancing, swearing, card playing, and especially drinking. The Wilkinson family went to church at Grace Methodist every Sunday and said grace before every meal. Mornings were for Bible study and earnest prayer.

As their breakfast sat cooling on the table, father, mother, and children would kneel down in unison, heads prone across the seats of their chairs. Many years later, long after he had sworn off religion altogether, Alan and Ada Wilkinson's youngest son, Frank, would still recall the breakfast prayers in vivid detail. The smell of leather upholstery lingered somewhere in the recesses of his sensory memory.

One morning, after prayers, Dr. Wilkinson warned his children about the recent influx of coyotes. The family was preparing for a long road trip to see relatives back on the shores of Lake Michigan.

"Be careful of strange animals," Dr. Wilkinson said before heading to the office. He took special care to look at Frank.

Douglas was a border town, sitting just across from Agua Prieta, Mexico, in the southeastern corner of Arizona. The principal industry in Douglas, like the rest of the region, was mining. Copper ore from the mines in Bisbee was shipped in by rail. Two hulking smelters loomed over the town, operating twenty-four hours per day, leaving the air perpetually thick with dust and smoke. The ore trains ran day and night. A few years earlier, during the tail end of the Mexican Revolution, Pancho Villa had attempted to raid Douglas, but he was stymied before he could cross the border in Agua Prieta. The Wilkinsons had come to Arizona at the same time as Abrana Cabral, and, like Abrana, they came to make a better life for themselves. But they came from different directions and lived in different worlds.

Dr. Wilkinson was partially deaf and walked around with a big hearing aid strapped around his shoulder. But this did not slow him down or diminish his hospitality. He served on boards and committees. He taught Sunday school. He tended to patients on both sides of the border. Despite his stern and authoritarian beliefs about the wages of sin and sinners, he was not a stern or authoritarian man by nature. He was a teller of stories and a lover of (appropriate) jokes.

A few hours after Dr. Wilkinson left for work that morning, young Frank found himself playing in front of the family home when out of the smelter haze emerged a large dog with a rope around its neck. Frank was a hardy and imaginative boy. He had thick, curly hair and a strong chin. His face was incapable of hiding even the slightest emotion, a trait that would follow him into adulthood. Frank had also inherited his father's congenital hearing condition, but unlike his father, he did not wear a hearing aid. When he was a little boy, he would lie under the piano in the family's living room to better listen to the music when his sister played. One time, a teacher had rapped him on the hand in class with a ruler for continuing to speak to the boy next to him, even as she called for silence. Frank had not heard her. He began to wet his pants out of fear that he might miss something.

But he had certainly not missed his father's warning: "Be careful of strange animals." The words echoed in his mind as he watched the creature approach. But this was no strange animal. This, he was convinced, was a police dog. There was something authoritative about it as it trotted down Twelfth Street, where the Wilkinsons lived near the edge of town. Plus, there was a rope around its neck. No strange animal would have a rope around its neck. Frank was only about six years old, and in his mind the plan that he concocted made sense: go catch the dog and return it to its owner. Frank Wilkinson would never be much for thinking about consequences. He ran after the dog.

When he finally caught up to it, the dog turned on him suddenly, fangs bared. There was no time to do anything but cower as the animal rose and sunk its teeth into his neck and elbow. Frank's screams drew neighbors out onto the street. What he thought was a police dog was in fact a coyote. The neighbors ran the animal off and rushed the bleeding boy two blocks to his father's medical office. Dr. Wilkinson, thinking fast, pulled out the strongest drug he had: bichloride tablets.

Bichloride, which had once been used as a syphilis cure, was a popular cleaning agent. Doctors would drop it into water before they washed their hands or operated on a patient. In the years to come, bichloride would be banned from medical practice because it was essentially pure mercury. But in the moment, Dr. Wilkinson saw bichloride as the best chance for his son. He ground a handful of pills into a blue paste and rubbed it deep into the wounds. The next day, with Frank more or less patched up, the family left for Michigan.

The Wilkinsons traveled north and east in their Buick touring car over slow desert roads until they reached a town called Trinidad, Colorado. There, after they stopped for breakfast, a local police officer approached the family.

"Are you Dr. Alan Wilkinson?" To the family's shock, the officer placed Frank's father under arrest. There had been a mix-up. Authorities back in Douglas had sent a message ahead to warn that the Wilkinsons were traveling with a local child who was in danger. The Trinidad police took this to mean that Frank had been kidnapped. This was not the case; as it turned out, the danger forewarned in the telegram was related to the coyote that had bitten Frank. Authorities in Douglas had captured it and discovered that it was rabid. They messaged ahead so that police along their route might be able to warn the Wilkinsons.

Frank needed to be subjected to Pasteur treatments as soon as possible. The nearest rabies vaccine was six hundred miles away, in Kansas City. This was long before the interstate highways were built. The drive would have taken a week, at least. So Frank was placed on a train with his oldest sister, Hildegarde, who was then about eighteen. Hildegarde would later go on to a career as a pioneering physician, the first woman to be accepted into Stanford Medical School. She would become a mother figure for Frank. But for now her job was babysitter.

As their parents and siblings drove behind in their Buick, Frank and Hildegarde traveled on to Kansas City by train. For six hundred miles, through Colorado and Kansas, over the mountains and the plains, Frank tormented his sister, howling and baring his teeth. Then they reached Kansas City, and Frank's own torment began. Six weeks of painful injections, three or four per day, a long way from home. Every day the large needle found its way into new parts of his body: arms, legs, stomach, and buttocks until the doctors were finally certain that Frank would remain the relatively normal boy he was, no foaming at the mouth, no painful illness or death. Just a lesson learned. Or not.

# 6.

On August 15, 1918, Abrana Cabral became a widow and a single mother. After three days under the care of a doctor, Nicolas Ybarra succumbed to what was diagnosed as "cerebral syphilis." On the death certificate, Ybarra was curiously listed as single. In the box asking "Was disease contracted in Arizona?" the attending physician wrote, in cursive, "probably not." In the box marked "Place of Burial or Removal," the physician wrote, "Mex Cemetery."

The Mexican cemetery was a few miles west of town. It was technically the Catholic cemetery, but almost all the Catholics in Morenci were Mexican. The cemetery is still there, on a hillside above the open-pit mine that exists where Old Morenci used to. Most of the grave markers are gone, and much of it is overrun with wild grass.

"At the time of the cemetery's inception, Morenci did not have a hearse or an official undertaker," wrote Al Fernandez, a newspaper columnist who lived in Morenci at the time. "Churches kept records of the deceased parishioners of their faiths, but no records were kept of the people that were buried in the cemetery. No one supervised or were in charge of it or of its maintenance, or that even had authority to enforce symmetry rules. All of this was left to the families or friends of the departed to select the location of their choice, and to dig their own graves."

If you were lucky enough to die on the job, which Ybarra was not, the mining company you worked for might send you up the hill to the cemetery by train. Otherwise, the coffin would be carried up the slope by wagon. But trains and wagons could travel only so far: the final stretch would have to be trekked on foot, up a harsh incline. The Mexican cemetery was a hard place to dig graves. It was a long walk if you were carrying a pine box with a body in it.

It would also have been a long walk for a young widow carrying a one-year-old girl to her father's funeral.

Abrana had journeyed a thousand miles through a country being torn apart by war, while pregnant, to start a new life with Nicolas Ybarra. She gave birth to their baby in a new land where business was conducted in a language she could not speak. She watched as her husband toiled away in a hot smelter. Then she watched as the syphilis he had contracted somewhere along the way spread to his brain and killed him. And now, almost immediately, she and her daughter were alone in America.

Abrana had almost certainly met Manuel Aréchiga before Nicolas Ybarra was buried in the Mexican cemetery in Morenci. She and Manuel came from the same town in Zacatecas. They lived in the same town in Arizona. At some point between Ybarra's death in 1918 and the census of 1920, Abrana and Manuel entered into a partnership that would last the rest of their lives, that would produce a large extended family, that would land them in newspapers and history books, and that would eventually land them in side-by-side burial plots in Resurrection Cemetery in Monterey Park, California.

# 7.

It's only a few hundred miles from Morenci to Douglas. That's either a great distance or a small one. They were on opposite ends of the same tiny pocket of America. Douglas was a small city, and the Wilkinsons' version of Douglas—white and well-to-do—was even smaller. The family social life was limited almost entirely to fellow Methodists—and, if not Methodists, fellow Christians at the very least.

During his childhood in Douglas, Frank was insulated not only from drinking, dancing, and card playing but also from the simmering and sometimes violent labor struggles that were ongoing around the nearby copper mines; insulated from the infamous Bisbee deportation, which saw thousands of union members arrested and sent off on a train to the middle of New Mexico without food and water; insulated from the harder lives of the Mexican kids he would sometimes see on his walks to and from school. But Frank's life was not devoid of adventure, or at least the kind of adventure that came with being part of a family of temperance advocates.

On a YMCA camping trip he was nearly caught in a wildfire in the Chiricahua range. A negligent camp counselor had left Frank and some other boys to their own devices as flames appeared in a mountain pass. It was just a brush fire, but Frank and his friends climbed a rock face, scrambled over sharp manzanita branches to avoid a large and unfriendly rattlesnake, and ran through an abandoned mine shaft, the entire time thinking that a wall of flames was at their back. Finally, before darkness fell, they found the light of a mountain cabin.

When federal prohibition was enacted in 1920, a family friend named Clarence Housel was appointed as the region's special agent in charge of enforcing the new law. Arizona had been a dry state since its inception in 1912, but suddenly Housel was tasked with seeking out bootleggers and moonshiners. For a bureaucrat accustomed to examining dry goods and applying tariffs, this was exciting work. To men like Housel and Dr. Wilkinson, it was also God's work.

"If the sewer sink in the post office building wobbles or squirms from its corner this afternoon it will not be its fault" went one story in the *Bisbee Daily Review.* "Announcement was made this morning by Deputy Customs Collector C. A. Housel that at 3 o'clock this afternoon approximately 50 gallons of confiscated liquor will be dumped into the sewer. The precious stuff is a mixture of beer, mescal and whisky. Housel will officiate at the ceremony."

Once, Housel invited Frank and his father along to bust a whiskey still in Willcox, a town a couple hundred miles north of Douglas. Frank recalled driving out over dirt roads with his father and Housel. The still was located in an old farmhouse, out in the middle of nowhere. Arrests were made. Booze was confiscated. For Frank it was all a great adventure. For his father it was something more: the fulfillment of his own vision for America.

One morning the Wilkinson family drove out of town to a church meeting. It was a long day and late night of fellowship, and it was a long, dark drive home to Douglas. It was dark when Dr. Wilkinson pulled the car up over a hill and dark on the way down, when the car suddenly smashed into an ore train that had been crawling along the tracks with its lights off. There was noise: screams, wheels spinning, bones breaking, the train screeching to a halt. Then there was silence. Frank, who had been asleep in the front seat, was flung through the canvas roof of the car and into the wheels of the train. He woke up covered in grease. He was still a little boy. He was fine. Little boys can take almost anything. It was dark when the family realized that Frank's mother, Ada, was not fine. She had broken her pelvis. It was dark when they sent her off to the Mayo Clinic in Rochester, Minnesota. It was dark for the four years she wore a concrete cast over her entire body, from her shoulders to her knees. It was dark when the Wilkinsons decided that despite the good schools and public parks and water-filtration system, Douglas, Arizona, was not equipped to deal with problems like hers. In 1925 the family set out for Los Angeles.

# 8.

By 1920, Manuel and Abrana were living at the same address in Morenci, along with Manuel's mother, his sister, and about a dozen other people. They got married, and on June 25, 1921, their first daughter was born. Her name was Aurora, but the people who knew her best would call her Lola. A year later, their son Juan would be born. But that would happen in their new hometown: Los Angeles, California.

Sometime between the birth of Lola and the birth of Juan, Abrana and Manuel made the trek west to California. After World War I, the demand for copper shrank, and the entire industry in Arizona crashed. Prices plummeted. Smelters shut down. Mines were closed. Jobs evaporated. Abrana and Manuel got out in 1922. Within a few years, the copper mines themselves would be radically different. During the depression, Phelps Dodge destroyed the entire ecosystem of shafts and tunnels under the town of Morenci and replaced it with a massive open-pit mine.

The open mine would grow and grow and grow. In the 1960s it grew to the point that Old Morenci, the place where Abrana and Manuel had lived, was dismantled to make way for its expansion. The copper buried under Morenci was worth more than the community itself. The mine is still growing. Where the town once stood there's just a vast man-made canyon filled with churning gravel and trucks driving busily back and forth. Rocks going up and down on never-ending conveyor belts. There are three pits now, but it's hard to distinguish them from ground level because they are so large and so sprawling. The mine, with its immense steppes and striations of color, feels like part of the natural landscape. When I visited Morenci, I found myself driving up the mountain to get a better look, higher and higher. I kept driving until I realized that I was never going to fully grasp it.

═══

THEY TRAVELED ALMOST six hundred miles due west through Tucson and Phoenix and Palm Springs. It was Manuel and Abrana and her daughter, Delphina, from her first marriage; their daughter, Lola; and their cousins, siblings, and in-laws. It seemed as if they were at the center of a traveling village, as if the little piece of Zacatecas that had moved with them north to Arizona was now following them west to California. And here it was: California, the golden object of manifest destiny. The final destination of the American Dream.

Abrana was twenty-eight years old when she reached the city that would become her home. She was thin. She had an angular face that made her seem old when she was young and then sort of ageless when she got old. Dolores Klimenko, one of Abrana's granddaughters, said that when she was a little girl in the 1950s, she used to think of her grandmother as looking like the heads side of a buffalo nickel. Manuel was only a few inches taller than Abrana. He was skinny too. He was a quiet man, with a sly charm and the ability to do hard work without letting it beat him down. He was always watching people, always observing. He was resourceful. Unlike Abrana, Manuel could read and write. But Abrana was the brains of the family, the engine that drove them through each passing day. She was the mouth too.

They went to Los Angeles because that was a place you could go. That was a place you could make a life for yourself. They were swept up in the currents of history. Los Angeles in 1922 was a city still coming into itself. The landmarks that would come to signify it as an iconic place to the outside world, and even to its own residents, were newly built, under construction, or still being dreamed up: Memorial Coliseum, UCLA, the Watts Towers, the Hollywood Bowl, even the Hollywood sign. City Hall was not yet built. Neither was County Hospital. The movie studios were still aligning themselves into a powerful regional industry: Warner Brothers, MGM, RKO, Paramount. But Los Angeles was filling up with dreamseekers as if in anticipation of what was to come. It was filling up with automobiles. With water piped in through vast aqueducts from distant rivers and lakes that would make it possible for even more dreamseekers and automobiles to follow.

It was also filling up with tens of thousands of Mexican people, crossing an invisible line that hadn't existed when their grandparents were born. Between 1920 and 1930 the population of Los

Angeles would double to more than one million people. LA would become the fifth-largest city in America. It would go from a place with a Spanish name and a Protestant sensibility to a place with a Spanish name and a Spanish-speaking population too large to ignore. But all those new arrivals had to find someplace to live. Neighborhoods that we would later come to associate with LA's pulsing diversity were still off-limits if you weren't white.

Abrana and Manuel found a place called Palo Verde. They bought a small plot of land there on Malvina Avenue. Really, Palo Verde wasn't even a place yet. It was a prayer tucked into the raw Stone Quarry Hills, just north of downtown. The hills had always been an afterthought: too rugged with gullies and ravines to build anything meaningful on and set apart from the city that surrounded them. These hills were a place where strange things happened. The first Jewish settlers in Los Angeles had buried their dead there. There had once been a smallpox hospital. When the Aréchigas arrived, there were brickyards, sending smoke out over the city below. And then there was Elysian Park, with its acres upon acres of wilderness, tamed and landscaped with colorful trees and hiking paths and creeks and even a baseball field.

Elysian Park gave you the feeling of being somewhere far away from city life. And that was the great thing about Palo Verde. Alongside the adjacent neighborhoods of La Loma and Bishop, it felt set apart from the city. It felt like the communities belonged to Elysian Park. In the 1920s the natural landscape of the region was still straining against the built environment of the growing city, was not yet fully consumed by bricks and concrete and wood and glass. Palo Verde belonged to the land.

Palo Verde was mostly owned by a self-aggrandizing lawyer and progressive activist named Marshall Stimson. Stimson parceled out subdivisions and sold tracts to poor Mexican families. He threw parties for them and considered himself to be a benevolent Santa Claus–type figure. In 1922 Palo Verde would have had only a few houses. It would have been a blank space. A canvas onto which one might begin to paint the outlines of a life. And so it was when Abrana and Manuel put up their tent that first night, when they went to sleep and woke up to begin building their new life. For a long time, this is where the Aréchiga journey seemed like it would end. In peace. Tucked away in the still-wild hills of Los Angeles, California.

# 9.

THE MYTHOLOGICAL ABNER DOUBLEDAY, THIEF OF SANTA ANNA'S leg, was not the first American man to take something from a Mexican. That was, after all, what the entire war was about. But the mythological Abner Doubleday does not resemble the real man or his real story in the least. The truth of Abner Doubleday is far more compelling. The true story of Abner Doubleday is the story of how baseball has always existed on the precipice between myth and fact, has always been simultaneously a force of genuine power and a theatrical contrivance, has always presented itself as one thing but really offered another. The truth is that like Abner Doubleday, baseball is a magic trick.

Abner Doubleday was indeed born in Cooperstown, and he was indeed a famous US soldier. But he was no sportsman. His crowning as the inventor of America's national pastime was the result of remarkable confluence of an obscure spiritual movement, nationalistic insecurity, and inspired marketing. In his book *Baseball in the Garden of Eden*, historian John Thorn paints a picture of Doubleday as a spiritual seeker: a "dream-filled" lover of poetry and mathematics.

In the months before Abner Doubleday was sent off to Mexico to fight in James Polk's war, he wrote a letter to the transcendentalist philosopher Ralph Waldo Emerson: "It seems clear as a general principle that the armed body should *act*, not deliberate. But when I think I may be employed to oppress instead of to defend, the case does not seem so clear." These hardly seem like the words of a man who would use a wooden leg as a baseball bat. However, they do seem like the words of a man who later in life would translate Sanskrit texts and would seek out the answers to life's unknowns in the world of alchemy. They read like the words of a man who would get involved in a nineteenth-century mystical society called the Theosophists, which is exactly what Doubleday did. And oddly these were the very pursuits that led to his posthumous anointing as the father of baseball.

The man who anointed Doubleday was Albert Spalding. Spalding once said that "baseball is a man-maker." But he knew that baseball was also a god maker and that for a smart enough businessman, it could be a kingdom maker. Spalding had been an exceptional pitcher in the mid-1800s in Rockford, Illinois, and then became a sporting-goods titan, slowly building an empire that he grew by proselytizing the sport of baseball itself and increasing the demand for his products. In the late nineteenth century, Spalding pushed baseball with the fervor of an evangelical preacher. This was a time when writers like Walt Whitman and Mark Twain were extolling the virtues of the sport. Spalding published baseball magazines and helped organize the National League. Perhaps most famously, he put together a legendary world tour of US baseball heroes: they went to Europe and Egypt and India and Australia. While Cap Anson was refusing to play against black players and helping create the unspoken color barrier that would last in America until Jackie Robinson, he was also happily taking Spalding's checks to stage exhibitions in the shadow of the pyramids. With every stop, Spalding hoped to open new markets for his sporting goods. Baseball became not just a game, and not just a product, but a symbol of what it was to be American. This was how Spalding wanted it.

Before he was married, in 1875, Spalding had been engaged to a woman named Lizzie Churchill. Lizzie chose instead to marry another ballplayer, named George Mayer. Lizzie and George moved to Fort Wayne, Indiana, where, as George floundered in business, she taught singing lessons and fell in with a spiritual group called the Theosophical Society, the same group to which Abner Doubleday belonged in New York.

Theosophy was founded by a Russian émigré who called herself Madame Blavatsky. She had deep-set eyes, round cheeks, and the aspect of a monk. In many surviving photos and illustrations, her chin is resting plaintively in her hands. It was easy to look at her and see a wise woman. "Theosophy is, then, the archaic *Wisdom-Religion*, the esoteric doctrine once known in every ancient country having claims to civilization," Blavatsky wrote. The group claimed three primary goals: promoting universal brotherhood, studying faraway religion and science, and investigating the unexplained laws of nature and other mysteries of man and the universe. In a sense the Theosophists were like a more mystical, Eastern-tinged version of the Freemasons. The central text of Theosophy was called *Isis Unveiled*, and much of it was plagiarized by Blavatsky. In 1890 Lizzie left her husband and set sail with her son for England to immerse herself in the world of Theosophy. When she returned, she moved to Chicago, where she quickly took up with her ex-boyfriend, Spalding.

Spalding and Lizzie carried on their affair for a decade. She grew increasingly involved with the Theosophists, and she likely came across Doubleday, who had briefly served as president of the US chapter of the group. Spalding carried on with his sporting-goods business, organizing the world tour, and in the 1890s, as baseball fell briefly in popularity, focusing on the latest craze: bicycles.

Meanwhile, Lizzie and Spalding had a son together. The boy was "adopted" by Spalding's sister. When Spalding's wife, Josie, died at the turn of the century, he and Lizzie were quickly married, and they adopted the little boy back into their lives. They moved to Point Loma, the site of a new Theosophical compound just outside San Diego, and built a house with an ocean view. The compound also held the papers and archives of prominent theosophists, including Doubleday. There were temples with amethyst domes that lit up at night, visible to ships passing by on the Pacific. There was a Greek amphitheater.

Spalding was not a spiritualist like Doubleday or Lizzie, but he saw nothing unseemly about Theosophy, living happily alongside its most-ardent practitioners. When the group came under criticism in a series of wild articles in California newspapers alleging orgies, child abuse, and weird occultist rituals in Point Loma, Spalding became one of Theosophy's most prominent public defenders.

In 1904, while living in Point Loma, Spalding became irritated by one of his own employees: the legendary baseball writer Henry Chadwick. Chadwick had been casually writing in Spalding's own magazines that the sport of baseball was a descendant of the English game of rounders. Spalding decided to turn Chadwick's claim into a marketing opportunity. He would pronounce baseball as uniquely American, even if he had to do it artificially. So Spalding put together a group called the Mills Commission, stocked with ex-ballplayers and baseball business types who owed him favors.

"Our good Old American game of baseball must have an American Dad," Spalding wrote, revealing his intentions for the committee. And the committee did not disappoint. A mining expert named Abner Graves who had grown up in Cooperstown came forward with the story of Doubleday inventing baseball in 1839: just early enough, based on available research, to be the definitive first instance of baseball played in America. And so the Mills Commission found that baseball was indeed an American game and that based on "best evidence obtainable to date," Doubleday, the dream-filled soldier, had in fact conjured the sport into existence.

John Thorn does not go so far as to accuse Spalding of a grand conspiracy in anointing the Theosophist Doubleday as baseball's "American dad." He merely points out that it was convenient. At the very least, Abner Graves's story must have seemed like a divine gift to Spalding. Here Spalding had the chance to anoint as the inventor of baseball a beloved US war hero who happened to have been a vocal Theosophist. In doing so, he could give a lift to the game that was his business and to the movement that was his wife's life work. And better yet, Doubleday was too dead to refute any of it.

And so, with an American dad, baseball became the American game, conjured by the forces of patriotism, capitalism, and mysticism. In this sense the rise of baseball in the American consciousness isn't that different from the rise of Los Angeles: both willed into existence by a bunch of opportunists printing the legend at expense of the fact and both growing into something bigger and messier and more interesting than their boosters could have ever imagined. Baseball became something people believed in. The illusion became real.

*Part II*

---

# SLEEP TO WAKE

# 10.

THE MOST STRIKING FEATURE OF ABRANA AND MANUEL'S NEW LIFE was how similar it was to their old one. They had traveled hundreds of miles and come finally to a place not so different from Morenci, Arizona. Another poor village. Another hill. Another neighborhood that was literally being carved away, extracted, stripped down to nothing in order that other, more valuable places could be built up. The brickyards were a huge industry in Los Angeles. They meant work for everybody who could stand it. They meant that in Palo Verde, Manuel and Abrana pitched their tent in the haze of toxic smoke and among the din of earth moving and whistles blowing.

This is where Manuel Aréchiga would build his first house. He would lay out a floor plan on the flat dirt parcel: an empty lot that carried with it all the possibilities of a life. This is where he would stand at the beginning of the day as the sun rose over the San Gabriel Mountains to the northeast or at the end of the day as the sun set orange and pink over the meager downtown Los Angeles skyline of 1922. This is where he could envision a home suitable for his children, a house he would want to come back to after a long day of work, because Manuel Aréchiga knew that work was what awaited him in this life.

The Los Angeles of the 1920s was a land of opportunity. It was a land of speculation and a place where hardworking salesmen and artists and even preachers could make themselves rich and famous. Los Angeles was land of opportunity in the 1920s, but opportunity was different if you looked like Abrana and Manuel Aréchiga. To them, opportunity meant simply having enough work that they would never go hungry, even if the work was miserable. It meant the chance to own something, even if it was something nobody else wanted.

Little by little, Manuel would buy the tools, the wood, and the nails. He would lay out the frames and hammer them together, studs sixteen inches apart. He would find a neighbor or a friend to help him raise the walls, one at a time. Imagine what it must be like to go to sleep at night in a tent and stare out across the dirt at your future home, to dream of the rooms, unbuilt, perfect in their possibility. And then, after the roof is shingled and the doors are hung and the windows are sealed, to finally fill those rooms with chairs and tables and beds, to put a picture up on your wall and see the plaster dust float down to your feet where the nail went in.

===

THE FAMILY GREW. Juan was born in February 1923, Celia in April 1924. In October 1926 Abrana had a second son, whom they named Manuel Jr.—they called him Mañito for short. He was a sweet-natured boy and a bundle of energy. Two years later, Abrana lost a baby in childbirth. Finally, in 1929, Abrana and Manuel had their youngest daughter, Victoria. They called her Tolina.

There was family everywhere. One of Abrana's cousins, Paulino Cabral, married Manuel's sister Antonia Aréchiga, and they lived across the street and had six children: four boys and two girls. Another of Manuel's sisters, Georgia, also lived on Malvina. Slowly, gradually, a community began to coalesce. Palo Verde was more or less a self-contained village, its streets laid out over the hills and gullies like a blanket thrown over a pile of stuff in the garage. The community abutted La Loma, Bishop, and Elysian Park. At the end of Malvina, the street where Abrana and Manuel had built their home, the Los Angeles Police Department would open its training academy in 1935.

There were only two ways in and out of Palo Verde. Paducah Street would eventually take you down toward Sunset Boulevard, and a diagonal called Bishops Road led out to Broadway, where you could catch a streetcar into downtown. Eventually, an elementary school would be built. A Catholic church called Santo Niño was erected next to the school on Paducah Street. There was a convent. A couple of locally run grocery stores. A cleaners and a pawnshop. There was a man in the neighborhood who dragged blocks of ice up and down the streets, sizing up chunks, chopping them off, and carrying them into each home with big metal tongs.

Death was always present, just as it had been in Morenci and before that in Zacatecas. Abrana's cousin Paulino died after a cut he sustained in a brickyard became infected. This was years before penicillin. The men of Palo Verde built furniture, poured gravel, and did whatever else it took to get by. Some of the women had jobs. Some stayed home. They planted gardens and raised animals. When new babies were born, the mothers buried their umbilical cords in the dry dirt behind their homes.

All around the Aréchigas, the village came to life with a generation of American-born kids, just like theirs. Other families named Zepeda and Nava and Elias and Colón and Díaz and Santillán. Not just in Palo Verde, but in the smaller adjoining communities of La Loma and Bishop. They filled the Palo Verde Elementary School and learned English from the white women who taught there. They wore underpants cut and sewn from the bags of flour their mothers bought to make tortillas. They didn't have any shoes, and the one boy whose family could afford shoes used to hide them in the bushes before class so he wouldn't stand out. They made kites out of newspaper and flour paste, and carts out of broken old wheelbarrow wheels to race down the hillsides.

The village grew house by house. New families came and settled into tents as the Aréchigas had. Abrana and Manuel watched them build houses and fix up crumbling old ones. They lent a hand, adding on rooms for new babies and lifting frames and digging foundations. They planted fruit trees. When cousins came up from Mexico with empty pockets, they let them sleep on their floor or on their couch or in their basement. Then, little by little, the cousins saved up, and soon they had a house of their own. Soon they were raising their own English-speaking boys and girls. This is the story of Palo Verde, La Loma, and Bishop, of families who made something from nothing.

The communities were in Los Angeles, but they were invisible: both physically, tucked away into the hills, and metaphorically. They were places that white city leaders preferred to just ignore. The population was about 85 percent Mexican or Mexican American; beyond that was a diverse smattering of African American households, white households, and immigrants, mostly from Europe. The city did not pave these roads or build streetlights. In the beginning, there weren't even street signs. One legend has it that Palo Verde got its name because the only identifying object that visitors could use to find their way into the neighborhood was a green tree on the side of the road: its trunk was the *palo verde*, the green stick. Imagine that you live against the backdrop of a great and growing American city: its goings on are your goings on, but also not. You are a part of it, but you are apart. You breathe its air, bus its tables, and mold the bricks that pave its streets and that form its centers of commerce, stores, warehouses, and banks, but you are still apart.

Abrana Aréchiga spent almost the entire 1920s pregnant or nursing. Meanwhile, the city government spent that decade fighting over the fate of the brickyards in her neighborhood. Ultimately, the brickyards were shuttered, not because of people like Abrana or her children but because the pollution had spread downtown.

If she had wanted to, Abrana could have kept tabs on the politicians from a distance. She could have climbed up the hill behind her house and watched the construction of the new Los Angeles City Hall, slowly rising to dominate the skyline. The building opened in 1928, white and regal, a triumphant art deco tower topped by a great pyramid like an arrow pointing upward to the infinite possibilities of Southern California—or perhaps like a giant middle finger aimed directly at Abrana and her neighbors.

# 11.

FRANK WILKINSON'S LIFE IN LOS ANGELES BECAME AN EXTENSION OF his life in Douglas. He delivered newspapers. The family went to church. His father crusaded for Herbert Hoover in 1928, and Frank and his older brother, Budge, joined him at speeches and rallies, selling little license-plate frames that said "Keep the 18th Amendment." The family lived in Hollywood and then Beverly Hills. They lived in the same city as Abrana and Manuel but not in the same place. Frank joined the basketball team and ran cross-country. He raced with his friends through the swamps and marshes that one day would become the shiny glass skyline of Century City. He played trumpet in the school band. Once, he went to a party and then left immediately because some of the other boys were smoking cigarettes out back. On weekends, he woke up early to mow the lawn. He spent hours making sure every blade of grass was aligned just so, every edge perfectly square.

When the Depression hit, Frank Wilkinson didn't know about it. Frank went roller skating with the other kids from Hollywood Methodist Church. His family joined the Edgewater Beach Club in Santa Monica. When he went swimming, the sky was clear, the water was blue, and everybody in the pool was white. Los Angeles was a booming city, but it was still a small town to the people who ran it. The Wilkinsons were part of that class. Frank helped take care of his bedridden mother, Ada. He learned to change bedpans and how not to complain. She wore corsets that required him to fasten dozens of buttons, and for years afterward the sight of loose buttons would terrify him.

When he was fourteen years old, he got his driver's license. He kept the family cars shiny and polished. Everything about his life was shiny and polished. "I was wearing tuxedos to Bel-Air cotillion," he remembered. Frank wanted only one thing in life, and that

*Frank Wilkinson*

was to go to UCLA. When he thought that getting a C in his chemistry class might prevent that, he begged his teacher for the *B*—and because this was Beverly Hills, and this was Frank Wilkinson, she gave it to him. Her name was Miss Marguerite Brinegar, and she would live to be 105.

At UCLA, Frank was recruited to join the Sigma Alpha Epsilon (SAE) fraternity, of which his brother and brother-in-law had been members. He was going to be student body president, they told him. And he liked the sound of that. He was on his way. He still couldn't hear a thing, but he learned to control the conversations he was in. He learned to cope. You could go a long way on moral conviction. You could go a long way on ambition. You could go a long way on the easy charm of not knowing how good you had it.

By the time he walked onto the brand-new UCLA campus in brand-new Westwood Village, Frank was tall and elegant and comfortable in his skin. The summer before his freshman year, a member of his fraternity got him a job as an usher at the 1932 Olympic Games. He stood at the fifty-yard line of Memorial Coliseum, with its high walls and imposing arches, and watched the greatest athletes in the world run and leap and heave their way to glory. It seemed like an omen, or a series of omens: here he was with a miracle of a job amid the pomp and circumstance, amid the literal physical manifestation of the hard work and clean living habits that were exactly what he stood for. Here was the campus being built, it seemed, just for him; here were boys at SAE who didn't drink or smoke or swear either—at least that's what Frank thought at the time. They had put him through hell with the initiation. But he swallowed his tears and got through it (onward Christian Soldier), and he joined the ROTC and the freshman crew team. He bounded across the quad and up the Janss Steps with their neat rows of bricks. One of his best fraternity friends was Lloyd Bridges, who would go on to become a famous actor and a known Communist.

Every Saturday night Frank would go dancing at the Cocoanut Grove nightclub in the Ambassador Hotel and order a cold glass of milk from the bartender. (By then, Dr. Wilkinson had come to grudgingly approve of dancing as an act that was, if not particularly moral, not an immediate ticket to Hell.) Frank loved to be there with his friends among the most glamorous people in the world, chattering under the arching fake palm trees, lounging at one of the perfect round tables with white tablecloths and little lamps on each one.

Frank's hearing was getting worse. The condition was degenerative, and the lectures at UCLA may as well have been happening a million miles away. But he took night classes in lip reading. He told himself that as soon as he won the election for student body president, he would tell the world about this burden. His deafness was the cause of his greatest insecurities, the creeping doubts that plagued him and drove him. As soon as he won, he would use his platform to exorcise the demon. Maybe somebody else out there was also hiding something. Maybe there was nothing to be ashamed about in the first place. Frank believed in the social gospel. He believed in salvation through good works.

In 1934 Frank wrote a letter to his mother, who was back home in Michigan for her own mother's funeral. In the letter he was totally unguarded about his insecurities and about his ambitions:

> I hope my hearing doesn't bother me any more than it does now; I keep my chin set in determination to make good in everything that I go into, but I think that I could be a greater man tomorrow if I did not have my bad hearing to trouble me. Still in another sense, I am encouraged when I look at all the great men in the past that have made the best of their handicaps and gone to the top. Please do not let folks read this back there, because after all, my youthful enthusiasm and ambition is nobody else's but just yours and mine, Mother.

The world was going to hell. Stalin, Hitler, and Mussolini were in power. Frank even wrote a paper about it. There were peace movements at UCLA. There was a group called Veterans of Future Wars, and one of the girls in it was named Jean Benson. She and Frank didn't see eye to eye, but they became friends. When a few of Frank's classmates wanted to host open forums on campus to talk it all out, he told them not to do it. When they did it anyway, he ratted them out to the provost and turned half the campus against him and cost himself the student body presidency. He thought he was doing the right thing. But it was OK. Frank was resilient. He decided he would leave politics behind. After all, he had never been that interested in economic systems or international policy. Frank's campus politics were about personal ambition, about social status, and about the fact that Frank loved people and wanted to be loved by them in return. He thought that perhaps if he devoted himself to the church, if he became a minister, they would.

# 12.

ABRANA COOKED *MENUDO* EVERY WEEKEND. SHE PREPARED OXTAIL.
Sometimes she would raise pigs to butcher. They ate *carnitas*
cooked over an open flame. She built a brick oven in the backyard,
where she and her friends and neighbors could bake bread and
roast meat. They grew fruits and vegetables. Cactus and corn and
grapes. Abrana would clean the spikes from the cactus—*nopales*—
and cook them up with chili and eggs. Manuel would cut up the
fruit of the cactus, called *tunas*, and serve them to his children.
Abrana made her own tortillas.

The porch, enclosed by a railing with vertical wooden slats that
looked like crooked teeth, was Abrana's domain: the crow's nest from
which she observed the goings on in Palo Verde. She would call out
to kids passing by and yell up and down the hillsides to her neighbors. She would peek through the empty lots across Malvina and see
what was happening on Gabriel Avenue, a block over. Abrana was
quick with her opinions and colorful with her language. For somebody who was a devout Catholic, and couldn't read or write, she had
a way of bending the Spanish language to express the full scope of
her disapproval. There were many things she disapproved of. Mostly
she disapproved of people who did not respect her or her family.

She always told the truth, as she saw it, and sometimes the
truth demanded swearing. If the kids were off somewhere and
she didn't like it, she would yell, call them names, see what they
were up to. *"Pá donde van cabrónes? A la calle?"* Most of her teeth
had rotted out by the time she reached her forties, but she could
still yell and curse with the best of them. When her son or one of
her nephews brought girls over to the house, she would interro-
gate them without shame. *"Yo sé quien eres,"* Abrana would say.
"I know who you are."

The neighbor kids called Abrana Two Guns Brooks, as if she was some kind of Old West outlaw.

Manuel had a milder disposition. He was sweet and patient on the outside, but he punctuated his quiet personality with a propensity for silly jokes. Sometimes he would play pranks on Abrana, sticking his head out the back window of the house and yelling insults to her as neighbors walked by, imitating their voices, so that Abrana, sitting on the porch, would call out to the street in a rage at the unsuspecting pedestrians.

"Take my hand," he would tell her. And after much goading, she finally would, only to have him stand up on a chair and lay a fart into her palm. His grandchildren used to call him Papa Comida because he was always dishing out something sweet—a piece of fruit, a slice of *pan dulce*, a candy—and because of a joke he would always make. "Papa es comida," he would say. "Potato is food."

In one of the cellars, Manuel made moonshine. He fermented grapes in big barrels. He had a copper still and pipes running every which way. The police academy was just a hundred yards down the street. Sometimes he would hire local kids to bottle the booze as it dripped out of the still. When a customer came by, Manuel would greet them at the cellar door and wrap a bottle up for them in newspaper. It wasn't much of a secret. Occasionally the cops would come for him.

"Manny," they would say, "it's time for us to take a ride." He'd be home within the hour. Sometimes he'd end up wrapping up a bottle for the arresting officer. He could make moonshine a block down from the place where cops were trained, and it wasn't even a secret. It didn't have to be. He called his concoction *matagente:* the people killer.

＝＝

FAMILY WAS SACRED in Palo Verde, but it was also fluid. People died. People moved. Families joined together, often in more than one place, then broke apart. It wasn't father, mother, and 2.5 children. Abrana and Manuel had five children together, and there was Delphina from Abrana's first marriage and the nieces and nephews, brothers and sisters, and cousins from back home who would come to stay with them on Malvina. Practically everybody was a cousin or a godfather.

Even though Manuel and Abrana were a thousand miles away from their village in Zacatecas, it was never far away. Siblings and cousins and old neighbors from Monte Escobedo passed through repeatedly over the years, working farm jobs and labor jobs before being occasionally deported, or leaving as their Bracero Program visas expired. Conditions were still tenuous at best for Mexican immigrants in Los Angeles. During the Great Depression, Mexicans were scapegoated for everything from stealing jobs to mooching off federal benefits. Anti-Mexican and anti-immigration groups sprang up in Southern California. National organizations like the American Legion and Veterans of Foreign Wars supported deportation, as did some labor unions. Ultimately, hundreds of thousands, if not millions, of Mexicans in America—many of them natural-born US citizens—were forced over the border in a concerted effort at repatriation. In some Mexican neighborhoods in Los Angeles, immigration officials went door-to-door checking people's papers.

Manuel's sister Georgia, who had joined him in Morenci in 1917 and had come with Manuel and Abrana to Los Angeles, was infamous for not remembering her birthday. When immigration officials would ask her when she was born, she would tell them "when the squash was getting ripe." It used to drive Manuel crazy and make him fearful that she would be deported. It wasn't enough to have your papers in order, he knew. You had to act the part.

"My grandma [Abrana] had three brothers who lived in Mexico," remembered Helen Lamp, the eldest daughter of Juan Aréchiga. "And they used to pray in Spanish. It was so beautiful. We were Catholic. We always were Catholic. I used to go to the church in Palo Verde, and I used to take flowers to the Virgin Mary."

===

THE ARÉCHIGAS SLOWLY saved money. They bought two additional lots and built two additional houses. They finally settled into the wood-frame house at 1771 Malvina Avenue. The house was set back from the street and perched above the driveway. There was a large pine tree out front, and there were stairs up to the front porch.

Inside there was wallpaper with geometric flower designs. There were little tchotchkes everywhere: family photos, religious icons, a painted piggy bank high up on a shelf. In her bedroom Abrana kept two matching wooden statuettes of the Pietà that she had picked up somewhere along the way. Each statuette contained a hidden drawer for sacred and sentimental objects. The house had running water and a rotary telephone.

Abrana went to church on Sundays and chatted with the neighbors in the street and in line at Don Francisco's grocery store, where everybody bought their bologna and Cokes and bags of rice and flour. She ran her house in her own particular way. The clothes hung up on lines in precise fashion—pants with pants, shirts with shirts. She kept a parrot and a mynah bird that used to repeat Spanish phrases.

In 1940 Manuel took out a permit to add an extra room. Sometimes cousins and grandkids would sleep on roll-away beds. On the lot next door, Manuel built a stucco home where the children lived as they got older: first Delphina, and then Celia, and then Tolina.

The three adjoining lots gave them space for their animals and space for their plants. There was a swing set. There were rosebushes. There were always Chihuahuas running around. Abrana kept chickens and goats and turkeys in a large enclosure. When it was time to make dinner, she would grab a chicken by the neck and swing it around in circles until it was dead. She used to give the chicken feet to her children and nephews and nieces, then later to her grandchildren. They could open and close the talons by pulling on the tendons running up the chicken's little legs.

One winter, it rained so much that there was a mudslide on the hill behind the house. The water came rushing down, and dirt and plants came with it. Abrana's chicken coops were ruined, and the chickens were drowned in the mud. It was like something mythological. A sign from on high. Dead chickens buried in the muck. Feathers caked with dirt. There was an eerie quiet at dawn, when the family was used to being awakened by the roosters. But nothing really changed. Abrana pulled the chickens out of the mud, one by one. She plucked the feathers and put them all in the icebox. The family ate chicken for weeks on end. They rebuilt the chicken coops. Life went on.

# 13.

THE FIRST PROFESSIONAL BASEBALL STADIUM IN LOS ANGELES WAS built inside an amusement park on the edge of what is now the city's downtown. Chutes Park opened at the turn of the century. This was after the railroads had been built and the oil tapped, after farmers discovered that irrigated well water made Los Angeles an appealing place to grow lemons and oranges. It was after the city's first land speculators began advertising its perfect climate in East Coast magazines.

Turn-of-the-century Los Angeles was a place for endless possibilities. The stadium was designed so that after the final out, the center-field fence opened up. Fans could stream down from the grandstand, trample over the infield dirt, and exit through the outfield into a wonderland of strange-looking buildings and unexpected attractions.

You could soar up over the city in a hot-air balloon and watch a live reenactment of the Battle of Hampton Roads, complete with ironclad ships. You could ride an early log-flume attraction called Shoot the Chutes (from which the park got its name). You could see monkeys and blood-sucking vampire bats. You could pass through a hall of mirrors called the Laughing Gallery and a haunted house called the Cave of Winds. There were contortionists, musicians, lions, sea lions, vaudevillians, and even a diving horse.

The baseball team in the middle of all this was the Los Angeles Angels of the nascent Pacific Coast League. The Angels were the brainchild of an entrepreneur named Jim Furlong Morley. Morley was a classic hustler. His father had opened the city's first shoe store a generation earlier. The Morley family were witnesses to, and beneficiaries of, the first great Los Angeles real-estate boom. Jim Morley did a little bit of everything. He promoted boxing. He opened bowling alleys and billiards halls (he was an ace pool player too).

He wore a straw hat with a wide brim. Baseball fit in among his other ventures. It was an amusement. Something to lose yourself in and lose your money on.

To promote his Angels, Morley turned his cocker spaniel into a mascot and signed famous players from the Major Leagues. One was the legendary pitcher Rube Waddell, who was known for racking up strikeouts, drinking to stupidity, and occasionally forgetting that he was actually playing ball. Waddell would sometimes find himself distracted from games at Chutes Park by the sound of passing fire engines and the sight of the hot-air balloons floating up over the stadium.

The Angels were an instant success. In 1903 they won the inaugural Pacific Coast League title with a band of ringers Morley had signed from competing leagues in baseball's wild, unregulated economy. These kinds of tactics would soon be outlawed. That very year, representatives from baseball leagues around the country signed on to something called the National Agreement, which meant that they would play by a mutually negotiated set of ground rules and submit themselves to government by a three-person panel called the National Commission.

The National Agreement set the stage for the rise of what has become Major League Baseball. It also created a mechanism by which leagues could suppress salaries by avoiding internecine bidding wars and more easily collude to maintain the sport's color barrier, which was unofficial but real. When the Coast League entered the agreement after the 1903 season, Morley was forced to return one of his star players, first baseman Cap Dillon, to the National League club from which he had been poached: the Brooklyn Superbas, who in the years to come would become more commonly known as the Dodgers.

Jim Morley's run with the Angels would soon come to an end as well. After the 1906 season and a heated disagreement about how the league handled the tragic San Francisco earthquake, the Angels were essentially taken from him in a coup by fellow owners and league executives. Morley had always spent bigger and talked louder than his colleagues. He was stubborn and hard to deal with. When they sent him away, he dug up home plate of his ballpark and took it with him. Chutes Park was briefly renamed Luna Park and then finally shuttered in 1914. The team then moved into a new stadium called Washington Park on the same site.

THE PACIFIC COAST League was blessed (and saddled) with an infinite supply of silly dramas and outsized personalities. It was technically a minor league on what was still then the geographic fringes of America. Yet it would grow to compete with the American League and the National League in terms of both talent and attendance. The men who ran the league and the men who invested in it were deeply committed to the idea that professional baseball could bring culture and respect to West Coast cities—and, with culture and respect, more money.

After Jim Morley was run out of the league, the Angels were taken over by a consortium of exactly such men. In 1909 they got some local competition. The expansion Vernon Tigers were based in a small city a few miles east of downtown LA. There was not much to do or see in Vernon, but unlike Los Angeles proper, you could legally buy, sell, and consume alcohol there on Sundays, which were big days for ticket sales. Not coincidentally, the team was owned by a beer magnate named Fred Maier.

Fred Maier soon died, and ownership was passed to his brother Ed. For a decade, Ed shuffled the Tigers around the region. The team was briefly renamed the Venice Tigers, and a new stadium was constructed near the beach. Then the stadium was taken apart and reassembled back in Vernon. Maier was eventually forced to sell the team after other league owners accused him of making side deals: secretly paying players beyond the official terms of their contracts to skirt league-wide compensation rules.

In 1919 the silent-film star Roscoe "Fatty" Arbuckle bought the Vernon Tigers. Arbuckle was a huge baseball fan, and at first his touch as an owner seemed to be golden. The Tigers dominated on the field and ultimately bested the Angels for the Pacific Coast League title, their second in a row. But soon the entire franchise would crumble. In the course of the 1920 season it was revealed that during the previous year's pennant race, members of the Salt Lake City Bees were taking bribes from gamblers to throw games to Vernon.

The whole thing had been arranged through Vernon's first baseman, Hal Chase. It was the biggest scandal to ever hit the Coast League, but it would soon be overshadowed. In September 1920 the news got out that the Chicago White Sox had thrown the 1919 World Series to Cincinnati. The Black Sox scandal practically erased the sleazy doings of the Salt Lake Bees and Vernon Tigers from popular memory. But there was also a common thread behind the concurrent fixes. One of the men accused of arranging the bribes taken by the Chicago players (and making a huge profit for himself by betting on the series) was none other than Hal Chase.

The Tigers would win a third straight title in 1920, but the luster was off. Arbuckle lost interest and sold the team. Prohibition put an end to beer sales during Sunday games or any other games. In 1926 the Tigers were moved to San Francisco, where they became the Mission Reds.

The city of Vernon's ultimate place in baseball lore would not be as the home of a ball club but, decades later, as the home of the meatpacking company Farmer John, makers of the iconic Dodger Dog. The Farmer John slaughterhouse is still located just a block from the site of the old Vernon Stadium. Inside, it is a place where pigs become hot dogs. Outside, it looks more like the kind of building you might have found in Chutes Park. The walls are painted with fat happy hogs, floating upward, unhurried, fleshy hot-air balloons in a bright-blue sky.

# 14.

IN 1935 A MAN NAMED DAVID GRAHAM FISCHER APPEARED, LIKE AN unexpected gift, in Frank Wilkinson's life. Fischer had the keys to the entire universe, or at least the entire globe. He was starting something unheard of at the time: a proto-semester-at-sea program called the Inter-Oceanic University. He had commissioned a 279-foot luxury steam yacht called the *Casiana*. The ship was owned by oil baron Edward Doheny and docked in San Pedro, where Frank had done his rowing on the crew team. Frank was now entering his senior year at UCLA and beginning to think about what might come next. Fischer offered the deal of a lifetime: if Frank could help him enlist a batch of students willing to pay for an education at sea, he would be given a cushy job onboard.

Along with a couple UCLA pals, Frank took Fischer up on his offer. He spent hours and days and weeks recruiting. He traversed Riverside and San Bernardino and the San Gabriel Valley. In the hot sun he trekked through the parts of Los Angeles that were still so far away as to not be Los Angeles yet. He sat down with rich fathers and mothers and convinced them to part with checks so that their children might experience the world beyond the orange and date groves and the neatly arranged tract houses. Meanwhile, Fischer threw parties on board the *Casiana*. He took out ads in the *Los Angeles Times* and held office hours at the Biltmore Hotel downtown, where he enrolled new students. The list of faculty was announced in the newspapers, and a route was drawn onto a map at the Inter-Oceanic University office. Then, all of a sudden, David Graham Fischer was gone. The money was gone. And all that was left of the Inter-Oceanic University was a few filing cabinets and a lingering police investigation.

Fischer, it turned out, had been a Hollywood con-man type for a decade. He had started a business in 1924 with the beautifully fake-sounding name, Author's Publishing Corporation. Three years later, he skirted a fraud charge after accepting $2,700 from the author of a crime novel called *The Hooded Asp* before failing to actually publish a single copy of the book. Fischer successfully argued that he was unable to publish the book because creditors had taken away his printing press. (*The Hooded Asp* was a contemporary LA gangster story featuring a minor crime boss and a mysterious device that could heal broken bones; it was published a couple years later to little acclaim.) There were clues that things might go wrong with Fischer: in June 1935 a Dr. Frederick Woellner resigned from his position as vice chancellor of the Inter-Oceanic University, concerned that Fischer was falsely implying that his program was sponsored by UCLA. But they were not the kinds of clues that most people would have noticed. By August, Fischer had disappeared. He would never be found.

All that was left of Fischer were his correspondence and his Rolodex. And this too was the kind of thing that happened to Frank Wilkinson. The dog running down the street with a rope around its neck turned out to be a coyote. But con man or not, Fischer had gotten under Frank's skin. He wanted now, more than ever, to travel: to see the world. During his final year at UCLA, Frank became increasingly certain that he would join the ministry. Around that same time, after her death in 1935, Frank also heard about a woman named Jane Addams: a pacifist social worker who won the Nobel Peace Prize for her work with Chicago's poor. She struck him as the embodiment of the social gospel, this woman who devoted her life to the most impoverished Americans. Frank decided that after he graduated, he would set off to Europe and the Holy Land with a fraternity brother named Del Harter. But first, Frank would go to Chicago and see the work that Jane Addams had begun at her Hull House. Then he and Del would make their way to the East Coast. Finally, they would set sail across the Atlantic.

Frank graduated from UCLA in June 1936 with a bachelor's in political science. "You will go far and you will always keep the right kind of flag flying above you," wrote Glenn Randall Phillips, the minister of Hollywood Methodist Church, in a note of congratulations. Frank figured he would see the world, then come home and enroll in a seminary somewhere. He had a small inheritance from an uncle who had died in a car crash and the help of his family to keep him going along the way. He had, in Del Harter, a friend and companion who was already a seasoned traveler. Frank had read books by the famous thrill seeker Richard Halliburton and decided that his own trip would be a grand adventure: he had notions of spending nights in a sleeping bag and getting by on only a dollar a day. And he had, finally, the advice of his father, the great beacon of virtue in his life. "My son, I only ask one thing," said Dr. Wilkinson as Frank pulled away toward Chicago and his grand tour. "Do not allow alcoholic beverages to touch your lips."

# 15.

THE CHILDREN HAD AN ENTIRE WORLD AT THEIR DISPOSAL. THE HILLS. Elysian Park, with its acres and acres of trees and bluffs and hidden secrets and winding mysterious paths to nowhere. They had room to follow their imaginations. Gradually, some of Palo Verde's streets were paved, so they could roller skate down the long grades and jump rope on the asphalt.

They had the city at their disposal as well. They could make their way downtown. It was only a few miles to walk or an easy ride on the streetcar. They could go to the movies. In the 1930s there was no better place in the world to watch movies than Los Angeles, the city where they were made. There were a dozen theaters within a six-block range on Broadway. At night they would be lit up in neon and packed with people from across society's wide spectrum: the richest of the rich in fur coats alongside the humble kids from Palo Verde in khaki pants and T-shirts. There were even a couple of actors who lived in the neighborhood: a tall, serious, blonde woman named Glen Walters, whose career had begun in the 1920s, and, more famously, Chris-Pin Martin.

Martin was known for starring as a sidekick in the Cisco Kid franchise. He had a mustache and a double chin and a big stomach. He lived up on a hill overlooking the neighborhood and used to call himself the "Self-Appointed Mayor of Palo Verde." He was a local character.

One day in the spring of 1935, a group of kids from the neighborhood went down to a theater on Spring Street, just off Broadway. During the Depression the Lyceum played nickel movies. It had turrets like some kind of medieval English castle and had battlements across the facade. The towers were lined with lightbulbs and illuminated at night. It was one of those buildings that could exist only in Los Angeles: architecture so outrageous and out of

*1771 Malvina Avenue*

place that it fit in perfectly. There was a high balcony where the kids liked to sit. They might have been seeing Boris Karloff's *Bride of Frankenstein.*

It was here that the next great tragedy of Abrana and Manuel Aréchiga's life occurred—or at least *likely* occurred. One version of this story, told by descendants of the Aréchiga family, is that the kids were sitting in the front of the balcony, playing around in the first row, when Manuel Jr. suddenly fell over the railing, just like that, all the way down to the seats below.

Another version is told by Gene Cabral, who says he was there that day at the Lyceum. Gene, who was a year younger than Manuel Jr., is the second-youngest son of Antonia Aréchiga (Manuel's sister) and Paulino Cabral (Abrana's cousin)—in other words, Gene and the Aréchiga children were cousins on both their mother's and father's sides.

As Gene remembers it, after the show Manuel Jr. tripped coming down the stairs. He tumbled all the way to the bottom. The boy who spent his afternoons in the hillsides unsupervised among cactus plants and tall climbing trees and loose cliffs overlooking steep ravines was wrecked not in any of those places but indoors, in a nickel movie theater downtown. "He never recovered," said Gene.

Manuel Jr. was a hyperactive but happy and good-natured kid. They called him *La Mosca*, the fly, for the way he seemed to be moving every direction at once. The details are hazy. But after he fell, he was driven back to Palo Verde, to his mother's house on Malvina Avenue. "At that time, *mi tia* believed a lot in *sobadoras*," Gene recalled. "Massage type of thing. And instead of taking him to the emergency room, they kept him there and brought in this sobadora. I think that did more harm."

As the sobadora worked on Manuel, massaging his broken bones and crunching them and not allowing them to set, Gene and the other kids stood outside of the house and listened to his screams. It would have been impossible to ignore. The neighborhood kids. Friends, cousins, brothers, sisters, standing on the pavement or in the garden, milling around with the turkeys and goats, listening. "We could hear. We were all outside listening, and he was howling in pain."

Abrana and Manuel would have been inside the house with him, doing the best they could to take care of their son: the beloved little boy who was perfectly healthy when he left that day for the movies. The rest of the world must have stopped, faded away, the entire universe reduced to one room in the house on Malvina Avenue where he lay, the entire world, from Zacatecas to Morenci to Palo Verde, reduced to the sound of his cries.

Mañito died, according to his death certificate, on June 1, 1935. His age was listed poignantly in its most complete form: 8 years, 7 months, and 28 days. His occupation was listed as "school boy."

The wake was held at the Aréchiga home. The casket sat in the living room as friends and family and neighbors piled in and stood out in the yard among the animals and fruit trees. These were the moments when the community of Palo Verde stood the strongest:

everybody intertwined, cousins married to friends and neighbors to siblings. Plates of food overflowing and tears spilling and people spilling out into the yard. The mass was held at the Santo Niño church on Paducah Street. The interment was at Calvary Cemetery in East Los Angeles.

But here is where we come across another one of those curious contradictions between the oral record and the written one, one of those places where the documented history of a life, even one as short as Manuel Jr.'s, feels insufficient. His death certificate listed his cause of death as pulmonary tuberculosis and his place of death as General Hospital: a condition that would have nothing to do with falling down stairs and a place that was relatively far away from Palo Verde.

The document is clear. You can see it scribbled in ink, in slanted thick handwriting. Yet I sat with Gene Cabral, in his garage office, the walls covered with photos of his family, of Frank Sinatra, of Elvis Presley, and listened to him tell me the story of his cousin. I sat with grandchildren of Abrana and Manuel Aréchiga as they recounted the story of the uncle they never got the chance to meet. The broken bones. The screams.

Is the family recounting a myth? Or is there some truth that reconciles the story and the paperwork? It is certainly possible that at the last minute, Manuel and Abrana rushed their dying son to General Hospital. Memory is fallible, of course, and perhaps this part of the story slipped away after so many years. But it seems unlikely that Manuel Jr. would have died from tuberculosis, which was extremely infectious and unfortunately common, only for the family to have mistaken the cause of his death at the time or to have obfuscated it over the course of generations.

There is another possibility. In the early part of the twentieth century, nativist groups in Los Angeles used tuberculosis as a way to justify discrimination against Mexican and Filipino immigrants. Hospitals that treated tubercular patients were among the few officially segregated public facilities in the city. It's not inconceivable that a lazy doctor could have just written the death of a young Mexican boy up to the disease and left it at that. It is doubtful that anybody would have checked a doctor's work or held him accountable on the details, especially at General Hospital, which mostly served LA's poorest citizens.

# 16.

In 1867 Antonio López de Santa Anna was broke and living in Staten Island, New York. It is remarkable that only two decades after the US invasion of Mexico, the commander of the Mexican Army found himself in exile in the country that had caused so many of his problems. Yet that is what happened.

How Santa Anna got to New York is a book unto itself: there was a chance meeting with US Secretary of State William Seward on the Caribbean island of St. Thomas, there were South American revolutionaries turned grifters, there was a ship purchased and a brief stay in New Jersey, and there was a great deal of money lost. After all that, there was another misadventure in Veracruz and a near execution, and finally the sweet relief of exile.

During his time in New York, Santa Anna hoped he could re-amass his fortune. One of his schemes for doing so involved a substance he brought with him from Mexico. It was a sticky latex that oozed from the bark of the sapodilla trees that grew in his native Veracruz, and it was called *chicle*. Pre-Colombian societies in Mexico had been chewing chicle for thousands of years. But Santa Anna thought it could be used for more than that. For instance, it might make a good alternative, or additive, to the vulcanized rubber from which buggy tires were then being made.

Santa Anna showed the chicle he brought to a local inventor named Thomas Adams. Adams tried for years to turn the chicle into something of industrial use: tires, shoes, anything that might make them a buck. Finally, after watching Santa Anna chew on the chicle as he tinkered futilely in his laboratory, Adams decided to try something simpler. He molded the chicle into little balls, wrapped them in colorful packaging, and began selling chicle at drugstores. By then, Santa Anna had departed from New York and left behind his dreams of chicle entrepreneurship. And so the chewing-gum industry began in earnest without him.

The plain chicle balls were a success, but Adams's company really took off when he began to experiment with flavoring. His licorice-flavored gum, Black Jack, was an especially big hit. He built a factory and put his gum in vending machines and started selling it in packs of precut slices. Suddenly, by the turn of the century, there were gum companies all over the country.

In Philadelphia, brothers Robert and Frank Fleer put out a product called Double Bubble: the first bubble gum. In Chicago, William Wrigley Jr. built an empire out of Juicy Fruit. In 1921 Wrigley became the majority owner of the Chicago Cubs and, with the Cubs, their Pacific Coast League affiliate, the Los Angeles Angels. In 1925 Wrigley opened a stadium for the Angels in Los Angeles. It had Spanish-style roof tiles and a clock tower behind home plate. Two years before the Cubs' iconic park in Chicago was renamed in his honor, Los Angeles had its own Wrigley Field.

As committed as American consumers were to chewing gum, they may have been even more obsessed with baseball. The 1920s were the time of Babe Ruth and Lou Gehrig: outsized heroes whose deeds were brought into homes for the first time over the radio, players who captured the imagination but who could still seem distant without the benefit of television or even color photos. For decades, cigarette companies had been including trading cards as promotional items. Cards offered the intimacy and urgency of color. They gave you that tactile sense of connection. That connection deepened as baseball became something more than just a game you played or watched people play: it became a realm for mythology and hero worship. You could hold Babe Ruth in your hands. You could look into his eyes and see the lines on his forehead.

In 1933 the Goudey Gum Company released a line called Big League Chewing Gum and became one of the first gum manufacturers to include baseball cards in its packs. The cards were beautifully rendered, with intimate portraits looming over bold colored backgrounds and short player biographies printed on the reverse side. Babe Ruth was marked card No. 1 in the set. Fleer, Bowman, and ultimately Topps would follow Goudey into the trading-card promotion, which would grow and grow until the card itself was the thing, the object of worship, and the player on it was an afterthought and the hard pink stick of gum itself a novelty, leaving only traces of white powder on the cardboard before disappearing altogether.

But this would all come later. This would all come a hundred years after Antonio López de Santa Anna brought his chicle to Staten Island and accidentally gave birth to an entire industry, a hundred years after Santa Anna once again became part of the weird, amorphous story that is baseball.

# 17.

MAXWELL STREET WAS ALIVE LIKE NOTHING FRANK HAD EVER SEEN before. There were people everywhere: poor, broken bodies struggling down the sidewalk, bartering anything they might have had. The smell of rotten fruit. The sight of old junk laid out on blankets. Blue jeans and rusted teakettles. People eating from trash cans and sleeping in the street. Frank was twenty-two years old, but he saw Chicago with the eyes of a child just coming into the world.

The poverty seemed to wrap Frank up. This was the first time in his life that he was free of the social structures that had carried him, almost like a raft coasting downriver through high school and college. This was the end of ignorance. "I was on my own, the world began, and Maxwell Street and Hull House was the beginning of life," he later said.

Frank stood there amid the junk as if paralyzed. And all he could do, all he could think to do, was to start feeding people. One by one. He went through all his savings, three months' worth, taking every person he saw around the corner to a diner. Then he went up to Northwestern University, to the local branch of his fraternity, and raised a collection. More meals. He went down to the lakefront and one of the fancy hotels and started asking there. "Do you know about Maxwell Street?" It was a question and also a plea. Here was this nice boy, and he looked as if he had seen a ghost—a city of ghosts. It was absurd, he realized later. He could not solve poverty in America by himself. But then again, maybe he could.

Soon Frank would go up to Detroit, where he would meet up with his traveling partner, Del Harter. They would hitchhike across the Northeast. Frank would see a whorehouse in Scranton (but not have sex, of course) and stay in a flophouse in New York City's Bowery. In the fall of 1936, Frank's sister Hildegarde came to New York to talk him out of his vagabond lifestyle. The letters he was sending home worried the family. She took him to dinners in fine restaurants and to plays on Broadway. "If you want to travel like this, do it as a Wilkinson should travel," she told him. She offered to let him drive back to Los Angeles in a brand-new Packard she had bought. She gave him a pair of wool pajamas. But Frank insisted on his flophouse. He insisted on his sleeping bag—even as inside it, stuffed among his things, he kept letters of introduction from the mayor, the governor, and the chief of police.

Before crossing the Atlantic, Frank and Del traveled the Eastern Seaboard. They visited Maine and Washington, DC. They showed up at the White House and presented their letters of introduction and were granted a peek at FDR himself, sitting in the Oval Office. They were given cards with Roosevelt's signature on them. They also saw New York City: the elegant Chrysler Building and the Empire State Building, the tallest in the world, completed just six years earlier.

Frank and Del shipped off for the Old World from New York Harbor on a blisteringly cold night in early November. They were aboard a Norwegian freighter called the *Ingria*, which was bound for Portugal. If everything went according to plan, they would be spending Christmas in the Holy Land. Frank had visions of serenity and peace. The Church of the Nativity. Desert landscapes. The manger scenes from front lawns and church entryways in Beverly Hills. It was a rough crossing, but they dined each night with the captain and his first mate. The floating university had never materialized, but this was something better. This was floating real life. Here was Frank Wilkinson on a working ship, steaming across the Atlantic, bound for real adventure with no curriculum, no restraint.

# 18.

Every summer, Palo Verde would empty itself. School would be over, and entire families would make their way north, to Simi Valley or Fresno or Stockton or Santa Clara, in order to work the fields, *las piscas.* Doors would be left unlocked. Toys would be left strewn about in front of houses. In 1935 the Aréchigas probably left not long after they buried Manuel Jr. Kids and cousins piled into the back of their Model T Ford, with everything quieter than it had been the year before, quieter than they wanted it to be.

They picked apricots, onions, grapes, and often walnuts. They camped out in big tents and woke up with the sun to make their way out to the fields and groves in waiting trucks. The children would carry pails like the ones another kid living in another world might use while playing on the beach. The men would shake the walnut trees with long, hooked sticks and watch the nuts fall from the branches onto the dirt, and the little ones would scurry under the trees, sunlight filtering through the wide, soft, green leaves, to collect them. Their fingers would be stained green afterward.

Everybody worked: husbands and wives, brothers and sisters. They would fill sacks of walnuts or boxes of grapes and take them to the stores to be weighed. In the afternoon the kids would swim in the San Joaquin River. At night there were campfires and guitars and simple meals of rice and beans. After a few months the families would pack their tents and collect their cash and make their way back to Los Angeles to tend their own more-humble gardens, to return to their jobs in the brickyards and train yards, to go back to school at Palo Verde Elementary and back to church at Santo Niño, where Father Tomas Matin awaited them with communion wafers and catechism classes.

Sometimes the harvest paid well, and sometimes the families barely broke even. But slowly, year by year, the families put their money away. They used it to pay rent or buy their homes or keep their cars in running shape. Working in the fields was both a return to the rural lives that many of Palo Verde's residents had left behind in Mexico and an embrace of the American Dream: the accumulation of wealth and security by any means necessary. The slow and steady process of putting down roots.

# 19.

ON CLIFFORD CLINTON'S SECOND TRIP TO CHINA, HE WITNESSED A line of men being held prisoner in a town square. "Their arms were behind them, and their necks were bared," he wrote many years later. "A man stood above them with a great two-handled blade, awaiting a signal." It was about 1910, and Clifford was about ten years old. He was a long way from Los Angeles, the city that he would change forever. But he would carry this memory to the grave: "As I stood, riveted to the ground, the signal came. The blade dropped on the first man. His head rolled to the ground, and blood spurted from his neck."

Soon the Clinton family would return to the Bay Area, where Clifford had been born. His mother and father were serious people who were devoted to having children, feeding the poor, and enlightening the unenlightened. They were Salvation Army missionaries. And soon his father would take on another kind of challenge: he would enter the restaurant business. Clifford watched his father struggle, opening cafeteria after cafeteria. He watched his mother die at forty-two after giving birth to her tenth child. School flummoxed Clifford, and his family thought he was slow. His father was a serious and hardworking man, but he was resentful. Clifford inherited the work ethic, but resentment did not suit him. He learned to love his fellow man. He read and took correspondence courses. He learned at his own pace. He observed. He waited for his moment.

Clifford Clinton loved ice cream, and he loved self-improvement. When World War I came, he enlisted. He joined Eisenhower's tank battalion and made it all the way to France, where he waited in the cold and mud and wrote letters to a girl back home named Nelda. He was still waiting there, watching the planes soar overhead and hearing the big guns boom, when Armistice Day at last came. Clifford made it only to the outskirts of the fighting, but while he was gone, he became a man. He developed convictions. He was slight of frame and wore glasses. Through them, Clifford Clinton saw the world. He came home to California sure that there was no calling more holy than to feed your fellow man.

Clifford Clinton was transfixed by the inefficiencies at his father's restaurant. He came to believe that running a cafeteria could in itself be a missionary act. There was a purity in it. There was an elegance. This was the 1920s. Anything was possible.

He married Nelda and bought his father out of the business. He developed the concept of uniform portion size and wrote thousands of recipes down on index cards and installed automated conveyor belts to carry dirty dishes back into the kitchen. He wrote manuals for his staff. He wanted only the finest for his customers. But he wanted even more. He wanted something bigger. So in 1931 Clifford Clinton did the unthinkable: he left San Francisco behind and drove down to Los Angeles in a large Studebaker to start a business in the middle of the deepest economic depression in the modern history of the world.

This was Herbert Hoover's Los Angeles, full of workers struggling to get by and the general feeling of "now what?" This was Los Angeles on the decline, on the precipice of falling back into the nothing place it had been before the water came and the real-estate developers bet everything on it. But Clinton's new place would be the opposite of depressing. There would be an ice cream counter. There would be an organ and an organist to play it. There would be only one rule at Clifton's Cafeteria—that's what he called the place, combining his first and last names—and that was the Golden Rule. At Clifton's you paid what you wanted. Clifford Clinton made his cafeteria into a home for his guests and made a family out of his employees. He called them associates. He put them on a medical plan. The critics told him he was doing it all wrong. They told him he was bringing unwelcome elements into Los Angeles. There were enough destitute, enough homeless already. And now you want to offer them free food?

When so many hungry people came to Clifton's that they overwhelmed the place, Clifton simply opened another cafeteria. He called it the Penny. You could get a portion of food for a penny and a full five-course meal for a nickel. Clifton's and the Penny became the kind of places where people of any race or social status might sit side by side at the counter. When the Twenty-First Amendment made it legal to sell alcohol, Clifford Clinton refused. He was a Christian man, and his cafeterias would remain family friendly, always. He wrote his own newsletter and put it out on the tables. It was called *Food for Thot*.

Clifford Clinton believed that there was no end to what a restaurant could be. He opened his most ambitious cafeteria yet, on Broadway. It had a barbershop and a beauty salon. It had an actual babbling brook inside, a waterfall, and bark on the walls. He called it Brookdale. A young writer named Ray Bradbury used to be a regular. A young animator named Walt Disney stared at the scene around him and imagined the possibilities. One day a county commissioner named John Anson Ford came through the door and asked for Clifford Clinton. He had a request for the man who fed the poor of Los Angeles: can you help us feed its sick as well? The General Hospital had just opened, and its food services were a disaster. Would Clinton straighten things out?

And so he did: he walked the halls of the hospital, which rose like an ocean liner out of the sprawling flatlands east of the Los Angeles River, and encountered a tangle of corruption and incompetence so vast that fixing it would require taking on the entire city's power structure, from the mayor's office to the police department to even the powerful Chandler family, owners of the *Los Angeles Times*. The cops were protecting and tipping off prostitution rackets, gamblers, and drug dealers. The mayor's office was in on it. The newspapers were just fine with that, as long as their business interests were protected.

After the hospital job, Clifford Clinton was named to the Grand Jury. And after the Grand Jury, Clinton made it his business to clean up the city, the whole mess of it. He joined with some fellow Christians to form a group called Citizens' Independent Vice Investigating Committee (CIVIC). They were prudish, seeing sin behind every parked car and under every park bench. But they were fearless in a way that only the divinely inspired can be fearless. The founding members of CIVIC included a fundamentalist evangelical radio preacher named Robert Schuler, an activist named Louise Blatherwick, a Methodist minister named Wendell L. Miller, and a Beverly Hills physician named A. M. Wilkinson, whose youngest son, Frank, had just graduated from UCLA and was off in Europe on a grand adventure.

# 20.

Frank Wilkinson was determined to rough it. To live humbly. To think deeply about the world and his place in it. When he and Del landed in Portugal, they were connected via the US Embassy with a group of Portuguese business titans who were on their way to Spain. The businessmen offered Frank and Del a ride to Seville and along the way took them out to a meal. Not wanting to be impolite, Frank drank the glass of wine that was poured for him. He had barely landed in Europe, and he had already disobeyed his father's sole admonishment: alcohol had already touched his lips. Frank was sick to his stomach. As Del slept that night, Frank scrawled out a long and tortured letter home.

They traveled across North Africa. They were robbed while sleeping under a bridge in Tunisia. They watched pilgrims making their way to local holy sites during Ramadan. The word of God had been the only word Frank ever knew. But now he saw faith manifesting itself differently, in a different situation, with different kinds of people and different beliefs. And it no longer made sense. Pitiful. Irrational. Absurd. Faith made sense if you were a rich kid in Beverly Hills, your life clearly blessed by a higher power. But for the destitute of North Africa, what did faith even offer? It was ridiculous to march across the desert for some assurance of holy redemption. Only a fool would do such a thing, Frank thought, even as he continued on his own pilgrimage.

In Alexandria, Frank saw a live sex show. A woman smoked a cigarette in her vagina. "I watched sexual intercourse for the first time in my life," Frank recalled. "And it was just disgusting." He was twenty-two years old. Every night, before nodding off, he read a chapter from his Bible. He would write the name of the city where he was sleeping in the margins. He was making his way closer to

Bethlehem: the heart of everything he was raised to believe. He was seeing the world as it really was.

Frank and Del took a train across the Sinai Peninsula to Jerusalem. Frank hummed "Silent Night" to himself and stared out the window. Years later, Frank's college friend Gilbert Harrison would say this of Frank: "He was not well educated, not brilliant, but he was sincerity from his eyeballs down to his toes." And so Frank looked out the window as the train cut across the same desert that Moses had once wandered, and he reminisced about his childhood. He remembered riding around Beverly Hills on the back of a pickup truck, singing Christmas carols with all his church friends.

At Jerusalem, they boarded a bus for Bethlehem. The bus passed through a field, and Frank saw Arab shepherds with tall canes. It was pastoral. It was beautiful. It was Christmas Eve just as he had always imagined. Until they reached Bethlehem. The city was packed with people. It was so crowded he could barely make his way to the outer doors of the Church of the Nativity. There were beggars everywhere. Outside the church doors, he saw a teenage mother in rags, nursing two babies at once and asking for money. Her eyes were dripping with sores. Trachoma, Frank could see, thinking of his father the doctor. The pus from the teenage mother's eyes dripped down onto the babies' heads. Inside the sanctuary, there were different sects fighting for space. It was all elbows and glares. It was chaos. Catholics, Greek Orthodox, Protestants all believing themselves the holy and right.

They stayed on in Jerusalem. Frank slept in a Turkish bath in the basement of the YMCA. He saw the sights. The Damascus Gate. The Wailing Wall. The Dome of the Rock. He began to think he was going crazy. Maxwell Street and now Bethlehem. He spent hours in the Church of the Holy Sepulcher, built on the site where Jesus was crucified, struggling with his faith. He contracted trachoma himself. His eyes scarred over, and, blinded, he was guided by kind strangers through the limestone passageways of Old Jerusalem to the British Ophthalmological Hospital. He visited the kibbutzim and the Sea of Galilee. He saw, in his own words, "the failure of our religions to practice their teachings in terms of social concerns."

Later, in Beirut, Frank went to the American University library and looked up the word *atheism*. Beverly Hills High School, four years at UCLA. But only now was he truly grasping this concept, this possibility. He began to write letters home: to friends, to mentors, to his mother and father. "There is no God," he wrote.

═══

FRANK AND DEL traveled to Syria, Greece, Italy, France, and England. They went to Germany and Poland, through Scandinavia and finally to the Soviet Union. The experiences shaped not only Frank Wilkinson but also the legend of Frank Wilkinson. His life would become a story unto itself. These were the anecdotes he would tell in the decades to come, tell them until they became rehearsed and polished things.

In Paris, Frank slept in the garden of a Russian Orthodox nunnery. Grass and trees and a locked gate that kept them safe at night. One night he was asleep, and it began to rain. He was awakened by a nun, who led him up to her room. And there, to his horror and ultimate thrill, she took off her clothes, and they lay beside each other in bed. They did not have sex. But it was enough to send him into a deep spiral of shame. He was twenty-three years old.

By his count, he visited five hundred churches in Europe. He was looking for God in Italy and Greece and Portugal and Spain. In Nuremberg he witnessed a terrible and impressive Nazi rally. He met an American woman there and had his first real affair. She was from Long Island. Finally, Frank and Del traveled north through Norway and Finland and into the Soviet Union.

The USSR was not like the other countries they went to. Their cameras were taken at the border. Their travel was coordinated by a state-run agency. And despite all of this, Frank saw something there that he felt was missing everywhere else. He saw a backward society trying to push its way forward. He saw a country free of the chains of religion. He saw a country where it all seemed to fit together, everybody in it for everybody else, so orderly and natural. This was a better world on Earth. This made sense to Frank. "We do not have anti-Semitism," his tour guide told him. "It is forbidden."

He marveled at the efficiency of a collective farm in the countryside. He marveled at the clean streets, old women sweeping everywhere with brooms made of twigs. There was poverty, yes, but this was not Maxwell Street. "There was no filth," he said later.

Frank saw what they wanted him to see; he saw what his own heart needed him to see. He entered Russia during a time of purges—of genocide and political repression—and although he may not have realized it yet, he left a budding Communist.

When he first came back to America, Frank wouldn't even celebrate Christmas. No gifts. No church services. No trees. There was no God anyway. So what was the point?

# 21.

Nobody really knows how Abrana Aréchiga became Two Guns Brooks.

One legend, passed down through the Aréchiga family, has it that Manuel was a womanizer: a good provider and a sweet man, but also prone to coming home with lipstick on his neck. One time, he allegedly encountered his son-in-law at a bar and, with women around both arms, said, "You want one too?"

Another time Abrana supposedly got wind that Manuel was out with a girlfriend and armed herself before leaving the house to chase them down. Two guns. One for Manuel and one for the woman he was with.

There's another story, courtesy of Beto Elias. Beto and his family lived a block over from the Aréchigas on Gabriel, and their next-door neighbors, the Novoas, lived in a house that was directly across from Abrana and Manuel's: all you had to do was cross Malvina, walk through the empty lot opposite the Aréchiga house, and you'd reach the back of the Novoa household, which faced onto Gabriel.

"Don Jose Novoa used to sit on the back porch and read the newspaper," Beto said. According to Beto, Don Jose and Abrana got into some kind of neighborly fight. She was not happy with the result. So one morning, while Don Jose was outside on the back porch reading his paper, Abrana raised a gun and fired a few times in his direction. The shots rang out in the quiet community and echoed off the hillsides, and Don Jose dropped his paper and scrambled back into the house. "I don't know whether she meant to scare him or to hit him," Beto said. "We'll never know. And that's the last time he ever sat there."

# 22.

EVERYTHING WAS CHANGING FOR FRANK WILKINSON. WHEN HE GOT back from Europe, he spent hours pondering the meaning of life, searching for what he liked to call a "basis for his ethics." He lost himself in household chores. Then the chores lost their meaning too. He tried graduate school at UCLA, but it didn't stick. He went to his very first picket line. He rekindled his friendship with Jean Benson, a UCLA classmate who had been a patient of his father's. Jean, whose politics had always been more progressive than his, seemed to get Frank, or at least tolerate him.

Frank finally got a hearing aid: a big old contraption that he wore around his neck like a purse, with a wire that strapped around his head and into his ear. As the years went by, Frank would go through a succession of smaller and smaller hearing aids. Eventually, he would find one that could fit into his shirt pocket. The hearing aids became a part of his life almost in the same way that his deafness had. They were always breaking down or getting lost, and he was always dealing with the fallout. His papers are littered with correspondence with hearing-aid manufacturers and insurers, appointments with audiologists, and repair receipts.

With his very first hearing aid on, he was overwhelmed by the background noise he hadn't heard before. The sound of a buzzing fly. The scraping of silverware against china. It was too much, but it was not enough. He brought it with him to a concert. For the first time in his life, he could really hear music. He didn't have to lie under his sister's piano anymore. For the first time in his life, he really heard his own voice, and it instantly dropped a full octave.

Frank put that voice to use as a public speaker. He gave lectures all over town about what he had seen on his travels: the beauty and horror of Europe and the Holy Land. But still, Frank could be hard to tolerate. One time, he was ticketed for speeding in Beverly Hills and then refused to pay the fine. He was determined to get himself thrown into jail. He wanted to see firsthand what conditions were like behind bars. Even this mission was almost thwarted by Frank's own privilege. When it came time for sentencing, the judge turned out to be a friend of his father's. The judge called Dr. Wilkinson and asked if he'd like to pay the fine so that Frank might avoid a sentence. Frank's father declined. He would not stand in the way of Frank's foolish personal growth, so Frank was convicted to two days in lockup downtown.

There was just one thing, Frank told the judge. He had tickets to a concert at the Hollywood Bowl. Could he report to jail after the show? The judge acquiesced. It was all delightful and easy. A little social experiment. But the next time Frank Wilkinson got himself thrown into jail, things would not be made so convenient.

# 23.

ALL DUKE SNIDER EVER WANTED WAS TO BE RESPECTED. HE WAS born that way, born big and strong and destined for adoration and destined to never be quite satisfied by it. He was born in 1926 in a small apartment in the back of a grocery store in the Boyle Heights section of Los Angeles. "It was a breech birth," he wrote in his autobiography, "so I entered the world by sliding home."

His given name was Edwin Donald, but his father called him Duke. His father worked in a tire factory, and Duke was his only child. The Sniders didn't make much money, but they made time for their boy. They gave him everything they could. His mother mended his shirts and patched up his shoes with cardboard. But no apartment in the back of a grocery store could contain a boy like the Duke.

One way you can think about Duke Snider is as the mirror image of Manuel Aréchiga Jr. The Sniders came to Los Angeles at about the same time as the Aréchiga family, and Duke was born less than a year before Manuel Jr. Like the Aréchigas, the Sniders didn't have much in the way of savings or in the way of education. But unlike the Aréchigas, they were white and spoke English. That meant they had a much bigger and more open city at their disposal.

The Sniders, like so many white families in the early twentieth century, had come to Los Angeles from the rural Midwest. They were drawn by the same promises as everybody else. They were looking for the same kind of prosperity. They moved from Boyle Heights to a quiet street with trees and sidewalks. They moved to a place where their son could fulfill his potential. They saved up and bought a house in a sleepy working-class suburb called Compton.

It's hard to imagine now, but the Compton of Duke Snider's youth was as white as he was, as white as a Dodger's home uniform. Compton, the Chamber of Commerce wrote, was a place

*Duke Snider*

"where workers may live close to their work in inexpensive homes of individuality, where flowers and gardens may be grown the year round. White help prevails." To keep it this way, Compton instituted some of the region's harshest restrictive real-estate covenants. This meant that if you wanted to sell a house in Compton, you were legally bound to sell it to a person who was white.

But it took more than legal language to keep the city white. Segregation was not just a matter of words on a page; it was an act of injustice that required constant vigilance by its perpetrators. The police force harassed black motorists even if they were just passing through. The city council passed legislation to enforce segregation.

The Federal Housing Authority denied loans to black families. The state government revoked the licenses of real-estate agents who sold homes to black families in white neighborhoods.

In the 1920s none of this made Compton remarkable in the context of Los Angeles or of the broader United States. Nor does it make the Sniders remarkable for moving there. Abrana and Manuel Aréchiga settled into Palo Verde because it was the best place they could raise their family. Ward and Florence Snider settled in Compton for that same reason. It was affordable. It was close to work. It was a good place to raise a son.

Duke grew into his nickname. He became obsessed with sports, especially baseball. He stayed home from school to sit by the radio and listen to the World Series. He closed his eyes and pictured Yankee Stadium in the Bronx and Ebbets Field in Brooklyn. When his folks could afford it, they took him to Wrigley Field to see the Los Angeles Angels and his favorite player, the speedy center fielder Jigger Statz.

There was no shortage of heroes for Duke to idolize. One of those heroes was an older boy from the other side of town named Jackie Robinson. When he was barely a teenager, Duke and his buddies would watch with awe as Jackie suited up for Pasadena Junior College and UCLA. Duke claimed in his autobiography that once he saw Jackie leave a ball game between innings, go race in a track meet on an adjacent field, and then come back to finish the game as if he had never left.

Like Jackie, Duke became one of those high school athletes who capture the hearts of their classmates and instantly seem too big for their towns. He played every sport, and he was the best at all of them. He could throw a sixty-yard spiral and score at will on the basketball court. But more than anything, Duke loved baseball. If Abner Doubleday was the sport's American dad, then Duke Snider was its all-American son. When the radio announcers told him to eat his Wheaties, he ate them by the boxful.

Ward Snider joined the navy when the war broke out, but Duke and his mother made the best of things in his absence. Duke fell in love with Beverly Null, the girl he would marry. He got a job in the nearby Shell oil refinery and saved enough money to buy a beat-up Chevy. He and Beverly took the Chevy to drive-in restaurants and drank malteds and listened to big-band music on the radio. They went to the movies. Duke especially loved watching Gary Cooper as Lou Gehrig in *The Pride of the Yankees*. He kept going back to watch it again and again. He may not have been the luckiest man on the face of the Earth, but he was pretty damn lucky.

When he was seventeen, in 1943, Duke signed with the Brooklyn Dodgers. He had one year of minor-league ball ahead of him before he would become eligible to enlist in the service. The Dodgers sent him to upstate New York for spring training, where he met Babe Ruth riding in an elevator. The Babe smiled at him and said, "Whattya say, kid?" He looked just like he had while playing himself in *The Pride of the Yankees*.

Duke spent the season in Newport News, Virginia. Then he joined the navy, just like his dad. He sailed for Guam. When he came home, he was bigger and stronger and faster than ever.

# 24.

Aurora Aréchiga was born back in Morenci in that hard moment after the copper industry collapsed. As a baby, she was chubby, and her older half-sister, Delphina, took to calling her "Bola," as in "Ball." Somehow, Bola became Lola. And to the people who knew her, Aurora became Lola.

Lola would grow up to be a charming and fun-loving person. She was taller than her parents, with softer features and a heart-shaped face. She had thick, shiny hair that seemed to fill up every picture she was in. Where Abrana was boisterous and harsh and quick to temper, Lola was reserved and easygoing like Manuel. But she inherited her mother's stubbornness, her inability to hide her feelings, and her streak of hard luck. Years later, Lola would have a sign on her refrigerator that read, "When I die, bury me face down so the world can kiss my ass."

Like her siblings, Lola grew up on Malvina Avenue. She picked grapes and walnuts with her family in the summers. She learned English at the Palo Verde school. The boys and girls her age saved up to buy pachuco and pachuca fashion: zoot suits, fedoras, fishnet stockings, and tailored skirts. The girls used to sneak down out of the neighborhood with their going-out clothes on underneath their regular clothes. They would do their hair in the scratched-up mirrors of service-station bathrooms down on Sunset and head from there to the dances and theaters.

But Lola didn't need to go far to find romance. When she was a teenager, she fell for a boy from Palo Verde. His name was Porfidio Vargas. The Vargas family had even deeper roots in Palo Verde than the Aréchigas. Porfidio's grandparents began constructing their home on Gabriel Avenue in 1913, a decade before Abrana and Manuel arrived. Porfidio was big, tough, and quick to anger. He had broad shoulders, a big head, and dimples, like a Mexican

John Wayne, with a shadow of a mustache across his upper lip. Everybody called him Pio.

At night in Palo Verde, especially in the winter months, the boys would gather on street corners. They would light up fires in metal trash cans and warm their hands against the flames. During the Depression they all wore the same dark corduroy jackets. The jackets had been provided as government aid, but the boys never admitted that this was where they got them. They just acted as if that was the style. As if everybody just happened to be buying the same dark corduroy jacket.

They would meet up in front of the Contreras Market or the Palo Verde cleaners on Paducah Street. There would be a different age group on every corner: the young kids together, just ten or eleven, wishing they were tougher and older; the teenagers thinking they already were; and finally the young men who were already greeting the hard work of adulthood or, later, life at war. There were no streetlights in Palo Verde, so the trash-can fires would be the only thing illuminating the streets. The neighborhood would glow in the moonlight and the firelight. The boys would gossip, talk trash, make big plans, and watch the girls pass by, even though they were the same girls they saw at school and at church and on the sidewalks and doing errands. There was a sense of pride and a sense of territorialism born of being so isolated.

═══

LOLA AND PIO were married on December 10, 1938. She was just seventeen years old, and he was nineteen. They moved into their own place in the neighborhood. Pio had quit school after eighth grade. He was a hard young man, and his hardness made him a legend among the youth of Palo Verde. He was known as a good fighter but known especially for his jalopy, a souped-up hot rod that he worked on all the time.

By the night of August 16, 1941, Lola and Pio had been married for almost three years. On that night—not a sweltering night, just a regular mild LA summer night—he found himself at a dance being held in a house in Lincoln Heights.

The dance broke up into a brawl. Then the brawl split open into something worse. It ended with Porfidio Vargas speeding down a curvy street in his hot rod, and a Lincoln Heights boy named Ramon Araujo driving toward Vargas from the opposite direction in a roadster. The *Los Angeles Times* would later describe the scene as a "Jalopy Duel." Araujo had two passengers in the car with him. As the vehicles approached each other, Araujo veered onto Vargas's side of the street, as if to issue a sort of challenge. It must have happened fast, neither side budging, the space between them shrinking double speed. Maybe the boys riding with Araujo begged him to stop. Maybe they begged him to keep driving faster, faster, faster. Maybe one of the drivers swerved at the last second—too late.

Both passengers in Araujo's car smashed their skulls and died. But somehow, Pio was able to drive off. He made his way back to Palo Verde in the wrecked hot rod. The car was found the next day by police on Malvina Avenue, a block up from the Aréchiga house. "Vargas said that he knew nothing of any gang wars, and that he didn't know any of the principals," reported the *Times*. Pio was charged with fleeing the scene and negligent homicide.

At one of the hearings later that month, the judge had to issue a public reprimand because somebody was making violent threats to potential witnesses. Pio was never convicted. But just three years later, he would find himself standing aboard a ship with a rifle in his hand, sailing across the Atlantic to war.

# 25.

ONE DAY FRANK WAS MOPING AROUND HIS PARENTS' HOUSE IN BEVerly Hills as usual, and the doorbell rang. The man standing outside was middle-aged and tall, but not too tall. He had a high hairline and a pointy nose. A pair of round spectacles framed his small eyes. But Frank saw none of this. What he saw was the man's black suit and his clerical collar. The stranger announced himself as Monsignor Thomas O'Dwyer, the parish priest at a small church in Boyle Heights and the head of Catholic Charities in Los Angeles. O'Dwyer spoke with a lilt brought over from his native Ireland.

As Frank later recalled it, this was during his most belligerently antireligious phase. He saw O'Dwyer's collar and wondered what this older man could want with an avowed atheist like him. If Frank hadn't been trained by so many years of cotillion and church dinners to be polite at all costs, he probably wouldn't have let O'Dwyer inside in the first place. After all, O'Dwyer represented everything wrong with the world. The opulent Catholic churches he had seen in Europe had stood in such stark contrast to the poverty surrounding them. Still, this was his parents' home. O'Dwyer came inside, and he set Frank Wilkinson on the path to the rest of his life.

It's impossible to know what exactly O'Dwyer had seen in Frank or what compelled him to knock on the Wilkinson family's door at 300 Oakhurst Drive. But somehow he intuited that Frank was restless, that he was capable of channeling all the angst and energy that had been building inside him into something productive. At UCLA, Frank had been an overachiever and a social butterfly. He had been ambitious, if oblivious. Frank was different now: he had been exposed to the world, and his convictions had evolved, but deep down he was still the milk-drinking do-gooder.

O'Dwyer appealed not to the trappings of Frank's religious up-bringing but to the social gospel that had underpinned his faith. O'Dwyer told Frank that he need not go to Palestine to see poverty or to get worked up about injustice. He took Frank to see poverty right in Los Angeles, poverty that even after traveling the world, Frank did not know existed only a few miles from his home.

O'Dwyer drove Frank around the city. He took him to Watts, where Simon Rodia's towers, otherworldly sculptures built from found rebar, tile, and glass, were rising over a poor, underserved community that was largely black, Asian, and Latino: populations restricted from living in other nearby areas like Compton and South Gate. What Los Angeles needed to do, O'Dwyer told him, was to clean up places like this. Clear out the slums and build adequate housing for its poorest residents. It was an ambitious goal, but there was a moral imperative for man to lift his brothers and sisters up. It was 1938, and the movement toward public housing was still nascent in America. Frank had echoes of the Soviet Union in his head. He remembered the great programs he had seen in Russia. The clean streets and the magnificent collective farms. There he saw a government helping a backward society right itself and an unequal society becoming, at least in his eyes, more equal. He saw a government making a better world.

Public housing appealed to Frank because it challenged the very notion of how people lived in America: in isolation, in competition, forever in service to themselves. He was questioning everything, and here was this priest questioning the idea of land as something to be owned or exploited. This was radical. Why should a house be something we owned, anyway? Frank remembered the kibbutzim he saw in Palestine, the cooperative communities where everything was shared and people lived their values. Public housing would not only serve the poor but would also challenge the status quo and perhaps help remake society at large. In 1938 this did not seem impossible. It was the era of the New Deal and of Upton Sinclair's End Poverty in California (EPIC) campaign, and the way people thought about government was changing. Frank, who had once picketed against Sinclair and EPIC, was changing as well.

Frank saw the poverty that O'Dwyer saw. He saw the urgency of the call for public housing. He picked a side. O'Dwyer would teach Frank to challenge the mainstream by engaging with it, instead of growing too cynical and high-minded and isolated from it as he had after returning from Europe. He would teach Frank to use his lifetime of training, his charm and his manners, to serve something larger than himself. O'Dwyer offered him a part-time job as secretary for an advocacy group he led called the Citizens Housing Council of Los Angeles. And so began Frank Wilkinson's career in housing.

==

IN 1939, TO the great relief of Dr. and Mrs. Wilkinson, Frank and Jean got married. That same year, he scrawled the words *conscientious objector* across his draft card. He worked a series of jobs that didn't stick: as a laborer at a pipe company, as a secretary for the Works Progress Administration, and ultimately as a social worker, where he got involved in the union. Jean was a schoolteacher. Meanwhile, Frank devoted himself to O'Dwyer and housing. Through O'Dwyer he met elected officials and fellow activists. He traveled to Sacramento to lobby at the capital. He gained a sense of purpose.

Frank may or may not have realized it, but he was falling into the same strain of activism as his father. Since founding CIVIC with Clifford Clinton, Dr. Wilkinson had become one of the city's most vocal and fiery anti-vice crusaders. The battle to take down organized crime in LA had spilled out from the grand jury investigations and onto the streets. In order to expose Mayor Frank Shaw's administration, the corrupt Los Angeles Police Department (LAPD), and the underworld figures propping them up, CIVIC turned to paid informants and vigilante investigations. Clinton railed about corruption in his weekly radio broadcast.

In 1936 a well-known gambling boss named Guy McAfee approached Dr. Wilkinson with an offer. He wanted to change his ways. McAfee came bearing a check for $4,400 to help fund a church pageant that Dr. Wilkinson was organizing called "The Last Days of Pompeii." Dr. Wilkinson took McAfee at his word and accepted the check. They got down on their knees and prayed together.

Soon, Dr. Wilkinson learned that he had been duped. McAfee's donation had been part of a plan to discredit urban reformers like himself by making them seem as corrupt as the mayoral administration they were trying to replace. In the late summer of 1937 Dr. Wilkinson testified before a grand jury and offered to resign his post in CIVIC. But CIVIC's opponents were doing more than laying political traps. In the fall of 1937 a bomb went off in Clinton's home. Then another bomb exploded in the garage of a former LAPD officer turned CIVIC informant named Harry Raymond. Clinton was unharmed, but Raymond suffered serious injuries.

The explosions, and the subsequent indictment of LAPD detectives for the Raymond bombing, were enough to turn public opinion against the department and the mayor's office. The following year, Clinton, Wilkinson, and CIVIC led a broad-based recall campaign to remove Mayor Shaw from office. In his place they inserted Fletcher Bowron, a superior court judge with a reputation for honesty and moderation.

The election of Bowron was a great victory for A. M. Wilkinson and, a decade later, would have a major impact on the life of Frank. But Dr. Wilkinson would not be around to see it. In 1940 he died of pneumonia. Frank was across town at work when it happened, and he rushed to the hospital but arrived to find his family gathered outside his father's room. It was too late. Dr. Wilkinson had quite literally worked himself to death. There had been a bad flu going around town, and instead of taking a break as he got increasingly sick himself, Frank's father just kept going from one patient to another until he couldn't function anymore. This was the way he had always lived his life: his values always in action, his purpose never in doubt. He was sixty-five years old, but until those final hours he had always seemed younger.

Frank cried. He was always a crier. And he was, in so many ways, his father's son. His father who had warned him about the coyotes and who had instilled in him the belief that Heaven could be made right here on Earth and the sense of duty to help make it. His father who, when Frank had sworn off God after his trip to Europe, instead of yelling, had simply called his good friend over to hear Frank's stories. His father who told his own stories and sang and never wore his piousness as armor. Frank was his father's son.

During the funeral at Hollywood Methodist, they sang and prayed. The minister from back in Douglas came to help with the service. Dr. Wilkinson was "a man who stepped from his path to give of his courage and vigor," said John Anson Ford. One of the speakers quoted the poet Robert Browning:

*One who never turned his back but marched breast forward,*
*Never doubted clouds would break,*
*Never dreamed, though right were worsted, wrong would*
  *triumph,*
*Held we fall to rise, are baffled to fight better,*
*Sleep to wake.*

*Part III*

---

# THE NEW TOWN IN TOWN

# 26.

JORGE PASQUEL SPENT HIS SEVENTH BIRTHDAY COWERING IN THE basement of his family's home in Veracruz. It could have been worse. It was a large home, and the basement had plenty of room for Jorge's parents, his seven brothers and sisters, and their servants, relatives, and neighbors. The Pasquel family owned Mexico's largest cigar factory and a thriving customs brokerage, but on that particular day, April 23, 1914, it seemed like everything might soon be gone: the business empire, the family, the entire city.

One day earlier, Woodrow Wilson had directed US warships in the Gulf of Mexico to conquer Veracruz. There are rarely good reasons to invade your next door neighbor, but the pretext this time was especially flimsy. The Mexican government had mistakenly arrested a few US soldiers in the city of Tampico, and Wilson did not find their apology sufficiently heartfelt.

By 1914, the revolution had torn Mexico apart ideologically and territorially; people were dying, and others, like Abrana and Manuel, were fleeing north. Mexico's nascent transportation and industrial infrastructure was collapsing, and the country was churning through presidents at an absurd rate. All this was happening, and here came the Americans again, pointing their cannons. Nearly seventy years after Winfield Scott, US soldiers were once again marching in the streets of Veracruz, their boots falling on the same cobblestones as their predecessors'.

Most of President Victoriano Huerta's troops retreated, which left the defense of Veracruz—in one of those tragic and somehow also beautiful historical echoes—in the hands of a group of military cadets from the naval academy. The cadets, along with some civilian volunteers and a few remaining troops, put up a brave but ultimately hopeless fight. The occupation of Veracruz lasted about as long as a typical major-league baseball season: from April to

October. The Boston Braves upset the Philadelphia Athletics in the World Series, and then the Americans departed. The experience of living through the battle and the ensuing occupation would stay with Jorge for the rest of his life.

In 1932, when he was twenty-five, Jorge married the daughter of former president Plutarco Elias Calles. He used his newfound connections to expand the family's business empire. He moved to Mexico City and built a mansion. Then he got a divorce. He didn't divorce the connections, though. Santa Anna had called himself the Napoleon of the West. Jorge became obsessed with the real Napoleon Bonaparte. He erected a statue of the general in his home and collected volumes of biographies about him.

Jorge Pasquel believed that his country needed to assert itself. Perhaps this is what led him to Napoleon, or perhaps it was Napoleon who led him to believe that Mexico needed to rise to the challenge of its imperial northern neighbor. Pasquel and his siblings grew the family fortune. They ran the state lottery in Veracruz. They imported American cars. They made even better connections. One of the neighbor boys who had hidden alongside Jorge in the basement in Veracruz was making connections too: his name was Miguel Alemán, and he was on his way to the presidency. Jorge had an idea about what could get him there, and that idea was baseball.

There are many stories about how and where baseball came to Mexico. There are the myths, like Santa Anna and his leg, but there is also the very real possibility that US soldiers in that war *did* introduce the game to residents. So much of the history of baseball is lost, especially in the inky predawn era before men like Albert Spalding came along to commercialize the sport. There is one theory about railroad workers at the Texas border and another about Cuban merchants sailing in and out of Veracruz at the turn of the twentieth century.

Regardless, by the 1930s, baseball was a beloved game in Mexico just as it was in the United States. Jorge Pasquel saw baseball diamonds the same way Napoleon saw continental Europe. He saw potential. He saw the sport's transformative powers. Pasquel was not the first man to believe that professional baseball could bestow a certain seriousness to a place. He would certainly not be the last. In baseball he saw an energy force that he could tap into like Mexico's oil reserves.

Under President Lázaro Cárdenas, Mexico had just taken back those oil reserves from foreign companies. But before that, Pasquel had watched Americans profit from Mexican resources for years and years. Why couldn't he do the same thing to them? What if instead of American businessmen taking Mexican oil, a Mexican businessman could tap into American baseball?

# 27.

By the end of the Depression, there was almost no vacant public land left near downtown Los Angeles. In a city that was born through real-estate speculation, all the blank, ripe spaces on the map were beginning to fill up. One site that remained empty was that of an abandoned smallpox hospital tucked into the hills beside Palo Verde, La Loma, and Bishop. The site on Chavez Ravine Road was centrally located and had the benefit of already being flat: it wouldn't require any regrading. Civic leaders wanted to use it to host a permanent trade exposition. They were going to call it the Pacific Mercado, and it was going to celebrate commerce on the West Coast of the United States, in Latin America, and across the ocean in Asia.

This was a time when expositions like world's fairs carried a great deal of weight. Would it be unseemly to build a triumphant trade expo beside a largely neglected community of immigrants and their families? That never came up. The Pacific Mercado would be LA's response to the 1893 Chicago World's Fair, which in its own time had been meant to honor the four-hundredth anniversary of Columbus's arrival in the New World. The Pacific Mercado, then, would commemorate the four-hundredth anniversary of the "discovery" of what would become the Pacific Coast of the United States by the Spanish conquistador Juan Rodríguez Cabrillo. In honoring Cabrillo the boosters behind the Mercado were trying to wish their own Columbus into existence. (This was, considering all we know about how malleable history is, not the worst idea, especially in Los Angeles.)

In the case of Cabrillo, fact and legend remain hard to parse. He was supposedly born in Spain—maybe Portugal—and served under Cortés in the conquest of Mexico. Little is actually known of Cabrillo the man, or his journey up the coast of California, because he did not survive it. In the final months of 1542, Cabrillo landed at Catalina Island and, while disembarking from his ship, supposedly tripped and fell on a rock. The wound became infected, gangrene set in, and he soon died. In the eyes of its planners, the Mercado would cement LA's place as the capital city of the entire Pacific Rim.

The Mercado was about as Los Angeles as it gets: a celebration of one conquering nation (Spain) by the conquering nation that supplanted it (the United States); a grasp toward a history that may or may not be invented; a business opportunity dressed up in a clumsy attempt at multiculturalism—"The name [Mercado] is of Spanish origin and thus is symbolic of our traditions," according to one brochure—and, perhaps most presciently, an attempt by members of the city's booster class to use public money and public land to advance what ultimately were private business interests.

But the Pacific Mercado would never come to be. Instead, after much consternation, the site was turned over to the US Navy to construct an armory that would house marines and midshipmen. And this is how, before Hitler conquered Poland and Japan bombed Pearl Harbor, the war first came to Palo Verde.

Tucked away between steep hills just like the communities that were its neighbors, the armory would be sheltered from potential enemy fighter planes. It was an art deco building, with a wide facade that gave it the look and shape of a mid-century high school. Its rooms were quickly filled with guns and rations, and with raw and red-faced boys from far-off places like Alabama and North Dakota and Kentucky. And at first, the communities of Palo Verde, La Loma, and Bishop got along fine with their new neighbors. Just as they did with their neighbors in the police academy. After all, what choice did they have?

==

WHEN THE WAR really came to Palo Verde, Camilo Arévalo was just a kid, living down the street from the Aréchigas on Malvina Avenue. He had an older cousin, Armand Muñoz, who came running over yelling about how the Japanese had attacked Pearl Harbor. Armand was obsessed with airplanes. Always had been. He had just graduated from high school the year before and then learned how to fly. He had a job at a little airfield working on prop planes. Armand joined the Army Air Forces. All the guys seemed to be joining up. It was the right thing to do: they were American, after all, born and raised. They saw the armory buzzing and the city getting ready to defend itself from Japanese attack. They heard the talk about submarines off the coast and the fearful whispers in the streets. They saw the city's Japanese community rounded up and sent off to internment camps. They might have lived in Palo Verde and spoken Spanish at home, but this was their country too.

Abrana and Manuel's nephew Cruz Cabral joined the marines. His younger brothers Gene, Paulino, and Rudy would also join up when they got old enough. Jesús Nava, the son of Manuel's sister Georgia, enlisted. Porfidio Vargas enlisted. When the war got going, even all the *viejos* in the neighborhood had to sign draft cards. For Manuel Aréchiga, this was the second time he had filled out a draft card in America. He was fifty-something years old—probably fifty-three. It's hard to say exactly how old he was because every time Manuel filled out a piece of government paperwork, he changed the birth year. He was born in 1893. Or 1889. Or 1888. But however old he was, he was American now. It had been three and a half decades since he had signed that initial draft card in Morenci, Arizona.

Back then, he and Abrana were not yet married. Back then, her first husband was still alive. Back then, Manuel was just getting settled in his new country. Palo Verde wasn't even a dream. Who knows what he saw his life turning out to be? But here he was, decades later and American now. Here he was, a grandfather. Was it likely that a fifty-year-old man who didn't speak much English would get called upon to serve in a war thousands of miles away? It wasn't. But the fact is that he signed the paperwork. He was willing to go. Manuel was invested in Palo Verde, in Los Angeles, in America. He had put everything into it.

The war effort in Palo Verde became a collective thing. Just like in towns all across America. The vegetable gardens in backyards were now Victory Gardens. They were already doing it in Palo Verde, of course, already growing their own food and making their own clothes and living like it was wartime all the time. The metal shortages, gas shortages, and food shortages were tolerated just fine. After all, the people of Palo Verde were used to making do with less.

"They had rationed everything," remembered Gene Cabral. "They used to have blackouts, where you had dark curtains on your windows. They had these tests. Sirens would go off. There were people to oversee each block. You'd come out at night, and I'd never seen the barrio so dark."

The city around them came to life with wartime manufacturing. People poured into Los Angeles from around the country to build airplanes and machine guns and whatever else Uncle Sam needed. Los Angeles was becoming a place where people built things. Even as fear simmered below the surface and enemy submarines lingered below the coastal waters, even as racial tensions heightened, the city worked.

The mothers and grandmothers of Palo Verde went to work. Even Abrana, the professional mother, aunt, caretaker, chicken-coop manager. We know this because during the war, Abrana journeyed to Mexico to visit her brothers. She came back to America on October 6, 1944. Immigration paperwork from the journey gives one of those rare documented glimpses into her life. Her occupation was "sanding furniture." She was forty-seven years old, five feet five inches tall, with a mole on the right side of her mouth and another between her eyebrows. Her address was 1771 Malvina Avenue.

During the war, the Aréchiga family made the newspapers for the first time in Los Angeles. The story, in the *Los Angeles Times*, offered a preview of how the paper and the establishment would treat them in the decades to come and into how they viewed the travails of the people in Palo Verde, La Loma, and Bishop. The item, just three glib paragraphs, was headlined "Goat Butts His 'Best Friend.'" It tells of Victoria Aréchiga—Abrana and Manuel's youngest daughter—getting butted by one of the family's goats while fetching it a pail of water. Victoria, called Tolina by the family, was just fourteen years old.

"The ungrateful goat knocked Victoria 30 feet down the hill where she crashed against the side of her house," the article reports. Then it notes, almost casually, that she may have fractured her back.

# 28.

THERE WAS SOMETHING ABOUT THE COMMUNIST PARTY: THE BIG ideas, the being on the right side of history, even the danger of it. In the early 1940s becoming a Communist wasn't so crazy. The party had been growing in America for a decade. Communists were deeply involved in labor and activism. They were freedom fighters and intellectuals in a city that was dominated by elite oil and real-estate magnates. Also, the United States and Soviet Union were now allies in Europe. To Frank Wilkinson, joining up made a certain level of sense. At heart, he was an institutionalist. He liked to feel like he belonged to something bigger. The Methodist Church wasn't cutting it anymore.

Frank and Jean were first approached about joining the party at Sunday breakfast in the home of Richard and Dione Neutra. The Neutras were the kind of people he and Jean wanted to be and to be around. They were plugged in, they were fashionable, and they were deeply concerned about the state of the world. Richard was a famous architect, and the Neutras believed that design could be sacred; design could save us. The Sunday breakfasts always seemed to be full of radicals and other interesting weirdos. They talked about housing. Richard had designed a project called Channel Heights in San Pedro. The Neutras invited Frank and Jean to move into the empty apartment upstairs. The home, which Neutra had designed himself, has since become a landmark of modernist architecture. It was here that Frank and Jean's first child, a son named Jeffry, was born.

In 1942 Frank and Monsignor O'Dwyer collaborated with other local groups to picket some new housing projects that had just been opened in Los Angeles. The problem wasn't the projects themselves, which Frank had helped lobby for, but the fact that the housing authority had decided to segregate them. For Frank, the issues of housing and racism were intertwined. Public housing was supposed to be a step *toward* racial equality. To segregate housing projects would be to undermine the entire enterprise and to set back the movement.

The protest that Frank led was not exactly headline news. After all, America was at war. There were other things to think about. The war had also changed the focus of public housing. Hundreds of thousands of workers were moving into Los Angeles as the city became an industrial hub in the war machine. Projects previously designated for poor citizens were being repurposed for soldiers and war workers and their families.

Frank recalled there being about ten people on the sidewalk in front of Hacienda Village carrying signs. Not much, but enough to make a nuisance. As Frank and his small army marched up and down the street, officials from the housing authority gathered inside the project before finally calling O'Dwyer in to confer. After a while, O'Dwyer came out with a public-relations official. "OK," the man told Frank, "we're going to mix them."

Here was Frank, back in Watts, where O'Dwyer had first shown him poverty in Los Angeles, where his journey in housing had begun. He had achieved a real victory: first fighting for the establishment of the housing project and then achieving its integration. But before he could bask in the achievement, the official continued: "If you love the colored so much, maybe you'd like to live with them. How would you like to be the manager?"

Frank accepted on the spot. And so the Wilkinsons moved into a brand-new housing project in Watts. The work he had been doing as a social worker carried over to his work managing the project. He threw himself into the job. To him, the word *project* didn't just mean a place. It meant an active thing; it meant possibility: the project of making a better world, of improving the lives of his residents, of being there for them.

As he organized adult-education classes and community gardens, Frank also began to think more deeply about the values that had led him to housing in the first place. He was afraid of giving up his independence. He was afraid of being told what to think or feel. But the Communists seemed to be saying everything that Frank was thinking and feeling. In 1942 Frank and Jean took the leap together and joined the Communist Party.

# 29.

As the weeks and months of war went by, the Santo Niño church in Palo Verde swelled with funeral crowds and emptied and swelled again. Mothers lit votive candles. There was a sense of urgency and a sense of helplessness. There was a lot of waiting, waiting, waiting for the ominous sight of Western Union messengers huffing their way up into Palo Verde on their bicycles. Each time one of the messengers arrived, the terrified family of a soldier had to wait as he approached the front door. Each time, they had to take the telegram, flimsy between their fingers but heavy with the weight of the news it carried. Each time, they had to open it.

Abrana and Manuel's nephew Cruz Cabral came home to Palo Verde for leave just before he was shipped off to the Pacific with the marines. While he was back, he married his teenage sweetheart, a girl named Adeline Guerra, from neighboring Bishop. Adeline then moved into the Cabral house on Malvina Avenue. Cruz's mother had died in 1940, and his father had died many years before from the infected cut he got at the old brickyard. Cruz and his brothers and sisters had been largely raised by Abrana and Manuel at the house down the street. Gene Cabral recalled sitting at home with his brother's new wife, staring out at the street through the living-room window. Cruz was his big brother. His hero. His inspiration to join the marines as soon as he was old enough.

"You would see this guy pulling up on the bike," Gene remembered. "And my sister-in-law started crying right away—you think of the worst."

In the war that's how the bad news came. No polite and stern officer wearing a dress uniform knocking on your door and consoling you and telling you what a hero your son was. Just a telegram. This is how Georgia Aréchiga—Manuel's favorite sister, the one who would tell the government officials that she was born

101

when the squash was getting ripe and hence drive her older brother crazy—got word that her son Jesús was dead. A telegram, written in English, by a person many miles away from Palo Verde.

When the bike messenger arrived at the Cabral house on Malvina, Gene and Adeline opened the door. They took the envelope in their hands. Cruz Cabral was wounded but otherwise OK. This was the best-case scenario.

Cruz came home for another leave before shipping out again. Then it happened again. Another bike messenger pedaling slowly up Malvina Avenue. Another wave of dread. Another envelope. This time, Adeline was pregnant with their first child. She met the Western Union man at the front door and opened the telegram and read the words inside. Cruz had once again survived: badly injured on the seventh day of fighting at Iwo Jima, but alive. He would come home.

# 30.

JORGE PASQUEL DECIDED TO CONQUER AMERICAN BASEBALL. IT WAS the kind of thing that only an absurdly rich man could dream up. But Pasquel was absurdly rich. He dreamed of a true World Series: one between the Mexican champions and the American champions. The first thing that Pasquel did was found his own club, called the Azules de Veracruz. The club was located in Mexico City, but he still named them after his hometown. Then he began taking long journeys to the United States to observe the game at its highest levels. This was easy for Pasquel because he owned an assortment of planes, including an air force bomber that he repurposed as a luxury jet (and once lent to Frank Sinatra and Ava Gardner). He was also a pilot himself. During his travels, Pasquel noticed something that many Americans were still choosing to ignore, which was that there was as much talent in the Negro Leagues as there was in the majors.

In the early 1940s, Pasquel began signing Negro League stars to lavish contracts. Josh Gibson, Monte Irvin, and Cool Papa Bell played for him. So did Cuban legends such as Martín Dihigo and Lázaro Salazar. He would fly their entire families down and hire tutors for the children. In Mexico these players were treated like celebrities—and, more importantly, they were treated like human beings. They got to eat in any restaurant they wanted to, stay in any hotel. The only catch was that they had to work for a man who worshipped Napoleon Bonaparte. Pasquel was a tyrant with a groomed mustache and a beautiful collection of pocket squares. One legend has it that Pasquel tore into Gibson after a game in which the catcher went four for four with a double and a triple: "I'm paying you to hit home runs." Irvin used to tell the story of how Pasquel waved him over to his box seat before he came to the plate in the extra innings of a big game. Pasquel offered him $200 to hit a home run, and Irvin, incredibly enough, actually did it.

Soon Pasquel became the president of the league, and soon after that the league began filling up with more and more Negro League talent. Teams in Mexico were limited to eight foreign players each, so Pasquel saw that they were evenly distributed. For instance, Roy Campanella played for Monterrey. During World War II, Pasquel arranged for Mexico to loan the services of eighty thousand laborers to the United States in exchange for keeping two of his star players out of the draft. Pasquel was making money and making headlines. He dated the Mexican movie star María Félix. He allegedly boxed with Ernest Hemingway, and even if he didn't, he seemed like he could have. He recruited washed-up legends to give an air of historical importance to Mexican baseball: Rogers Hornsby spent nine days as a player-manager. Babe Ruth came for a visit but was in no shape to stick around. Pasquel gave the image of a mogul, and in fact he was one. Thanks to him, the league was profitable, and it was increasingly popular. He bought the controlling interest in Parque Delta, Mexico's premier ballpark.

In 1945 Pasquel sent a lackey to Daytona Beach, Florida, where a young man who had recently been signed by the Brooklyn Dodgers was spending his first spring training with their minor-league affiliate. That young man was Jackie Robinson, and for Robinson and his wife Rachel, just getting to Daytona through segregated Louisiana and Panhandle Florida had been an ordeal. Pasquel offered an alternative. Forget Florida and forget Brooklyn. Come to Mexico. He offered to put them up, to pay their room and board, and to triple Jackie's Dodgers salary. But Robinson said no. He wasn't one to look elsewhere for dignity or respect. For Robinson, who had an opportunity that none of his fellow Negro League stars did, the challenge of playing in the Brooklyn system *was* the point. Comfort didn't have anything to do with it.

After the war, Pasquel decided to set his sights not just on Negro League talent but on major leaguers as well. At the time, major-league ballplayers were still restricted by something called the reserve clause. This effectively meant that they were bound forever to the team that owned their rights. It was an unfair system, and it took decades—until the 1970s—for ballplayers to overcome it and earn free agency. Pasquel found a work-around. The players could simply leave the country and sign for more money with him. As Pasquel's brother Bernardo put it, he wanted to "destroy the United States' monopoly on baseball." Before the 1946 season, Pasquel signed seventeen major-league ballplayers to deals in Mexico. Among them were the Giants' Sal "the Barber" Maglie, Cardinals pitcher Max Lanier, and Dodgers catcher Mickey Owen.

The American press made Pasquel out to be a thief and a raider, a notion that one of Pasquel's brothers later rejected: "We paid better money, that's all." Pasquel set his sights on the game's biggest stars. He went after Joe DiMaggio. He supposedly offered Ted Williams, whose mother was half-Mexican, a hundred thousand dollars a year. "Pasquel had diamonds on his tie, diamonds on his watches, and diamonds on his wrist," Williams remembered. One of Pasquel's representatives supposedly thrust a briefcase full of cash on the bed in Stan Musial's hotel room in Florida. Musial somehow managed to resist the temptation. The threat of losing top-tier players was enough to send major-league owners into hysterics. The Brooklyn Dodgers tried to get a court injunction to prevent players from crossing the border into Mexico. Commissioner Happy Chandler banned any player who signed with Pasquel from playing in the majors for five years.

Meanwhile, Pasquel's gambit had worked. The Mexican League may not have reached the same level of prestige as the American League or National League, but it did demonstrate itself to be a legitimate threat to those leagues. And with talent from across Latin America and the United States joining Mexican ballplayers, it could certainly compete on the field. In 1946 Pasquel's friend Miguel Alemán won the presidency.

Then, just as quickly as it ascended into glory, the Pasquel-run Mexican league began to decline. Chandler's threats of suspension stopped major-league players from coming over, and the gradual integration that followed Jackie Robinson's debut in 1947 dried up the well of black stars. This was bittersweet for Pasquel. After all, his own ambitious recruitment of players black and white had helped make the case to the racist and fearful lords of US baseball that integrated ball clubs could play together. Now his own success was undermining him.

In 1949, Danny Gardella, one of the white players who Pasquel had recruited to Mexico, brought the first successful lawsuit against baseball's reserve clause. By then, having been stripped of a great deal of its talent and prestige, and also of Pasquel's blank checkbook, the Mexican league had collapsed into chaos. Pasquel officially gave up his stake in the league after he was struck in the head with a rock hurled by a fan at a game in 1951 (it's unknown whether he was the rock's intended target). The Azules de Veracruz were dissolved, and Pasquel entered his own sort of Napoleonic exile. He was rewarded for his service by President Alemán with a monopoly on oil distribution, and he took off to enjoy his wealth on a series of extravagant hunting safaris in Africa.

Perhaps Pasquel would have returned to baseball, but he never got the chance. On March 7, 1955, the private plane he was piloting crashed into a mountain range north of Mexico City, killing Pasquel and five passengers. He was forty-eight years old. A month later, the remaining owners of the Mexican league voted to incorporate themselves into American organized baseball, much like the Pacific Coast League had done half a century earlier. Pasquel's dream of an independent league equal to the majors was as dead as he was. Six months after that, the Brooklyn Dodgers won their first and only World Series behind Duke Snider, Jackie Robinson, and Roy Campanella.

# 31.

JUAN ARÉCHIGA NEVER WENT TO WAR. WHILE HIS COUSINS AND neighbors were shipping off for Europe and Japan, Manuel and Abrana's only surviving son was getting married to a girl from Alpine, the neighborhood down the hill that was Palo Verde's biggest rival. Juan was eighteen when the Japanese bombed Pearl Harbor in 1941. He was nineteen when he got hitched to Nellie Tavison in November 1942. She was nineteen as well.

Juan Aréchiga never went to war, but sometimes it seemed like he lived life like a war. He could be funny and charming and also mean and mercurial. He was always looking for something, looking for his place in the world. He was a seeker—of adventure, of money, of meaning—and a fighter against injustice when he saw it. Juan was not formally educated, having dropped out of school before he could even properly read. But Juan saw the way that people like him were treated in this country. He heard the way the politicians talked about people like him. Why should he die for a country like this? When it came time for his army physical, he played deaf. "Repeat after me," the officers said. "What?"

Nellie was born in San Diego, and her folks had been born in Mexico like Abrana and Manuel. She was a quiet, lovely girl. She was patient, which served her well with a husband like Juan, but not endlessly so. She was organized and meticulous; he was a pack rat. When the family went out to the fields, Nellie would stay back at the campsite and cook.

On the wedding certificate, Juan listed his place of employment as a steel foundry and his position as chipper's helper. A chipper is responsible for removing excess material from the large castings made in the mill, usually with a jackhammer or some other big, loud machine. As a helper, Juan was probably doing hard, hot labor,

*Juan Aréchiga*

dragging broken pieces of steel off the shop floor. It was the kind of job that his father, Manuel, might have held back in Morenci.

Juan worked a lot of jobs. He worked in a tannery and ran a restaurant with Nellie in Chinatown. He was always pushing back against society's rules, written and unwritten. "My dad was very obstinate," said his daughter Jeannie. He used to get parking tickets and then refuse to pay the fine. "I have more time than money," he would tell the judges, and they would throw him in jail. He was always in and out of jail, in and out of solitary. All the cops and judges knew him. In jail Juan became a Jehovah's Witness. In jail

Juan taught himself to read. He was insatiable. He would sit for hours with a book and a dictionary. He had more time than money. He would look up every word.

By 1941, the discomfort with Mexican immigrants had evolved into panic about the children of those immigrants—the first generation of American-born kids who were wearing zoot suits and speaking perfect English and expressing themselves. People like Juan Aréchiga. The *Los Angeles Times* had taken to running paternalistic stories about juvenile delinquency among Mexican youths.

During the war, Abrana and Manuel's nephew Gene Cabral would write his older brother Cruz letters. Gene was a teenager. He wasn't old enough to fight yet like Cruz or old enough to skip the fight like his cousin Juan. But he was old enough to understand the fight. He saw the sailors in the armory nearby. He saw the way they looked at him and his cousins, his friends, his neighbors, especially when they put on their pachuco clothes: their pleated pants and their sharkskin jackets. They used to save up money to buy the zoot suits. They all went to the same tailor downtown on Main Street. They'd run into the guys from the other barrios there, the guys they sometimes fought with on Friday nights, everybody doing their best to look the part: to express something that was easier to say with clothing than it was with words. A sense of being American but also something else.

The trouble started slowly. It wasn't just California but also New York, Illinois, Pennsylvania. It wasn't just Los Angeles but also San Diego, Oakland, Delano. In Los Angeles the papers made a tabloid story out of the murder of a young Mexican boy in East Los Angeles—the trial saw seventeen Mexican American kids wrongly charged with a gang-initiation killing. It became known as the Sleepy Lagoon murder, after the name of the swimming hole where the victim, José Gallardo Díaz, had been discovered beaten and dying. The reports stirred the darkest fears of white Los Angeles. Something about the way the Mexican American kids dressed, the way they carried themselves. Too much pride, maybe. Some people say that it was the very fact of wearing baggy, long-fitting clothes at a time when the country was short on raw materials. As if by dressing up, these boys were undermining the war effort. The Japanese had already been sent to internment camps. All that fear, all that resentment, had to find some place to go.

The word *riot* does a disservice to what actually happened, beginning on June 3, 1943. For five days sailors spilled out of the armory on Chavez Ravine Road in a convoy of taxis and into the streets of downtown and East Los Angeles, though not Palo Verde itself. The white servicemen brought clubs and sticks, and ganged up with civilians and off-duty law enforcement to attack young Mexican Americans—and eventually African Americans and Filipino Americans too. They beat them and stripped them of their clothes. They urinated on the torn zoot suits and burned them in the streets. Meanwhile, the newspapers continued to treat the victims like perpetrators and the perpetrators like heroes. The violence increased with each passing night. The police watched idly, then arrested the victims. All of it happened against the backdrop of the biggest armed conflict in the history of the world. When, in the aftermath of the violence, Eleanor Roosevelt condemned the attacks, the *Los Angeles Times* responded by calling her a Communist.

Mario Zepeda lived in Palo Verde. He was a young man when the riots occurred: a new husband and a new dad. The oldest of five brothers. He dressed up in a zoot suit. A flower in his lapel. Neckties. It wasn't meant to provoke, he said, but it did. "It was the design of the clothes," he said, as if there was nothing that could truly explain the mysteries of resentment and racism. "And that's that."

Zepeda remembered being downtown in the theater district with his wife. "We were coming out of the theater and everything, and there was a bunch of sailors and army guys and all that. Our first child was just born, and I was carrying him. They were gonna sort of jump me. They figured out I was carrying the baby, so a few of the guys pulled the other ones back. They let us go."

Zepeda and his wife and baby escaped onto a streetcar and made it back to Palo Verde. But with the armory right next door, getting in and out of Palo Verde was not easy either. You had to steer clear of the servicemen. The story of Vincent de Nava took on a kind of fable quality: he was caught downtown by sailors from the armory and stripped of his suit and beaten and bloodied. "They tore him right up," said Gene Cabral. They took his pants and everything. To get back home to Palo Verde, he had to get around the armory itself. He ripped a sheet off a clothesline and wrapped himself in it. He climbed through the hills and scrambled up over scrubs and bushes, dodging cops and sailors, humiliated but alive.

# 32.

THE PACIFIC COAST LEAGUE WAS NEVER QUITE MAJOR LEAGUE. IT never had been. It was baseball by and for the West, by and for the types of people who settled in far-flung places like Seattle and Salt Lake City at the turn of the twentieth century. As those cities grew, the league grew too, but it never lost its weirdness. It was where the washed-up old pros went to live out their golden years in the sunshine and where up-and-coming talent like the DiMaggio brothers of San Francisco lingered before heading to Boston or New York.

One of the up-and-coming players who emerged from the Pacific Coast League was Mel Almada. Almada and his older brother Louie were born in Mexico but grew up in Los Angeles. Their father had been a high-level political ally of the one-armed general Álvaro Obregón during the Mexican Revolution, and when the political winds shifted against Obregón, the family fled to California. After he graduated from high school, Louie Almada signed with the Seattle Indians, where he became a local hero. A few years later, Mel (also known as Melo) followed him to Seattle.

It was clear from the start that Mel was too talented for the minor leagues. In 1933, at just twenty years old, he signed with the Boston Red Sox. The team was moribund, as it had been since 1919, when owner Harry Frazee sold Babe Ruth to the New York Yankees. But when they finally called up Almada, he was a revelation: athletic, exciting, and good-looking. He was the first Mexican-born player in major-league history. And on the final day of that 1933 Red Sox season, Almada became the last player to ever record a hit off Ruth in what would be the legend's final appearance as a pitcher.

Almada spent seven years bouncing around the majors, from Boston to Washington to St. Louis to Brooklyn. His final season came in 1939. He was just twenty-six years old. Almada had always felt that his place in the big leagues was tenuous. There were other Latino players, but like Almada, they were all light-skinned. The truth was that the color line that barred African American and Afro Latino players could be bent, as long as you had what scholar Adrian Burgos Jr. called the "right combination of ancestry, physical features and talent." Almada had it. But that didn't mean the league wasn't hostile to him.

Almada believed that he was being targeted by pitchers. According to his brother Louie and at least one of his teammates, the brushback pitches got into his head and ultimately drove him from the game. "Melo couldn't stand being thrown at," Louie Almada told the researcher Carlos Bauer. "'Louie,' he once said to me, 'they're throwing at me because I'm a Mexican!' 'No, Melo,' I told him, 'they're throwing at you because you're a *batter*!'"

After his big-league career ended, Mel Almada spent a few months back in the Pacific Coast League with the Sacramento Solons. But he batted just .232. The dream was fading. He played briefly in Mexico and then joined the Army Medical Corps during World War II.

After his pro career was over, Almada came back home to Los Angeles, where he became a small speck in what was by then a vast semipro and amateur baseball landscape that stretched from the border with Mexico to the central coast. For many Angelenos, these games were more urgent and more meaningful than anything happening in the distant major leagues or the nearby Pacific Coast League. There were dozens of teams, representing everything from movie studios to local businesses and fraternal orders.

But the most famous team of this era was Carmelita Provisions. Carmelita Provisions was founded in East Los Angeles by a local businessman named Mario López. López had worked in meatpacking and saw a market among LA's growing Mexican community for pork products from back home. The team became known as Los Chorizeros: the sausage makers. They were a dominant force on the field, winning championship after championship, and a community institution whose impact extended beyond it. The Sunday home games they played were a point of pride and became a gathering point for the Mexican American community.

In the 1940s and 1950s, baseball became one of the places where the Mexican American community in Los Angeles could feel the most like itself. The games were pure mid-century Americana, all the way down to the gender roles. Women and children picnicking in the local park as the fathers and sons played ball at the end of a hard week of work. It was swimming pools and barbecues, dirt infields and picnic tables. But it was also a distinctly Mexican American thing, with Spanish music on the transistor radio and chorizo giveaways and even occasional pregame speeches from activists and local politicians such as Edward Roybal, who became the city's only Mexican American elected official when he was elected to the city council in 1949. It was the national pastime, remade for a new version of the nation. Jorge Pasquel wanted to conquer US baseball. Los Chorizeros didn't need to; they just wanted to claim their share.

# 33.

IN 1944 FRANK BEGAN TO RECONSIDER HIS CONSCIENTIOUS-OBJECTOR status. He was beginning to see the war as a necessary evil, and perhaps more importantly, he had come to believe that the housing authority was needlessly protecting employees from the draft.

When Frank first got into the housing fight, Los Angeles was facing a housing shortage and a series of structural problems that made fair and comprehensive housing seem impossible. That was beginning to change, in part because of the war. The demand for wartime housing made the notion of government-subsidized homes more palatable (as long as those homes were being constructed to support the war effort).

Still, the movement for public housing faced both internal and external challenges. Internally, there was the simple fact that building and operating public-housing projects was hard. In theory, architects such as Richard Neutra could design efficient and beautifully planned communities. In practice, they were constrained by budgets and political will, and the people living in these communities knew it. As good as they might look in renderings, housing projects were always starving for resources and were constantly being stigmatized by their political opponents.

The very concept of public housing had many such opponents. On a fundamental level, there were competing ideas about how to live. And although the federal government did begin to invest in housing projects during the Great Depression, it was never in a definitive way: support for public housing came hand in hand with support for home-ownership initiatives. In 1934 the National Housing Act created the first federally insured mortgages, making private home ownership more accessible. Three years later, the Housing Act of 1937 solidified funding for the first federally subsidized low-income housing projects.

Public-housing advocates such as Frank argued that their projects allowed families a foothold to reach the home-ownership class.
Home builders and developers believed that tax money spent on
subsidized housing was a threat to their industry and an insult to
the notion of America as a haven for the rugged individual. Housing projects, quite simply, were socialistic. The fundamental question was of collective versus individual. Frank had made his choice.
But he also knew that if he was open about his membership in
the Communist Party, opponents of public housing would use that
against him and against the entire program.

This quandary left Frank feeling trapped. He couldn't be open
about his political beliefs. And as the war progressed, his discomfort with being protected only grew. The United States and the Soviet Union were allies now. He loved being a manager, but his job
could be filled by somebody else: somebody older, or a woman.
Frank thought he ought to be in Europe. He ought to take a stand.
So in typical Wilkinson fashion, he dramatically quit his job. They
had a going-away party for him at the housing project with a cake
and everything.

He kissed his children good-bye, removed his hearing aid, and
went down to the draft board. Still as deaf as ever, he hoped to lip-
read his way through the enlistment process. He passed through
one room, then another. Finally, he was called into the recruiter's
office. The man was a mumbler, and Frank could not make out
what he was saying or fake his way through the conversation. It is
harder to pretend you *can* hear than pretend you can't. He found
himself repeatedly asking the officer to speak up until finally, suspicious, the officer sent Frank to have his hearing examined. That
was the end of that.

And so before it even began, Frank's military career was over.
Soon he was back at the housing authority, and soon after that, he
was promoted to the main office as special assistant to the housing authority's executive director: a ruthlessly effective bureaucrat
named Howard Holtzendorff.

# 34.

PORFIDIO VARGAS ENLISTED ON JUNE 10, 1943. HE WAS AN INFANTRY-
man, assigned to the Second Division, Ninth Regiment, First Battalion, Company C. In October 1943 the division landed in Great
Britain, where it would spend ten months in Northern Ireland and
Wales training and waiting. Finally, on June 7, 1944, the day after
D-day, Vargas and his fellow soldiers landed at Omaha Beach. The
division made its way slowly southwest to Brest, where it helped
take the port city from the Germans, and then east through France
and into the Ardennes Forest. This is where on December 18, 1944,
in the early days of the Battle of the Bulge, Pio Vargas was killed in
action. He was twenty-five years old.

We don't know the circumstances of Pio's death, and we don't
know where Lola Vargas was when she got the news. Perhaps she
watched from the porch with her mother as a Western Union man
pedaled his way up Malvina Avenue. But at twenty-three she was a
widow, as her mother had been nearly thirty years before.

In February 1950, Lola applied for a military headstone for Pio.
Perhaps his body had finally made it home from the snowy forests.
Perhaps she realized that it never would. But in his death, Lola
was able to correct an error that had plagued Pio's military records
since the date of his enlistment: all of his official paperwork, even
after his death, had his name misspelled as Profidio, not Porfidio.
His headstone at Calvary Cemetery would not make this mistake.

Armand Muñoz, Camilo Arevalo's cousin, became a bomber
pilot and first lieutenant in the Army Air Forces. The prop pilot
from Los Angeles would go on to fly one of the biggest planes in the
world—the B-17 Flying Fortress—on the other side of the world.
First, he was sent to Rapid City, South Dakota, for training, and
then to Germany in early 1945. In the pictures you can spot an
earnest, fresh-faced kid. He's shorter than most of his crew and

looks younger than his twenty-four years, with thick eyebrows and a vague wariness underneath his smile, like you can tell that his mind is elsewhere.

Armand led a crew in a B-17 called *The Latest Rumor*. Their first mission came on February 6, 1945. "Being the first mission, everybody was tight. The flak was moderate but very accurate. Tail section was damaged," Armand's copilot wrote in his diary after their first run together, to bomb munitions factories in the German city of Chemnitz. "A long, tiring mission," he concluded. "Nine planes of our group failed to return." Muñoz flew more than twenty-five missions: mostly bombing runs, but also food deliveries and prisoner transports. He flew in Germany, France, and even northern Africa.

"When the war ended, he was OK," remembered Camilo. "When the war ended, he was stationed up in England someplace, and when he was coming back home, his plane went down. I remember my aunt told me, his plane went down some place up in England up in the mountains. That's it. He was flying back home, and he never made it."

# 35.

When Jackie Robinson was an officer in the army during World War II, he was nearly court-martialed for refusing to move to the back of a transport bus. The incident resulted in his discharge. A few years later, Jackie Robinson would become a tall tale. He would desegregate baseball before the country could officially desegregate its armed forces.

Jackie was an American hero, but that didn't mean he wasn't hated by millions of people. He was an American hero, but he still had to live in America, a fact that he was reminded of every day, on the field and in the clubhouse and in the streets.

Soon he would be reminded again. On New Year's Eve in 1948, a man named Alvin Stokes contacted Dodgers President and General Manager Branch Rickey. Stokes was a black man like Robinson. He was also a Republican and an investigator for the House Un-American Activities Committee (HUAC). Stokes wanted, more than anything, for Jackie Robinson to come to Washington and testify before HUAC.

The House Un-American Activities Committee and its precursors had been a fixture in US politics since 1918, when a Senate committee was opened to investigate allegations that there were German sympathizers in the beer industry and Bolsheviks hiding in alleyways after the Russian Revolution. This was a time when the fear of Communists was real, even if the threat that they posed wasn't.

In Los Angeles that fear played out in Hollywood. In 1941 no less a man than Walt Disney took out an ad in the film industry newspaper *Variety* claiming that Communists were behind a recent strike by animators. In 1944 Disney cofounded an industry group that offered advice on how to avoid putting Communist propaganda in films: "Don't deify the common man." Then, in 1946, the publisher of the *Hollywood Reporter* wrote an editorial listing the names of alleged Communists in the movie business. This led to the arrival of HUAC. The committee had carte blanche to publicly investigate anybody whom it suggested might be a Communist. It didn't matter that being a Communist was not even technically a crime. Walt Disney and Ronald Reagan testified as friendly witnesses.

A group of ten writers and directors refused to answer the committee's questions. All ten were convicted of contempt of Congress. All ten were sent to jail. And all ten were part of the much larger and more sweeping Hollywood blacklist when they got out.

Stokes had come to believe that black celebrities would benefit from preemptively clearing their names and that their doing so would reflect well on black people across the country. "My father convinced himself that what he was doing was totally in the black interest," Stokes's son Alvin Jr. told the writer David Falkner, "because he understood the double curse of being branded a communist. Black people had enough trouble as it was to then have to deal with that—that was his point of view."

On behalf of HUAC, Stokes negotiated with the Dodgers to convince them that Jackie ought to testify. It helped that Branch Rickey, who had signed Jackie in the first place, was a resolute anti-Communist. The parties came to an agreement: Jackie's testimony as a favorable witness to HUAC would not only serve Stokes's version of the black interest; it would also serve the committee and the broader mission of anti-Communism. Plus, it would serve the Dodgers. The movie business may have been full of Reds, but baseball? Baseball was the national pastime. In 1951 the Cincinnati Reds even briefly changed their name to the Redlegs to make sure that this was abundantly clear.

The opportunity to testify before HUAC may have suited Robinson, too. Jackie was a conservative person who, despite everything he had put up with, was still perhaps a little bit naive about America. He had grown up on an integrated block in Pasadena. His older brother had won a silver medal running right behind Jesse Owens in the 1936 Berlin Olympics. Jackie believed in the institutions of his country. In 1960 he would even endorse Richard

Nixon for president over John Kennedy, to the puzzlement of his wife, Rachel.

But it's not as if Robinson really had a choice. Stokes helpfully reminded the Dodgers that as the organization that had integrated baseball, they might fall under suspicion too. What if one of their star players was associating with Communists? How would that look? Arthur Mann, a sportswriter who covered the Dodgers at the time, put it this way: "He [Stokes] was particularly helpful in conferences relating to the proximity of subversive influences to Negroes in the Dodgers organization."

If the word got out that the Dodgers had refused to cooperate with HUAC, the great experiment would have been tarnished. And the personal stakes for Jackie were even higher. If he refused to testify, in addition to the pressure he already felt as perhaps the most visible black person in America, he would have to live with what Alvin Stokes Jr. called the "double curse."

Now all the committee needed was a pretense to call on him.

# 36.

Frank's new boss Howard Holtzendorff *looked* like a political operator. He was a stocky man with a high hairline and slicked-back hair parted down the middle. He wore pocket squares and chomped on cigars. When his work called him outdoors, he put on a fedora and a pair of tortoiseshell sunglasses. Holtzendorff wasn't on the take like many of his colleagues in local government, but he did understand that there was a game to play, and he played it to win. It was Holtzendorff, behind the scenes, who called Frank inside from that picket line at Hacienda Village, not because he believed especially in equality and integration but because he recognized their political expediency. Now it was Holtzendorff who promoted Frank to be his deputy.

Holtzendorff recognized from the get-go that the only way to neutralize Frank's ambition and channel it into something productive was to keep close tabs on him. Frank was a true believer. Even after he was promoted to the main office, Frank and Jean kept living in housing projects: first Aliso Village, then Estrada Courts in Boyle Heights. As Frank rose in the department in the middle and late 1940s, and made himself increasingly indispensable, Holtzendorff deployed him all over the place. They became a common sight, strolling through the city side by side: the shorter, wider Holtzendorff and the taller, more plainly dressed Wilkinson, giving the air of a Secret Service agent with the wires from his hearing aid running down from his ear under the collar of his shirt.

Frank did a little of everything. He was the housing authority's public-information director, and he became integral in cooperating with other government agencies. At one point he joined representatives from the planning and health departments on a driving tour across every city block of Los Angeles, hanging out the window and taking photos to get a sense of where future public-housing developments might fit. One of the neighborhoods they visited was Palo Verde. Frank also became the point person for interacting with all of the political and activist groups that were organizing in city-run housing projects. Chief among those groups was the Communist Party.

Frank's membership in the party was still a closely held secret, and the party was structured to maintain secrets like his. Members were divided into clubs by the nature of their industry. Hollywood types would be grouped with Hollywood types. Teachers with teachers. Frank was part of a club of social workers named after John Peter Altgeld, a crusading former governor of Illinois. Frank's official contact with fellow party members came at surreptitious club meetings held in the living rooms of private residences. A handful of party members gather in the living room of a house in Los Feliz. They draw the curtains. To anyone else, it looks like a normal get-together among friends or colleagues.

The paranoia was understandable. Even before Joseph McCarthy and J. Edgar Hoover began whipping up a frenzy of fear in the late 1940s, the LAPD was notorious for its Red Squad, and the city's business leaders were viciously opposed to Communism or anything that resembled it. At one point, Frank was so nervous about anti-Communist sentiment in LA that he took his membership card into the backyard and lit it on fire.

Frank's goal as an organizer was always, above all, to be effective. That was the word he used, too. Ef-fec-tive. He would enunciate all three syllables. The way he dressed, the way he spoke, the way he carried himself: everything was in service of effectiveness. Being outed as a Communist would have been, to say the least, ineffective. So even though he was in the party, Frank maintained his old high-society Wilkinson ties. For instance, although his immediate family—by 1947, Frank and Jean had three children: Jeffry, Tony, and Jo—joined a radical Unitarian Church branch, Frank still maintained his membership at Hollywood Methodist, where the family had a pew. His father had died in 1940 and his mother in 1946. His older sister, Hildegarde, had a growing practice as an ob-gyn. His brother, Budge, was a doctor as well. His sister Betty was a high-society woman up in Berkeley.

Frank was recruited to run for an open congressional seat. The only thing that stopped him was the fear of his Communist Party membership being revealed. The risk was too great. Another opportunity presented itself as well. Hollywood screenwriter Dalton Trumbo and director John Huston recruited Frank to run an organization called the Hollywood Independent Citizens Committee for the Arts, Sciences, and Professions (HICCASP).

HICCASP was a sort of activist collective that supported progressive causes and candidates. Huston and Trumbo took Frank out to lunch across from Paramount Studios and laid it all out. This would be a good opportunity for Frank to advance his career and use the organizing skills he had developed at the housing authority on a wider slate of issues. He accepted the job on the condition that the film stars could help find his family private housing, but they never could.

HICCASP would soon collapse anyway when the organization came under fire for its Communist Party ties. Trumbo himself was blacklisted as part of the Hollywood Ten. One of the final fractures came when one of its members, an actor named Ronald Reagan, demanded that the group put out a statement denouncing Communism. By not taking the job, Frank avoided this mess and preserved his reputation—for the moment.

=

THE REASON THAT a pair of Hollywood titans like Dalton Trumbo and John Huston could not find a modest apartment for the Wilkinson family is that Los Angeles was brimming with people. Wartime manufacturing jobs had drawn tens of thousands of African American families west. Returning soldiers passing through Southern California decided to stay. Japanese American families, rounded up and sent to internment camps during the war, came home needing new places to live. Between 1940 and 1950, the city's population grew by a third: from about 1.5 million to 2 million. Not even the most ambitious real-estate developers could keep up. There were simply not enough homes.

The answer to this problem, according to Frank, was obvious. But public housing was just one part of a broader social-engineering mission that came to be known as urban renewal. To Frank, urban renewal did not mean simply refurbishing old buildings or improving city services. It meant finding slums, clearing them out, and replacing them with something else. There was opportunity in urban renewal: opportunity for government organizations like the housing authority to justify their existence with ambitious housing projects, opportunity for private developers to make a buck, and opportunity for politicians to remake the landscape of the city in a way that would benefit them politically and monetarily. Generally speaking, the debate in Los Angeles wasn't over whether "renewing" neighborhoods was the right or wrong thing to do; the debate was over whether it should be a public or private endeavor.

The housing shortage gave Holtzendorff and Frank leverage to make their case. Frank became something of an urban renewal evangelist. He threw himself into the cause of convincing his fellow citizens that public housing was not just smart policy; it was a moral imperative as well. Frank began offering what he called "slum tours." He would charter a Greyhound bus, fill it with teachers or housewives from the wealthier parts of town, and direct the bus through LA's worst neighborhoods. He took thousands of Angelenos on these tours, including college students. Imagine what it must have felt like for the residents to see a bunch of strangers get off a bus and gawk at how poorly they lived. Frank's son Tony recalled that he would even drive the family car through slums if they happened to be nearby, just to show the children. He would slow to a crawl and fall into speechifying about rat rates and infrastructure as they made their way down streets where they were clearly not welcome: "We all expected a brick through the window."

Frank was convinced that if people saw what he had seen, and what he had been so ignorant of for so many years, they too would understand the need for public housing. In his oral history, Frank tells the story of hiring the Goodyear blimp and taking his boss, Holtzendorff, and the mayor, Fletcher Bowron, on a slum tour of the entire city.

The word *slum* was and is a pejorative way to describe somebody's home, and there is no doubt that the people who lived in these neighborhoods took offense to it. But this was exactly why Wilkinson and his allies chose it. They wanted to move public opinion; they wanted to evince an emotional reaction in the white home owners and City Hall decision makers who were their audience. *Slum* also became an official classification, albeit one with vague and shifting definitions. If a neighborhood was designated as a slum, it could be a target for clearance to make way for public housing.

IN 1948 IT seemed like public housing was on the verge of either total victory or total collapse. On one hand, real-estate interests across the country were furious about it. On the other, there was still momentum for big social programs in Washington left over from the New Deal. Congress was pushing President Truman to sign a bill that would guarantee housing as a basic right to every American, would provide funding for slum clearance, and would give hundreds of millions of dollars to local authorities to build new public-housing projects across the country, including ten thousand units in Los Angeles.

To make the case for housing, Frank joined with a pair of USC film students to turn his slum-tour concept into a short film called *And 10,000 More*. He recruited a popular news announcer named Chet Huntley to do the voice-over, and studio executives donated some of their musicians to score the thing. The film, which runs twelve minutes long, is an incredible time capsule: pure propaganda, complete with dramatic violins, close-ups of insects, and a totally nonsensical plot. But it also provides some insight into the kind of arguments that Frank and his colleagues were making.

The film follows a newspaper reporter as he investigates the city's housing shortage. He meets Howard Holtzendorff and peeks at some maps and charts. Then he decides to see the slums for himself. What the reporter finds, of course, is the worst kind of squalor. A child nearly falls off a fire escape. Little boys playing baseball are chased out of a narrow alley by a vindictive neighbor. "I suppose a kid gets to feeling like he doesn't belong anywhere. So he just cuts loose," the reporter says, before citing statistics about juvenile delinquency. The slums, we learn, breed disease, disease that we pay for with our tax dollars at County Hospital.

So what's the solution? The writer remembers that some public-housing projects were built before the war. He decides to pay them a visit. They are, of course, immaculate. A woman waters her lawn. A family sits down to eat. The music changes. The claustrophobic close-ups give way to lingering wide shots of children playing in a field. Why, these kids aren't delinquents at all!

"Decent housing builds self-respect," the narrator/reporter says, falling out of character. After one more look at the slums (to really drive his point in), the reporter returns to the newspaper office.

"So," says the newspaper editor, "do we really need ten thousand units of public housing?"

"Brother," says the reporter before the screen cuts to black, "and ten thousand more."

# 37.

ON SATURDAY NIGHT, JULY 10, 1949, THERE WAS A DANCE AT THE SAN Bernardino Municipal Auditorium. It was the kind of dance the kids from Palo Verde would have gone to: a live band, a ticket taker at the door. San Bernardino is about sixty miles east of Los Angeles. These days it sits at the far end of a single unrelenting urban landscape that begins at the ocean. But in 1949, San Bernardino was disconnected, its own place, population sixty thousand, on the other side of the citrus groves at the base of the mountains. In 1949, sixty miles was a long way.

Just after midnight, a group of local boys gathered outside the auditorium. There were sixteen of them, according to the newspaper reports, and they stood by the entrance, loitering, not committing any crimes, not doing anything wrong, but just kind of getting in the way. One of the boys had been kicking at the side door earlier and had been asked to stop. He scuffled with the off-duty police officer working security. One of the other boys was named Ramón Ríos. He was twenty years old. He was just standing around.

To clear the boys out, the dance organizers turned to the off-duty police officer. This was Johnnie Epps. Epps had just two years on the force. He was twenty-three years old, and he was the only black officer in all of San Bernardino. He was working that night to pick up some extra cash. Words were exchanged. The boys didn't want to leave. Epps had a job to do.

"You can't charge me for standing here," Ríos supposedly said. "You don't have to do that."

"Oh yeah?" Epps replied. "You want to make something of it?"

Epps drew his revolver, a .38 special. He cocked the weapon. It had been a hot day in San Bernardino, up in the nineties, but the temperature dropped fast when it got dark. The music was still playing inside. Patrons were shuffling in and out. Ríos turned his back. He began to walk away. It was then, witnesses said, that Epps reached up and shot him through the neck.

Some of the boys who saw the shooting said it looked like Epps was trying to strike Ríos with the gun, not shoot him with it. But because he had forgotten to disarm the weapon, it went off. Ríos died instantly. He left behind his mother, four brothers, and four sisters. Not so long ago, he had been a football player at San Bernardino High School. Now his body lay awaiting an official autopsy at Kremer's Funeral Home.

The story was front-page news the next day and traveled especially quickly through the Mexican American community. Epps was suspended, jailed, and then released on bail. The cause of justice for Ramon Ríos fell to one man: a newspaper publisher named Ignacio Lutero López. In the vast agricultural region east of Los Angeles, nobody was more influential or more vocal when it came to the fate of Mexican and Mexican American people than López. In the years to come, López would make his way west and become just as influential in the lives of the people of La Loma, Palo Verde, and Bishop.

=

LÓPEZ WAS BORN in Guadalajara but was brought to Southern California by his father, a minister, when he was a young boy. The family settled in Pomona, roughly halfway between San Bernardino and Los Angeles. López finished high school and then college, and in 1933 he began to publish a newspaper, *El Espectador*, out of the living room of his home. The paper quickly grew popular, featuring a mix of muckracking investigation, sharp opinion writing, and practical advice. López found his voice speaking not only to first-generation immigrants like his parents but also to second-generation Mexican Americans like his peers.

López was handsome, with a thin black mustache and ears that stuck out. He was a storyteller, a cigarette smoker, and a social drinker, but intolerant of drugs and petty crime. His friends called him Nacho. "He was well-read, a very sharp person, very witty, an excellent writer, a good political strategist, a marvelous speaker, and had a good sense of humor," recalled the Chicano activist Bert Corona. "Above all, Nacho was very bold about taking on tough issues, especially when it called for confronting racists."

López's audience was not the racists but the victims of racism. His essential driving motivation was to cement his people's equal place in US society. Even as temporary-worker programs and anti-immigration policies made life unstable, he prodded his readers to fight for their share: a notion that, in his writing on López, the scholar Mario T. García called "permanency." To López it was urgent that Mexicans and Mexican Americans recognize the value of their own experiences, organize, and claim their stake of the American Dream. He pushed and encouraged and even scolded his readers to take action, and when they didn't, he led by example.

Ignacio López led campaigns and boycotts striving to integrate public spaces like movie theaters, and he published lists of discriminatory businesses. In 1944 he successfully sued the mayor of San Bernardino over a segregated public-pool policy. The decision in his favor was a precursor to the influential *Mendez v. Westminster* case in nearby Orange County and later the landmark *Brown v. Board of Education*. He organized campaigns to get Mexican American candidates elected to local office. His writing inspired the beginnings of the Chicano movement of the 1960s, and his organizing helped build the foundations of the movement.

López was not a radical seeking to destroy the institutions of US society. Rather, he wanted to force those institutions to work for everybody. During World War II, despite the Zoot Suit Riots and ongoing violence against Mexicans and Mexican Americans in Southern California, López left the newspaper in the hands of his wife and went to work for the Office of War Information, crafting propaganda, pushing to engage Latinos across the country in the war effort, and then devising strategies to highlight their contributions to a white audience.

In the case of Ramón Ríos, López continued to insist that it was his own people's responsibility to change the system because to rely on the system to change itself was futile. "Johnny Epps is not to blame," López wrote in *El Espectador*. "The guilty ones are all of us, who permit the police to become the executioners of the people they are supposed to serve. . . . We are the criminals."

His tone changed when the court found that Epps had acted in self-defense. "His office," López promised, in reference to the district attorney, "will have to be judged by society."

# 38.

In 1949 time slowed down in Palo Verde. Everything became surreal and strange. There was something almost spiritual about it. The changes began in January, when the neighborhood awoke one morning to find the houses and streets covered in bright white snow. Six years earlier, the first recorded smog had descended upon Los Angeles, throwing the city into a mild panic. But this, the snow, was even harder to explain. The eucalyptus branches in Elysian Park bent under the weight of the accumulated frost, and the dogs in Palo Verde barked up at the sky.

Snow fell on Los Angeles for three days. It fell up in the hills and even down in the flatlands where Frank Wilkinson lived. The Wilkinson children had a snowball fight in their front yard. Children across the city built snowmen for the first time in their lives. Their parents' cars slid off the roads and into buildings. The streetcars, when they still ran, looked otherworldly floating through the fog and ice. A newspaper writer encountered a family in Elysian Park "gazing wonderingly at the blanket of snow." They had been there for seven hours.

═══

There is a certain kind of beauty that is inherent to the Southern California landscape. It's the way the city and its natural environment seem to blend into each other. The vines hanging over the freeway overpass. The little shoots of grass rising up from between the asphalt on city streets. The bougainvillea climbing up fences. The way the colors of the buildings seem to rhyme with the colors of the trees. The way the trees and the dirt and the sky meet one another. This was the beauty of Palo Verde, La Loma, and Bishop. They were beautiful in a wholly Southern Californian sense. The outsiders who visited liked to say that the communities were lost in time, but really they were just a little bit closer to nature than outsiders were used to.

Abrana and Manuel and their families lived in a place where humankind had not totally conquered the natural world because there was no reason to do so. In Palo Verde, La Loma, and Bishop you could see the gray and green of the trees. You could see the silhouettes of the houses against the setting sun. You could turn one way and see a typical US suburb, houses shoulder to shoulder and set back from the parked cars on the street. Then you could turn another way and see the cascading hillside, homes growing organically out of the Earth like some haphazard version of ancient Jerusalem. You could see goatherders and their goats grazing in Elysian Park. You could see the police cars crawling along, leaving tire marks in the dirt roads. It all seemed to fit together.

It wasn't always easy to live in the police academy's backyard. All these kids growing up on the margins, and sitting right beside them was a building with swimming pools and basketball courts and hot-dog stands. Where there were waterfalls landscaped into the grounds. A building where there were *grounds*. The kids from Palo Verde would sneak in and skinny-dip in the waterfalls. They'd collect spent bullet casings. But as they got older, their relationships with the cops changed. They'd become more than just neighbors. Sometimes that was a good thing. It was a good thing to be on friendly terms with detectives.

But sometimes, it just meant the truth revealing itself. The LAPD was not always a force for justice, especially if you were a person of color. There was one notorious cop who came around the neighborhood. His name was Brooks. He was a legend. You saw him coming, and you went in the opposite direction. He used to beat people with his billy club and really, truly, enjoy it. Gene Cabral remembers a story that his cousin Louie Carranza told him. Brooks pulled his car up next to Louie and a few of his buddies. He rolled down his window. "If I had my ways," Brooks said. "I'd chain up all of you fucking Mexicans and march you into the ocean. All of you."

There was another legendary cop in Palo Verde, but in a different way. His name was Julio Gonzales. In the years after World War II, Julio became a liaison between the youth of Palo Verde and his fellow cops at the academy. Julio went door-to-door and built a youth club. He started taking the boys on overnight trips to the mountains and to cookouts at the beach. He found corporate sponsors to pay for school buses and snacks. He organized baseball and football teams.

Because of Julio, the academy, which had previously been off-limits, slowly revealed itself to the kids in Palo Verde. The academy became a window into another world. There was a room inside with a piano in it. There was the pool. There were ice cream socials and Christmas parties. There were honorary dinners for important officials with famous guest speakers like the actor Ricardo Montalbán. There were dentists who set up shop there and eventually tended to the neighborhood kids. There were new bathrooms with beautiful new fixtures.

Julio Gonzales joined the small pantheon of outsiders who earned the trust of Palo Verde. And strangely, the police academy became one of the few mainstream institutions to embrace the community. The other two pillars of Palo Verde were located next door to each other on Paducah Street: the Santo Niño Church and the Palo Verde Elementary School, led by Father Tomas Matin and Principal Silvia Salvin, respectively. Matin was Austrian, and Salvin was Jewish. But both had earned the respect of the community. In the priest's case it was more like love.

Matin was legendary for hosting undocumented immigrants in the church basement and for living as humbly as his parishioners, with holes in his shoes and his black suit faded into gray. He spoke fluent Spanish and wore thick, round eyeglasses. He kept diligent records of baptisms, marriages, and deaths in immaculate cursive handwriting, but more than that, he became an everyday presence in the life of the communities. When kids were carted off to jail, it was Matin who came to talk the officers into releasing them into his custody. When families didn't have enough to eat, it was Matin who scrounged together a meal. He hosted movie nights on Fridays. His parish extended beyond its own walls and into the streets of Palo Verde, La Loma, and Bishop. His services were joyous and welcoming. After he died, a group of former Palo Verde residents even tried to get him canonized.

Whereas Padre Matin's church represented a link between the communities and their roots in Mexico, the school was a constant reminder to the residents of the communities that they were different. In 1927, soon after the school opened, a group of white citizens who lived nearby had petitioned the district to have their own children removed from the Palo Verde School and placed some-where with white students only. "Experience has shown it is almost impossible to Americanize those people," they wrote.

Salvin understood that "those people" were already American. She organized multicultural festivals and Mexican folk-dance per-formances. To her credit, she appears not to have condescended to the community. Even though the teachers in her employ were all white and non-Spanish speaking, she recognized the resources Palo Verde had: the tight-knit atmosphere, the culture that was proudly both Mexican and American. Salvin made home visits. She published a school newspaper that went home to parents in English and in Spanish. At one point she even invited the Nobel Prize–winning poet Gabriela Mistral, who had recently moved to Los Angeles from Chile, to address the school community. (Mistral politely declined.)

In 1955 a USC graduate student named Helene Hoelzel Gumbin-ger published a master's thesis that focused in part on Salvin's work. The school became a breeding ground for local activism. The PTA morphed into a local coordinating council that lobbied the city to build a recreational facility in Elysian Park, a place, as Gumbinger notes, that "had originally been connected with the home of the Pachuco gangs. It is said that when the recreation park was being built, former gang members stood guard at night on regular shifts to see that none of the building materials was disturbed." The Elysian Park Recreation Center opened in December 1949 with a dance performance by the children at Palo Verde Elementary School and speeches from local politicians.

# 39.

In 1946 Ignacio López wrote the foreword to a book called *Not with the Fist: Mexican Americans in a Southwest City* by a friend of his named Ruth Tuck. The book was an anthropological examination of the Mexican American experience. Tuck, a professor, had lived in San Bernardino's Mexican neighborhoods to research it. But López's foreword was something else: a screed, a mission statement, a fierce argument that systemic racism is not passive and that its cost is not invisible. He begins with a description of the Zoot Suit Riots: "the terrible Quixotism of the mob." As he wrote, "It was not a 'Mexican' problem. It was an American one."

Sure, López pointed out, there was an outpouring of support after the riots and after white Americans realized how many people with Spanish last names had given their lives in the war. But what did it solve? What changed? "Still, when the emotional fever and the defensiveness subsided, few real gains had been made for or by the Mexican American group. They were basically where they had been for twenty-five years, and the flare of faddish interest was dying."

López published his foreword about twenty-five years after Abrana and Manuel Aréchiga had moved to Los Angeles. Twenty-five years that saw Southern California explode, that saw Los Angeles inflate with its own air of destiny and grow from a town into a city into a destination, a world-famous metropolis. Twenty-five years, and what could Abrana and Manuel do now that they couldn't before? What could their children do? They were rooted to their land, and they were proud of it. But that didn't change the fact of what had happened in 1943 with the sailors from the naval armory. It didn't change the fact that their daughter lost a husband, Manuel's sister lost a son, and their relatives still could not buy homes in the neighborhoods they wanted to. "The conflict between Anglo and Hispanic groups in the Southwest is not as much the working of unconscious forces as [Tuck] makes it seem," López wrote. "There is deliberated action and premeditated cruelty."

# 40.

WHILE CONGRESS DEBATED THE HOUSING BILL, FRANK AND HOLT-zendorff began to plan for what the ten thousand units of new public housing might actually look like in Los Angeles. The units would have to be located within commuting distance of job centers, especially the area around downtown. Many neighborhoods classified as slums and slated for clearance were in industrial zones. Building new housing in those zones was out of the question. The new projects would also have to be sited in a thoughtful way to fit with planned freeway construction, potential rezoning, and, perhaps most importantly, the remaking of downtown LA into a business and cultural hub befitting the ambitions of the city's ruling class.

By the late 1940s, there was only one place in LA that was near downtown, with living conditions that might make it amenable to urban renewal, and with enough empty space to house a large number of people. The city had burned through everything else: every buildable field and empty lot.

Simon Eisner, a city planner at the time, drove up to Palo Verde for the first time with Frank. He recalled seeing the remnants of the old brickyards, the places where the clay had been removed from the mountains. He recalled the landscape of shrubs and dirt. He recalled the animals and the family gardens. But mostly, he recalled the community itself: "There was a very strong association of people in the area, centered about two institutions: the elementary school and the Catholic Church. They had festivals, they had things going on that were so rich culturally that you couldn't believe it."

To the decision makers at city hall and the architects and planners thinking about urban development, the selection of Palo Verde, La Loma, and Bishop felt inevitable. The great minds of the city had never quite known what to do with the land up there in the hills. There had been the cemeteries, the pesthouses, and the brickyards.

*Los Angeles City Hall*

There were the police academy and the armory, which made sense. There was Elysian Park. And then there were these communities, which were small and insular and Spanish-speaking and which the English-speaking men downtown had tried their best to ignore.

By the time Truman got around to signing the Housing Act in 1949, it was clear that the communities could be targeted for redevelopment, not that anybody was asking the people of Palo Verde, La Loma, or Bishop about it. Around this time, the nonprofit Haynes Foundation hired an architect named Robert Alexander and his colleague Dayton Bryant to write a book called *Rebuilding a City: A Study of Redevelopment Programs in Los Angeles.* Alexander and Bryant offered a thorough and statistical examination of the communities. They found high rates of tuberculosis but also high rates of home ownership. They found substandard housing conditions but also low rates of juvenile delinquency. They found the same vibrant civic culture that Eisner had encountered.

Alexander and Bryant recommended redeveloping the communities with a mixture of private single-family homes, private rental apartments, and public housing. They argued that doing so would account for the economic diversity of the current residents: the home owners and the poor renters alike. They also pointed out that most residents of the communities would not be eligible for public housing, which at the time prioritized war veterans, families with children, and US citizens.

Reading the report, you can almost feel the authors' ethical gears turning. From a big-picture planning perspective, Alexander and Bryant believed that the land was too valuable to remain sparsely populated, but they also saw that simply dismantling the communities would have been inhumane and counterproductive. Palo Verde, La Loma, and Bishop might have been poor and underserved, but they already had many of the traits that successful urban planning was seeking to provide: a rich pedestrian culture, an engaged populace, a sense of community. Toward the end of the book, Alexander and Bryant offered a warning: "Active opposition of the site occupants could conceivably delay a redevelopment program for many years."

# 41.

THE PACIFIC COAST LEAGUE MAY NOT HAVE BEEN ABLE TO HOLD onto big-league-caliber players like Mel Almada, but it had big-league amenities. The seasons were longer because of the milder weather, the salaries were relatively high, and the owners had no particular use for the high-minded, haughty traditions of the East Coast game; there would be no Doubleday worship or pointless nostalgia. The league existed on its own terms, and it even developed its own uniquely civilized schedule, with Mondays off and Sunday doubleheaders (in the spirit of that civility, the second game was always just seven innings).

Nothing in the league was sacred, not the length of ball games and not the bonds between franchises and their cities. For instance, after they left Los Angeles, the former Vernon Tigers would languish for a dozen seasons in San Francisco as the Mission Reds. But in the meantime, the very year they left, Los Angeles got a replacement club to compete with the Angels. The Salt Lake Bees, the team that had thrown those crucial games to the Tigers in 1919, moved west and replaced them. They became the Hollywood Stars.

The Hollywood Stars. What a name for a baseball team. It evoked the best of what Los Angeles wanted itself to be, all glamour and mystery and movie magic. But the Hollywood Stars played in South Los Angeles at Wrigley Field. They were a long way from Hollywood, and they were a long way from popular. They lasted only from 1926 through 1935, after which they took off for San Diego, changed their name to the Padres, and signed a local teenager named Ted Williams to play the outfield.

But just three years later (and this gives you an idea of how little stability there was in the league), the Mission Reds returned to Los Angeles from San Francisco, not to reclaim their old identity as the Vernon Tigers or to become the Los Angeles Reds but to take over as the new Hollywood Stars. The name was too good to pass up, especially in Los Angeles, especially in Hollywood, the land of invention and reinvention: a place where nothing is what it seems and nobody is quite who they say they are.

The new Hollywood Stars played at a new ballpark called Gilmore Field, which was near enough to Hollywood to actually justify the team's name. Beyond the right-field fence was a drive-in movie theater. If you sat in exactly the right spot up in the bleachers, you could catch a movie and a ball game at the same time. One of the club's owners was Robert Cobb, who had invented the Cobb salad at his Brown Derby restaurant. Cobb sold shares of the club to actual Hollywood stars like Gary Cooper and Gene Autry, and this time the club developed into a popular rival for the Angels.

The teams grew to truly hate each other. The players fought constantly. Once, in 1953, things got so bad during a brawl at Gilmore Field that Los Angeles Police Chief William Parker, watching the game at home on television, picked up the phone and called in riot squads to break things up.

It wasn't major league, but this was the baseball that LA had. In an essay for *Sports Illustrated* the writer John Schulian recalled growing up in the 1940s and 1950s, the time of Stars and Angels, of silly antics and journeymen revered like gods in a parallel baseball universe:

> But the town, if you judged it by its tastes, was still shamelessly small-time. Forget all the hoorah about college football at Southern Cal and UCLA. Forget all the cigar smoke that got blown about the club lights at the Olympic Auditorium and Hollywood American Legion Stadium and the title fights at Wrigley and Gilmore fields. The L.A. I choose to remember devoted far more passion to professional wrestling, both live and televised, from the Olympic, from Legion Stadium, from South Gate, from Ocean Park Arena (with none other than Steve Allen at the ringside mike). So great was L.A.'s hunger for these sweaty morality plays that Channel 11 had to pipe even more of them in from Las Vegas. How lining for a city where a good Sunday afternoon of TV sports meant watching semipro football and the Jalopy Derby from Culver City Stadium.

When I think back to all that raw exuberance and unbridled tackiness, it seems the Coast League gave L.A. sports a rare touch of . . . well, dignity isn't the word, not with the shorts the Stars insisted on wearing in the '50s and the call-the-cops brawls they had with the Angels. But normality, maybe, because no matter how outrageous the two teams got, they still played baseball, they still did something connected to the rest of the country and not confined to Planet California.

# 42.

As the 1940s gave way to the 1950s and Los Angeles grew larger and denser, Palo Verde, La Loma, and Bishop came to be more connected to the rest of the city but at the same time feel less like a part of it. It wasn't just the rec center or the police academy. The first generation of kids who were actually *from* the communities, the ones who had been born or brought there in the 1920s, were parents now. They weren't immigrants. They spoke English and had commuted to high schools in East Los Angeles. They had served in the war and come back to work regular jobs downtown. They had children who wore blue jeans rolled up over their sneakers and played stickball in the streets. They understood exactly how unique the communities were.

The city had modernized at a faster rate than the communities themselves could. The streetcars had been ripped up, and the freeways had spread their tentacles across neighborhoods and even tunneled under Elysian Park. At night you could see the brake lights hugging their way around the base of the hills. You could hear the hum of traffic like waves on a beach. As the scholar Ron López has pointed out, the construction of the 110 freeway served to physically separate Palo Verde, La Loma, and Bishop from downtown. This meant that even though in the quiet mornings, it almost seemed as though you could reach out across the freeway and touch the downtown skyline, the communities became easier for outsiders to write off as backward, distant, and irrelevant. "From the City Hall to Chavez Ravine is a five-minute drive by modern traffic-time; sociologically, the two points are separated by a time-span between fifty and seventy-five years," wrote Carey McWilliams, the great chronicler of Southern California.

141

White city leaders (even well-intentioned progressives like McWilliams) viewed Palo Verde, La Loma, and Bishop as antiquated and backward, despite the fact that they were close-knit and politically organized. McWilliams himself chronicled the way that residents of Palo Verde, La Loma, and Bishop banded together after World War II and successfully demanded bus service from city leaders. "We have been walking for years and years, and now we're very very tired," a resident told him.

For years and years, the people of Palo Verde walked. For years and years, Palo Verde made do with less: less attention from the city, fewer government services, less representation at City Hall. Abrana stood on the little hill in her backyard and looked down on the skyline as it filled in beneath her. The buildings grew higher and higher, closer and closer. She watched the freeway built and saw the river paved. She saw progress all around her but almost always somewhere else. When the people of Palo Verde finally made their voices heard—when the rec center was built and the bus finally came—it was already too late.

═

FOR ALL THE services that Palo Verde lacked, one that it did not was US mail delivery. The mail came every day, rain or shine, sleet or even, that one time, snow. Abrana and Manuel picked up their mail a couple blocks down from their house at the intersection of Malvina Avenue and Effie Street, where there stood a cluster of mailboxes perched on rails and poles that looked, at a glance, like a group of children standing and waiting for a school bus.

In July 1950 the people of Palo Verde, La Loma, and Bishop opened their mailboxes to find a letter that would change everything. This letter was the culmination of a series of rumors that had been whispered about for years. There had always been talk about the city doing something with their land. There had always been the fear that they were somehow expendable. After all, wasn't that why the city had ignored them? Isn't that why they had such a hard time getting electricity and gas and pavement for their streets? There had always been rumors. But this was not a rumor:

## HOUSING AUTHORITY OF THE
## CITY OF LOS ANGELES

*July 24, 1950*

To the Families of The Palo Verde and Chavez Ravine Areas:

This letter is to inform you that a public housing development will be built on this location for families of low income. The attached map shows the property that is going to be used. The house you are living in is included.

Within a short time surveyors will be working in your neighborhood. Later you will be visited by representatives of the Housing Authority who will ask you to allow them to inspect your house in order to estimate its value. Title investigators will also visit you. You should be sure that any person who comes to your house has proper identification.

*It will be several months at least before your property is purchased. After the property is purchased*, the Housing Authority will give you all possible assistance in finding another home. If you are eligible for public housing, you will have top priority to move into any of our public housing developments. *Later you will have the first chance to move back into the new Elysian Park Heights Development.*

Three offices are being opened in this area to give you information and answers to your questions. They are located as follows:

Santo Niño Parochial Hall at 1034 Effie St., (rear of Church)
San Conrado Mission at 1809 Bouett, (near Amador St.)
Tony Visco's old grocery store at 1035 Lilac Terrace

You are welcome to come in at any time. We will be open day and night this week, July 24 through July 28, and during the day Saturday, July 29. Next week we will be open during the day and in the evenings by appointment. Telephone Angelus 2-1963 for any information.

We want to assure you that it is our intention to help you and work with you in every way possible.

*Yours very truly,*

Sidney Green
Management Supervisor

Imagine opening your mailbox and getting this letter. You don't even have to read it to know what it says. The official government font and the big blue heading give it all away. But still, you chase down one of your children to translate the words into Spanish. You hear the words, but how can you really listen? Your neighbors are standing around talking about it, stray phrases bouncing off the houses and ringing out in the church and the schoolyard. But the houses, the church, the schoolyard are doomed. In a sense the community is already gone.

Strange men began to appear. The men who made this happen, who, while the residents of Palo Verde were working and sleeping and raising their children, were determining that their lives would be offered up as a sacrifice to the great purpose of housing. A better world does not make itself; it requires sacrifice. One of these men was Frank Wilkinson.

*Part IV*

---

# BILLION DOLLAR
# BLACKJACK

# 43.

IN 1971 AN EARTHQUAKE RATTLED THE SAN FERNANDO VALLEY. THE damage spread across the city. Freeway interchanges crumbled, and a pair of hospitals collapsed. About sixty people died in the quake and its aftermath. One other consequence of the 6.5 magnitude earthquake was that a retaining wall fell on an old movie ranch, allowing a herd of white reindeer to escape their enclosure and wander into the community of Sylmar. As the city panicked, the reindeer made their way down residential streets and through busy intersections, prancing obliviously through the ruins. And as Los Angeles began its slow recovery, Fritz B. Burns, one of the men who had willed the city into existence, or at the very least into *this* existence, the one where exotic animals walking down paved streets is not even that weird, had to make sure that they were rounded up and returned to his ranch.

There is a notion that Los Angeles is an accidental city, not even a real place, just a bunch of suburbs thrown together and then later ripped apart again by freeways. Disparate parts that don't actually make up a functioning metropolis. But LA was not an accident; it was an idea, and before the freeways were built and the backlash came and the sprawl spilled out of the basin, before strip malls and smog, before the reindeer, and before big-league baseball, Los Angeles was sold to America and to itself by people like Fritz Burns.

Like his future rival Frank Wilkinson, Fritz Burns was born in the Upper Midwest. Whereas Frank was brought to Arizona and Los Angeles as a child, Fritz Burns came as a young man. When he arrived, he had one goal: to become a millionaire. In 1921 that was the kind of thing a man could dream about, especially a man like him: twenty-two years old with a Wharton education, good years of wartime service behind him, a square jaw, and a single-mindedness that was so intense it often broke through into unbridled grandiosity of vision.

When Fritz Burns came to Los Angeles, he was already well acquainted with the business of buying and selling land. He worked for an outfit called Dickinson & Gillespie, traveling the hard, cold midwestern plains, snatching up wide, flat properties, turning them into subdivisions, and then selling them again in pieces. He wore dandy suits and burst through the cities of South Dakota and Minnesota glowing with his own ambition and with the charisma that would also carry him in Los Angeles. If there was one thing that Southern California had, it was land. Beautiful, naked, and empty, just waiting for men with vision, men like Fritz Burns.

He told the world that he would be a millionaire at thirty. And from the moment he set foot in Los Angeles he did everything he could to make it happen. Dickinson & Gillespie sold the dream: lots in subdivisions with optimistic names like Orange Blossom Manor. He gave the people what they wanted. He offered potential home buyers rides in repurposed World War I prop planes, and he piloted them himself. He bought a stake in the city's first professional football team, the short-lived Los Angeles Buccaneers of the NFL. He got married, had a son, and just as quickly got divorced.

For Fritz Burns, selling was not just a job; it was a lifestyle, a purpose, an organizing principle, just like his Catholicism. Fritz Burns was a philosophical man. He thought deeply about what he did. He bought land on the hills overlooking the beach at Playa del Rey, and he bought land along the beach itself. In the morning, beachgoers strolling on the sand would come across Burns beginning his daily sales meeting. They would see him standing before his team of young, clean-shaven, and hopeful men, miniature Fritz Burnses all, in military formation performing calisthenics as the waves crashed and their ties flapped in the breeze, gearing themselves up into rigorous and virile form in the salty air before they set off to sell Los Angeles. This city was not an accident.

In the middle of 1929, Fritz Burns bought the controlling share of Dickinson & Gillespie. On October 9 of that year, he turned thirty years old, a genuine millionaire. He had achieved his goal. Then, three weeks later, the stock market crashed. So did the Los Angeles real-estate market. Fritz Burns was a millionaire at twenty-nine, and at thirty he was divorced, broke, and living on the beach at Playa del Rey in an abandoned tent.

The book on Fritz Burns is called *Fritz B. Burns and the Development of Los Angeles* by James Thomas Keane. This title dramatically understates how weird and fantastical his life was, how much the Fritz Burns story reads like a fable for the city he made. Burns lived out the Great Depression in his tent, writing poetry and staring at the stars, waiting for his fortunes to change. He clung to his last bit of property at Playa Del Rey, and he leveraged the last of his money to buy abandoned cottages from the 1932 Olympic Village and roll them out there so that he might later resell them as beachfront homes. This was a time when houses moved from place to place, a time when it was still possible to view a map of Los Angeles like a game board, with the buildings and the people as little pieces to be rearranged on the whims of the players.

Then Fritz Burns caught a break. He struck oil in Playa Del Rey. His face was covered in it. Suddenly, there was a way for him to get off the beach and out of debt. Little by little, one venture at a time, he re-amassed his fortune. Then, as Keane lays out, the New Deal brought forth the passage of a series of bills "creating and protecting a nation of homeowners." Suddenly, mortgages were standardized and insured. Suddenly, the government wanted to *help* people buy houses. Fritz Burns decided that if that was the case, he ought to sell them, and before he could sell them, he had to build them.

Fritz Burns became more than a salesman and a subdivider. He became a home builder. Before famous suburbs such as Levittown, New York, were constructed and celebrated on the East Coast, Burns pioneered methods to mass-produce houses that were cheap, fast, and sturdy enough to stand up to the elements. He built communities all over the city, from Inglewood to the San Fernando Valley. He became a voice for individual property rights. After all, that was the dream of Los Angeles. A lot of your own with a yard and with flowers. A home of your own. The choice of whether you wanted that home to have the "Cape Cod" exterior or the "Californian." The chance, rich or poor—so long as you were white—to own a little piece of America. "It is no less important now than in days gone by," he wrote, "for people to have their own 'vine and fig tree,' their own bit of this earth, where they are at least to some extent masters of their fate."

# 44.

To Frank Wilkinson, this vision—the vision that was powering the region's booming real-estate market—was absurd and dangerous. Vines and fig trees were well and good, but housing was much too important to turn into a commercial product while the poorest among us slept in hovels and on the streets.

The ten thousand new units of public housing would be a start. Public housing units were bare bones; they were cheap by necessity. Closets had no doors, only curtains. Surfaces were slick, durable, and easily cleaned, to account for the high turnover between tenants. In his oral history, Frank discussed the fact that many of the tenants in the projects he ran had never lived in finished housing before, had never experienced plumbing or electricity. At one point, he had to threaten fines because children kept flushing their toys and clogging pipes: they hadn't had toilets before.

But although the units were humble, Frank believed that the communities did not need to be. The biggest and most ambitious new development would be the one slated for the site of Palo Verde, La Loma, and Bishop: Elysian Park Heights. Holtzendorff tapped two leading local architects to lead the project. One was Frank's old mentor and landlord Richard Neutra. The other was Robert Alexander, who had cowritten the ominous report on the area's suitability for redevelopment.

Neutra and Alexander had worked together before. Both were highly respected in Los Angeles, and both had worked on innovative, modernist housing projects, drawing on the vision of French architect Le Corbusier. Their design for Elysian Park Heights would have space for retail, schools, and, at the center of it all, churches. "The new town in town," Holtzendorff had called it.

The Elysian Park Heights project did not go off without a hitch. Neutra and Alexander hired Simon Eisner, formerly of the city planning department, as the project's chief planner. But almost immediately, Eisner uncovered major obstacles. The soil around the communities was not suitable for the kind of construction the city wanted. Even with extensive grading and a total remaking of the landscape, large swaths of the land around Palo Verde simply were not buildable. The alternative that Neutra and Alexander hit upon was to include a combination of low buildings and thirteen-story towers; this would allow for an equal number of units but a narrower footprint. The notion of building high-rise apartments was abhorrent to many public-housing supporters; even Eisner himself had problems with it. But the city had signed a federal contract to build the units, and at the very least, Neutra and Alexander's design was architecturally impressive.

The towers, minimalist and sleek, would be perched on a series of steppes carved into the hills, and they would loom over the downtown skyline. It would have been the opposite of Palo Verde, La Loma, and Bishop, communities tucked away to the point that many Los Angeles residents didn't even know they existed. The towers would have stood proudly overlooking downtown and the entire city. They would have changed the entire feel of Los Angeles. Eisner likened the design to the ancient Greek Acropolis: "It would have been a hell of a thing to look at."

===

FRANK WILKINSON WAS not afraid to deliver the good news face-to-face. This project was the culmination of his career in housing. It was an ambitious, city-changing step toward the better world on Earth he had always dreamed of. Towers on a hill overlooking the city. A city without slums. The site selection had been up to him. All the public relations. Everything in his life had built toward this moment, so of course he was out on the front lines.

Frank spent much of 1950 in Palo Verde, La Loma, and Bishop. He showed his film at the schools and at the church. The appointments are still there in his old planners. On September 29 he screened *And 10,000 More* at the Palo Verde school. He displayed aerial photos and government charts.

To connect with the locals, Frank hired a Spanish-speaking organizer he had met along the way. Afterward, this organizer would be written into Frank's story as a mere assistant or interpreter. But

Frank knew better than that. The interpreter was Ignacio López. Later, Frank recalled that he and López had knocked on every door in all three communities and spoken to every resident they could find.

It would not have been hard to find Abrana Aréchiga. She would have been home; she almost always was. And with the way gossip traveled through Palo Verde, she would have known that this tall white man with the hearing aid was coming. She and Manuel would have looked out at Frank Wilkinson, still a stranger to them, through their venetian blinds. They would have watched as he climbed the steps, the same steps that they had carried Manuel Jr. up as he ached in pain after falling in that movie theater fifteen years earlier and the same steps that they carried his coffin down after the wake. Manuel might have put a hand on Abrana's arm to calm her as Frank approached.

Frank would have been accompanied by López, and López would have done the talking. López had credibility that Frank didn't: after all, he wasn't just a Spanish-speaking employee of the housing authority but was also a seasoned civil rights activist and organizer. He knew how to speak to people and meet them on their level. The fact that López was willing to work with Frank and advocate for the Elysian Park Heights Project shows not only his commitment to the project but also his humility and willingness to get in the trenches for the causes in which he believed.

This would have been a complex decision for López. After the war he had turned increasingly to the issue of housing. Mexican American soldiers were coming home and finding themselves turned away from new subdivisions. Local municipalities were refusing to enforce building codes and hold slumlords accountable in Mexican American neighborhoods; elected officials were also dragging their feet when it came to applying for the federal funding that could support Mexican American communities. López believed that fair and integrated housing could lay the foundation for a fair and integrated society: "It is not the anglo-saxon who will reap the repercussions . . . of segregation . . . it will be those of us who have yet to understand that the only way to end discrimination and segregation is for us to integrate fully into society . . . making us part of the community and not trying to live in an exclusive world reserved only for ourselves."

López had been an advocate for self-determinism and empowerment among Mexican and Mexican American families. Yet here he was going door-to-door in Palo Verde and telling families who had achieved those things—or thought they had—that they were going to have to give it up on the altar of housing desegregation, telling them that soon this land that you built from nothing into something will once again become nothing. Dust to dust. Soon you will have to leave the community you made.

To Frank, the people of Palo Verde might have seemed ignorant for getting angry when he was simply trying to *help* them, simply trying to lift them up. And even if they didn't need the help, surely they could see that their community needed it, that their city needed it. It would be painful to leave, but it would be worth it, he argued. This, of course, is the kind of attitude that's much easier to have when it's not *your* house being razed, when the "slum" is only something you see through the window of a bus.

For López, the pain would have been more acute. He understood that communal pride was at stake but decided that for him, desegregation—and the possibility of housing more families in humane conditions and perhaps lifting them from poverty—were worth the cost.

Frank quickly learned that the people of Palo Verde would not be compliant. They would not be easily convinced. The people of Palo Verde had already been politically engaged long before the housing authority letters were mailed. Now they had a cause to rally around.

On August 8 the city's plans for Elysian Park Heights broke in the *Los Angeles Times*. Ten days later the residents of Palo Verde, La Loma, and Bishop gathered in protest at the Elysian Park Recreation Center that they had helped build. Now it seemed like a monument to their naïveté. What was the point of a park if nobody lived nearby to play there? The fight for the communities was just beginning.

# 45.

THE BROOKLYN PRESS TOOK ONE LOOK AT DUKE SNIDER AND SAW greatness. He had those big cowboy-actor teeth, and his hair was already turning silver. When he made contact from the left side, everything seemed to slow down, and the ball soared and just kept soaring. The press couldn't help themselves. Nobody could. Not even his general manager, Branch Rickey, who told the world that the Snider kid had steel springs in his legs and that he was "potentially the greatest hitter I have ever seen." Duke spent 1946 in the minors in Texas, and in 1947 he made the big club. He was just a backup, a young prospect with a chance to be something special one day, but not today. Today the story was the other rookie, Jackie Robinson.

Somehow Duke Snider had grown up and left Compton and gone all the way across the country and found himself a few lockers over from a person he had once idolized. Jackie Robinson was a man now. He had lived twenty-eight hard years and seen things and heard things and felt things that Duke couldn't understand even if he wanted to. But Duke knew what he didn't know, and he took his seat on the bench and watched in awe as Jackie Robinson changed the world.

It would take two more years for Duke to become the Dodgers' full-time center fielder. When he did, in 1949, he became an instant star. The Dodgers reached the World Series that year, and Duke found himself playing in Yankee Stadium on the same field that his idol Lou Gehrig had once walked. He wore number 4, just like Gehrig. The Dodgers lost. Snider struggled. But after it was over and he went home to Compton, the city threw him a parade.

Duke Snider was a walking advertisement for baseball. Brooklyn loved him unconditionally. He learned to lay off the high fastball, and he grew to love Brooklyn back. There was Mantle, there was Mays, and there was the Duke. He and Beverly started a family. He would play stickball with the neighborhood kids in Bay Ridge. He would come to embody exactly what the Brooklyn Dodgers were all about: fierce local pride and deep-seated insecurity, utter greatness that was never quite great enough. The Dodgers *were* Brooklyn. Even their name was a product of the borough's rough history. Dodgers was a shortening of Trolley Dodgers, a nickname that dated back to the 1890s, when Brooklyn switched from horse-drawn streetcars to electric trolleys and experienced a spike in fatal pedestrian collisions.

By Duke's prime, the Dodgers were under the operating control of Walter O'Malley. In the history of baseball there had never been an owner like Walter O'Malley. He was a big, imposing man who draped himself in fine suits. He looked like an old-time political boss, which was just as well because his father had been an operator in New York's Tammany Hall machine back in the 1920s. He was charming and funny. He saw angles that other people didn't. At spring training in Vero Beach, Florida, O'Malley was known to invite reporters to play cards with him after dinner. If he liked what they had been writing about the club, he would intentionally throw hands to them. It was his way of passing out unspoken monetary rewards for favorable coverage and gently reminding them who their friend was.

O'Malley had been an engineer and an attorney before his career in baseball started. Perhaps this was why he was able to think about the sport in a more dynamic way than other owners. Whereas the Dodgers' initial run of on-field success had been driven by O'Malley's former partner, Branch Rickey, who was himself a visionary as the inventor of the farm system, the challenger of the color line, and one of the sport's earliest statistical freethinkers (Rickey was dismissing the value of runs batted in decades before it was cool to do so), the team's business success owed everything to O'Malley. He was a man of great pride and great foresight. Before any of his peers, O'Malley grasped the vast potential of baseball as commercial entertainment.

O'Malley also understood by the 1950s that the Dodgers desperately needed a new ballpark. Ebbets Field was quaint, but it was falling apart. Squeezed onto a small lot in Flatbush, there was no room to expand beyond its 32,000 seats. (Not that the Dodgers typically sold their games out anyway; in 1955, when they won the World Series, they averaged about 13,000 fans per game.) There was no room to add parking either, which O'Malley saw as vital to future attendance.

Nobody loved Ebbets Field more than Duke Snider. As the Dodgers' best left-handed hitter, Snider benefited from the stadium's dimensions. There was a short fence in right field. Duke happily bashed towering home runs clear over it and onto Bedford Avenue. But to his critics, that fence was a mark against him: Snider was just lucky to play in Brooklyn, lucky to play in Ebbets Field, lucky to have the protection of a lineup full of great right-handed hitters. Of course he hit all those home runs.

The critics got to Duke. He was a victim of expectations, his own and other people's. As a boy he never learned what it was like to fail. Now, even in all his majesty, he had to reckon with the individual failures that strung together to form the long big-league season, with the fact that to some people, even his triumphs weren't good enough. He was ungraceful with the press when things were going bad and oblivious to his teammates. Snider could be sullen even after Dodger wins. Carl Erskine, who was Duke's best friend on the team, told the writer Peter Golenbock that it had to do with Duke's own insecurities: "No matter how good he was, they'd say, 'His potential is so great, he can do even better.' And this was a real frustration for Duke. He saw himself as not measuring up."

Duke worked hard and lived clean and loved his family. He put together one of the great careers in baseball history. But it was never enough. He was lucky, but he didn't feel like the luckiest man on the face of the Earth.

The Dodgers finally won the World Series in 1955. Snider was in the middle of the best run of his career. He had achieved his wildest dreams. Despite himself, he was beloved and vindicated. But he was tired. The following year, he collaborated with the writer Roger Kahn to publish an article in *Collier's Weekly*. The headline was "I Play Baseball for Money—Not Fun." Snider and his boss O'Malley may not have had much in common, but they both had a clear understanding that baseball was a business.

In weary, searching prose, Snider tries to figure out what went wrong. He lays out all the burdens of the big league life. The travel, the pressure, the fans hurling insults and objects at him in center field:

> I remember when I was a boy around Los Angeles I used to dream about playing in a World Series. It was my biggest and most important dream.
>
> Last autumn when I played in my fourth World Series, I was still dreaming. Only the dream had changed. While we were beating the Yankees, I was dreaming about being a farmer. I'm looking forward to the day when baseball will allow me to settle down to raising avocados in the California sunshine.

# 46.

BEFORE THE EVICTION NOTICES WENT OUT, FRANK AND HIS ALLIES had worked to recruit partners in the community. Their main targets were Father Tomas Matin and Principal Sylvia Salvin. Frank's mentor Monsignor O'Dwyer used his pull to talk Matin on board. The church and a parish in nearby Solano Canyon were used as temporary offices by the housing authority.

In the case of Salvin, architect Richard Neutra took matters into his own hands. Eisner remembers that Neutra invited Salvin to his home in Silver Lake, the same place where a young Frank Wilkinson had been convinced to join the Communist Party. Neutra spoke rapturously of how the new community would not only replicate the cultural richness of Palo Verde, La Loma, and Bishop but would in fact expand on it. Salvin was convinced.

Suddenly, the very institutions that had underpinned the three communities were being leveraged to unmake them. The neighborhoods had always been isolated. Now it felt like they were under siege: not just from without but also from within. You don't normally think about your community simply ending, disappearing, or being replaced. But this was a possibility. To many, it felt more like an inevitability. The school had been at the center of community organizing. The church had been the place where you went for solace. Now it was a staging area for strangers who wanted to take your home away. But you still had to go to services. Babies were still being born. Easter was still coming around on the calendar. You were still Catholic.

There were obvious problems with the housing authority's offer. As Alexander and Bryant had pointed out, home owners were not eligible for public housing. Noncitizens were not eligible either. What good was first choice of units in the new housing project if you couldn't technically live in the new housing project?

*Manuel Aréchiga*

The resistance was organic: an outgrowth of decades of close living, an outgrowth of the fact that the parents of Palo Verde had sent a generation of their children off to war. But it was not unanimous. Palo Verde was like any other community: everybody had an opinion; everybody had their own motivation. Some families sold right away. One resident, Beto Elias, remembered that his father took the first offer and then turned around and bought a duplex in Lincoln Heights.

"There was a lot of tension between people who wanted to sell and people who didn't," said Camilo Arévalo. "The older people wanted to sell. They were thinking 'We can buy a home. We'll be better than where we are now.' But it was wrong. Because they didn't have to pay the taxes they paid when they bought again—the high money they had to pay. A lot of people, I don't think they even finished paying off their homes."

There was social pressure not to sell. Every time somebody sold, it became that much harder to argue for the integrity and cohesion of the community. For Abrana and Manuel Aréchiga, there was no consideration of ever selling. This was their home. This was the life they had journeyed a thousand miles to make. This was the life they had suffered for. Their children had been baptized and married at the Santo Niño church. They had literally dug the foundations themselves. They had planted gardens.

The people of Palo Verde, La Loma, and Bishop had been prepared by years of fighting for city services to defend their rights. They knew how to go to City Hall and make their voices heard. The communities organized into a group called the Civic Center District Improvement Association, led by a husband and wife named Manuel and Agnes Cerda and represented by an attorney named G. G. Baumen. The Cerdas lived in Palo Verde, and Baumen owned property there. In their opposition to Elysian Park Heights, landlords and tenants were united as allies.

But even though the association was well-organized, it was hard to mount an effective resistance to a government that spoke another language, that held the legal right of eminent domain, and that was willing to do whatever it took to convince you to sign your home away. It wasn't just the government either; it was also local elected officials, Mexican American community leaders, and everybody who ostensibly should have been there to support a place like Palo Verde. It was the church and the Communist Party, also miraculously united by this cause. It was Ignacio López and other Mexican American activists. It was City Councilman Edward Roybal.

Abrana and Manuel were not experts in civics, but they understood the fundamental promise of America, and they had kept up their end of the bargain. They had worked and worked. They had bought a home. They had paid their taxes. They had saved money and gone to church. They were lowercase "c" conservative people who simply wanted to be respected and otherwise wanted to be left alone.

And this is how they and their neighbors would become the unlikely face of opposition to public housing in Los Angeles and unlikely allies of the city's richest and most powerful interests. Theirs would be an alliance of mutual interest, not necessarily mutual respect.

In April 1951 Palo Verde residents packed a planning commission hearing on the project. All the key players in the development spoke, from Frank Wilkinson and Richard Neutra to Manuel and Agnes Cerda. Whereas the witnesses on behalf of the project discussed with great academic precision the need for housing and the reasons why the site was selected, the residents themselves appealed to the American Dream. When it was Manuel Cerda's turn to address the commission, he pointed to a display of photos taken of Palo Verde homes: "If you call this a slum, I don't know what would be a good house. We have plenty of facilities in there. We have gas, water, lights. The streets are very poor, but that is due to the City Engineer and the Council. They have not done anything for us."

Agnes Cerda was even more pointed. She told the story of Palo Verde and the city's neglect of the community:

> These are our homes they are taking away from us. I represent all the people, the majority of the people in the area, the Mexican people, those who have come here from Mexico. Maybe they did not have a home and they came out here to the land of liberty and justice for all to build their homes and they started that in the Chavez Ravine area. There was not a building there. It was full of rocks, full of sand, nothing but hills. They started one by one to build to the best of their ability and, after all these years the City Health Department never thought about coming in there to see that these homes were up-to-date and standard. Now, when they have them built, with the sweat from their own brow—they have worked, these poor people who came in from Mexico to see that they have liberty. The Housing Authority comes in now to take their homes away from them. It is not justice and not American policy.

The story Agnes Cerda was telling was not just one about a momentary failure. It was also about a generational failure. These communities had been the victims of neglect and systemic racism for decades. And then the government compounded that racism with the ultimate insult: declaring them slums because of lack of upkeep.

The following week, the planning commission approved the project.

==

BUT THE PROTESTS continued in the months that followed. In May about forty residents held a sit-down strike in Mayor Bowron's office. In June they filled the chambers of the city council as it heard appeals on the planning commission's selection of the site. The council meeting was bedlam. As members of various civic groups stood up to speak on behalf of the housing project, residents in the chambers booed them loudly. Over the noise, housing authority director Howard Holtzendorff tried to explain that the federal grants for public housing depended on swift action. Swift action was what he got. Five days later the council reaffirmed approval for the site, and demolition in Palo Verde, La Loma, and Bishop was approved to begin.

The council's approval also gave the housing authority the runway to advance condemnation proceedings against the property owners who refused to sell. One of those owners was the Aréchiga family. Their land on Malvina Avenue, consisting of the three adjoining lots and two houses, was initially deemed by an independent appraiser to be worth $17,500, but that total was overruled by a judge, who declared the property's value to be $10,050. This valuation would be binding. And it would change everything.

# 47.

Ed Davenport was a brilliant politician and an unscrupulous, power-starved drunk. It made sense that he would be instrumental in deciding the fate of public housing in Los Angeles. He was technically a Democrat. He was a powerhouse on the city council, and early in his career, a proponent of public housing. But Davenport's real passion was Red-baiting; he never met a Communist plot that was merely imagined. At one point he even proposed forcing all Communists entering the city limits to register with the police. The resolution passed with a 13–1 vote—the lone dissenter was Edward Roybal—before being ruled unconstitutional.

In August 1949 Davenport flew to Washington with Mayor Bowron and Holtzendorff to secure the public-housing contract. In the years that followed, Davenport continued to be a reliable vote in favor of public housing. The councilman even let Frank Wilkinson write speeches on housing for him. Davenport voted to approve the various sites, and he voted to begin condemnation proceedings. His support of public housing continued despite protests from residents in Palo Verde and other communities across the city, even as the council slowly shifted from 14–1 in support of the program to 9–6 in support.

How did support for a popular program collapse so dramatically and so quickly around Davenport? Was it something that Frank Wilkinson did? Was the revolt of the Palo Verde home owners changing the hearts and minds of constituents in other parts of the city? The answer begins with the developer Fritz Burns.

By the middle of World War II, Fritz Burns had transcended Los Angeles. He was running his industry's biggest lobbying group, the National Association of Home Builders. He was traveling the country, giving speeches on this dream of vines and fig trees. And at home his empire was growing. He bought the movie ranch of the film mogul D. W. Griffith for his personal pleasure. He partnered with the shipbuilding industrialist Henry J. Kaiser. He would attempt, in his new development, Panorama City, something more ambitious than a mere subdivision: a "total community" with shopping and banks and schools. This was when he bought the reindeer so that Christmases for his residents would be something magical. He kept the reindeer at the ranch. He concerned himself with the smallest details.

In the scope of his ambition, Fritz Burns was not unlike the public-housing advocates politically aligned against him. Even their language was similar. Burns had called Panorama City "a city within a city." Holtzendorff had called Elysian Park Heights "the new town in town." The idea that wise men knew the best way to live—well, that was something everybody could agree upon. The question was which wise men we should listen to. Burns was selling the dream of rugged individuality. Frank Wilkinson was selling the dream of a society of brothers and sisters lifting each other up, even at the cost of some of that individual freedom. What is the purpose of the home? What is the best way to live?

When the war ended, the need to answer this question became fundamental. Public-housing projects were antithetical to real-estate developers' interests. The projects were not only morally offensive—communal space? apartments?—they were unfair competition. The government didn't have the handcuff of a profit motive. The government could do things like evict entire communities with eminent domain to gain control of desirable real estate.

Fritz Burns was still the single-minded builder, the hard worker, the devout Catholic; he was still the showman, parading elephants across sheets of drywall to demonstrate how strong his new homes were; but now he was also the face of private home construction in America. In Los Angeles that meant he was on the front lines in the battle against Frank Wilkinson and public housing. Rallying behind him, and putting pressure on politicians like Ed Davenport, were the city's business, banking, construction, and real-estate interests: the robber barons.

# 48.

THE BROOKLYN DODGERS OPENED THEIR 1949 SEASON ON APRIL 19 at home against the crosstown New York Giants. Jackie Robinson went three for five, with a home run, and the Dodgers blew out the Giants 10–3. The game was an auspicious sign. In 1949 Jackie had the greatest year of his career. He hit .342, tops in the National League, and stole thirty-seven bases en route to being named the league's Most Valuable Player. The Dodgers won the pennant, and he played in his first World Series. (The Dodgers would lose to the Yankees, of course.)

While the Dodgers and Giants were squaring off in Brooklyn, the singer and civil rights activist Paul Robeson was standing on a dais in Paris. Robeson had been invited to address a group called the World Congress of Partisans for Peace. Robeson was a big and charismatic man with a voice that could fill an entire city. He was also a singular figure in American history. His father had escaped slavery on the Underground Railroad. Robeson was one of the country's greatest athletes (a back-to-back all-American football player at Rutgers), a first-rate thinker (he worked his way through Columbia Law School while playing pro football), and a superstar entertainer whose mere presence on the playbill could sell out a Broadway show for months on end.

But as he became more radical in his politics and assertive in his activism, he also became a target of anti-Communist politicians and media outlets. Robeson was exactly the kind of person that HUAC members lived to investigate. In 1949 he may have been even more famous than Jackie Robinson. The conference in Paris was not an official function of the Communist Party, but it drew delegates who were members and others, like Robeson, who were sympathetic to the Soviet Union.

Robeson sang solidarity songs, and he delivered off-the-cuff remarks for an adoring audience. However, before Robeson actually spoke, the Associated Press correspondent at the event had already filed a dispatch home. The story would be published in the following day's papers, and one of the quotations in it would be life changing: "It is unthinkable that American Negros would go to war on behalf of those who have oppressed us for generations against the Soviet Union which in one generation has lifted our people to full human dignity."

The problem is that these words were never uttered by Robeson. The *New York Times* reporter at the conference buried Robeson's appearance at the bottom of his report and made no mention of his speech. In his biography of Robeson, the historian Martin Duberman dug up French transcripts of the conference that also debunk the AP report.

But it was the AP report that caught the country's attention. It didn't matter what Robeson actually said. Quickly, civil rights groups, including the NAACP, were falling all over themselves to condemn him. And just as quickly, HUAC took notice. After all, what could be less American than Paul Robeson saying that it would be "unthinkable" to go to war on behalf of the United States against its greatest global enemy? And who better to disavow such an absurd notion than Jackie Robinson?

WHATEVER HIS POLITICS, Jackie had second thoughts about testifying against Robeson. He was justifiably worried that no matter what he said, the media would hear only his condemnation or his words would be wrung so tightly that all subtlety dripped out.

"I was not sure about what to do," Jackie wrote in his autobiography. "Rachel and I had long talks about it. She felt I should follow my instincts. I didn't want to fall prey to the white man's game and allow myself to be pitted against another black man. I knew that Robeson was striking out against racial inequality in the way that seemed best to him. However, in those days I had much more faith in the ultimate justice of the American white man than I have today."

Robeson's comments were troubling to Jackie. At the same time, Robeson was a man who deserved the benefit of the doubt.

Robeson's experience as a barrier-breaking stage star was not so different from Jackie's as a ballplayer. In fact, Robeson had been a pioneering black athlete himself. Robeson had actually worked to integrate baseball before Jackie Robinson initially signed to play in the minor leagues with the Dodgers.

On December 3, 1943, Robeson had addressed the gathered owners of the American and National Leagues at New York's Roosevelt Hotel. His purpose was explicitly to encourage them to sign black players. In his speech, Robeson recalled playing against (white) future Hall of Famer Frankie Frisch as an undergraduate athlete at Rutgers and then coaching baseball at Columbia during law school when a young first baseman named Lou Gehrig was on the team.

Among other arguments, Robeson appealed to the patriotism of his audience and to baseball's place in the popular imagination. Breaking the color line was especially important, he argued, because of the ongoing world war: "We live in times when the world is changing very fast, and when you might be able to make a great contribution to not only the advance of our own country, but of the whole world, because a thing like this—negro ball players becoming part of the great national pastime of America—could make a great difference in what peoples all over the world would feel toward us as a country in a time when we need their help."

Integrating baseball was not just the right thing to do; it was the right thing to do because baseball was supposed to represent the best of the country, the version of America that we ought to be showing to the world. We might still be a country that treats black people like second-class citizens; we might still be a country of lynchings and Jim Crow. But baseball, of all things, should be better than that.

Speaking many years later in a television documentary, Robeson's only son, Paul Robeson Jr., said that when Jackie debuted for the Dodgers, he had asked his father to get him Robinson's autograph. However, Robeson declined. He told his son that his own reputation was too controversial to risk sullying Jackie's by approaching him in public. If somebody snapped a picture of them together, the resulting scandal would have meant the end of Robinson's career in the major leagues. As much as Robeson admired Jackie, he also understood that the best thing for him, and the best thing for baseball, was to keep a wide berth.

ON THE MORNING of July 18, just six days after he played in his first All-Star Game, Jackie appeared before HUAC in Washington, DC. The gallery was jammed. He stood and raised his right hand to be sworn in. Surrounded by photographers, Jackie sat at a heavy wooden table. He bent over a microphone and began to read. In his usual, somewhat high, sincere voice, he said that he was "an expert at being a colored American, with thirty years experience at it." He said that if Paul Robeson had indeed made such statements, "it sounded very silly to me." He said that no one man—not Paul Robeson and not Jackie Robinson—could speak for fifteen million. But beyond that, he said that this whole hearing, this whole spectacle, was beside the point:

> The white public should start toward real understanding by appreciating that every single Negro who is worth his salt is going to resent any kind of slurs and discrimination because of his race, and he is going to use every bit of intelligence such as he has to stop it. This has got absolutely nothing to do with what Communists may or may not be trying to do. And white people must realize that the more a Negro hates communism because it opposes democracy, the more he is going to hate any other influence that kills off democracy in this country—and that goes for racial discrimination in the Army, and segregation on trains and buses, and job discrimination because of religious beliefs or color or place of birth.
>
> And one other thing the American public ought to understand, if we are to make progress in this matter: The fact that it is a Communist who denounces injustice in the courts, police brutality, and lynching when it happens doesn't change the truth of his charges. Just because communists kick up a big fuss over racial discrimination when it suits their purposes, a lot of people try to pretend that the whole issue is a creation of communist imagination, but they're not fooling anyone with this type of pretense, and talk about communists stirring up Negroes to protest only makes present misunderstanding worse than ever. Negroes were stirred up long before there was a Communist Party, and they'll stay stirred up long after the party has disappeared unless Jim Crow has disappeared by then, as well.

Of course, nobody listened to that part.

In the *New York Times* the front-page headline was "Jackie Robinson Terms Stand of Robeson on Negroes False." In the *Los Angeles Times*, it was "Jackie Robinson Brands Robeson Claims Silly." Jackie may have given a nuanced and impassioned speech, but the coverage was far from nuanced.

The HUAC hearings furthered the public case that Robeson was a Communist and a threat to the American way of life. Just a month after the hearing, a riot broke out in Peekskill, New York, when it was announced that Robeson was set to perform a benefit there on behalf of the Civil Rights Congress. Robeson was blacklisted from mainstream theaters and concert venues. His records were banned from stores. The FBI confiscated his passport, which prevented him from touring internationally. Despite the fact that he was still beloved by millions, he was essentially erased from mainstream public life.

In the wake of Jackie's testimony, Paul Robeson suffered the fate that he had tried to spare Jackie from two years earlier by refusing to get that autograph for his son. However, Robeson never lashed back. He knew that doing so would undermine the end goal of civil rights. Everything Robeson had said back in 1943 before the room full of owners was still true. The integration of baseball had been an important symbolic step for the country, and Jackie Robinson had become an important symbolic figure, but the process was by no means over. And according to his son, Robeson was not bitter at Jackie anyway; he was bitter at the system that pitted people who should have been allies against one another. "Dad wasn't surprised that Jackie Robinson, the first black player in baseball, would be called down to make a statement denouncing Paul Robeson," Robeson Jr. said. "As a matter of fact, he told me that if Jackie had refused and forced them to subpoena him, he would have never had a baseball career."

Both men were caught in the same trap. It was just that at the time, Robeson had a better understanding of its scope. In 1953 Robeson wrote an open letter to Jackie that made no mention of HUAC. Instead of rehashing, Robeson encouraged Jackie to embrace the fight: "People who 'beef' at those of us who speak out, Jackie, are afraid of us. Well, let them be afraid. I'm continuing to speak out, and I hope you will, too. And our folks and many others like them all over the world will make it—and soon!"

Toward the end of his life, Jackie would come to think differently about his testimony before HUAC. It was one of the many political choices he reconsidered: "I have grown wiser and closer to painful truths about America's destructiveness. And I do have an increased respect for Paul Robeson who, over the span of that twenty years, sacrificed himself, his career, and the wealth and comfort he once enjoyed because, I believe, he was sincerely trying to help his people."

# 49.

THIS WOULDN'T BE A BOOK ABOUT LOS ANGELES IF THERE WERE NOT a good conspiracy somewhere in it: powerful forces working in the shadows to manipulate the lives of oblivious everyday people. But the thing about the plot to kill public housing in Los Angeles is that there was nothing particularly secretive about it. For decades the city's richest industrialists, executives, attorneys, and landholders met in private clubs and boardrooms with leather chairs and shiny oak tables and cigar smoke in the air.

At the head of those shiny tables sat Norman Chandler, whose family had owned the *Los Angeles Times* for three generations and now also ran the afternoon *Mirror*. The papers were not just a business in and of themselves; they were also a tool to advance the Chandler family's other business interests, especially real estate. In the 1950s a former councilman named William Bonelli published a book about the Chandlers and the Times-Mirror Company called *Billion Dollar Blackjack*, the title referring to the fact that the family wielded the paper as a blackjack, a medieval cudgel, demolishing all opposition to get what it wanted. The (ghostwritten) book consists of hundreds of pages of invective and accusations, some of which are backed up by fact and many others with circumstantial evidence or none at all.

"For almost three quarters of a century, the Times-Mirror hierarchy has stolen from the many to enhance the power and fortune of its few. Impudence and hypocrisy have been its weapons; arrogance and vindictiveness its trademarks," Bonelli writes in the introduction. He continues: "The corrosive effect of the Chandler creed to rule or ruin reaches into every home; touches the life of every person in California."

In the late 1930s the *Times* dismissed the civic crusading of people like Clifford Clinton and Dr. A. M. Wilkinson in order to uphold a corrupt mayor, Frank Shaw, who did its bidding. By the 1950s, the mayor who replaced Frank Shaw, the incorruptible former judge Fletcher Bowron, was still in power and was a willing builder of public housing. The paper became the fulcrum of an organized effort to oust Bowron and kill public housing in one fell swoop by tying the mayor, the program, and all of its supporters to Communism. This effort also included Police Chief William Parker and business interests led by Fritz Burns.

Burns and an attorney named Frederik Dockweiler, himself the scion of one of LA's founding families, started a group called Citizens Against Socialist Housing (CASH). The group's acronym was also essentially its cause. CASH was a vehicle to organize opposition to public housing among the city's business interests.

CASH hired a public-relations firm called Baus & Ross to run the actual campaign against housing. Baus & Ross took out billboards and newspaper ads. Their slogan was "Don't Pay Somebody Else's Rent." Meanwhile, Baus & Ross worked hand in hand with the *Los Angeles Times*, especially its City Hall reporter, Carlton Williams. "We conferred daily or many times daily," recalled Herbert Baus. "Our campaign figured heavily in the Williams coverage. Some people would have called it propaganda."

Burns himself was out on the front lines in the fight against public housing. In a direct shot at Frank Wilkinson and his film *And 10,000 More*, Burns gave a talk to apartment owners called "10,000 Socialist Housing Units Would Compete with You." Burns and Wilkinson were paired up for debates on television and radio. Once, Burns came to a debate equipped with a police report that purportedly showed juvenile delinquency as being higher in housing projects than in nearby slums.

The report, Wilkinson knew, was a complete fabrication. The "nearby slums" were in fact areas that had already been cleared for future construction. There was no delinquency there because nobody lived there. The facts didn't matter. The report, which had been delivered on orders from Chief William Parker's office, became another tool in the fight against public housing. It was even used in a newspaper ad published in—of course—the *Los Angeles Times*.

———

THE NATIONAL POLITICAL climate was on fire. In 1950, in the aftermath of China's Communist revolution and the beginning of a US war in Korea, a young senator from Wisconsin named Joseph McCarthy brandished a list of purported Soviet spies who had infiltrated the government. There was no such list. But it didn't matter. McCarthy dragged American politics further into a state of fear and hysteria by claiming that there were traitors all over the government and that only true patriots like him could root them out. In March 1951, Julius and Ethel Rosenberg were convicted of spying, only furthering McCarthy's case. Meanwhile, the FBI ramped up its already massive counterintelligence campaign, seeking to identify every US Communist or sympathizer. In interviews, J. Edgar Hoover spoke with religious fervor about the evils of Communism. "I would never fear Communism in America if all Communists were out in the open, peddling their wares in the market place of free speech and thought," Hoover told *U.S. News & World Report*. "But they are not. We cannot meet them on an even basis. They are working behind the masquerade of hypocrisy. For this reason America must be vigilant to recognize Communism for what it actually is—a malicious evil which would destroy this nation."

The quest to root out these secret communists became a national obsession, and for politicians who were willing to sacrifice their principles, it became a means to accumulate power. One such politician was Ed Davenport.

By November 1951, support for public housing was narrowly hanging on, at just 9–6. Then Davenport switched sides. His reversal was shortly followed by that of a colleague named Harold Harby. (Harby would later become known for his hatred of abstract art and jazz music.) Suddenly, just two years after it had heard the call for ten thousand more units of public housing, the Los Angeles City Council was now aligned in opposition to the program.

After Davenport and Harby's defection swung the council to 8–7 against public housing, a fellow councilman named Kenneth Hahn publicly questioned whether anti-Communist fears were the only thing at play in their decision making. Specifically, Hahn wondered whether they had accepted bribes. It's important to note that Harby and Hahn hated each other. Harby was especially fond of calling Hahn a "political prostitute," an insult that he lobbed at various times throughout their careers. But it's also worth noting that maybe Hahn had a point.

In July 1953, just after narrowly winning reelection to a third term, Ed Davenport went out to dinner with a friend. The friend later recalled that Davenport ordered a glass of milk and mixed his vodka into it. This was unusual. Davenport normally liked his booze neat. But Davenport complained that he was feeling worn out. This was unusual too. Davenport typically liked to boast about his fitness. The next morning, Davenport was discovered dead.

Not long after his death, Davenport's wife, Harriet (who was later appointed to fill his seat on the council), found $30,000 in cash in a safe-deposit box, plus another $27,570 in various checking accounts. The money, she later told the IRS, had been "gifts of cash" to her late husband and had thus not been reported in tax filings. In 1957 the syndicated columnist Drew Pearson made the accusation that this money was actually bribes from the real-estate industry. In the archives at UCLA there is an unsigned, undated, and unverifiable memo about Davenport that reads like something out of a detective novel. The memo, which rests among the papers of his former campaign managers, Ed and Ruth Lybeck, consists of gossip, interviews, and notes relating to Davenport's corruption and to his drunkenness.

"Davenport is on the chisel for anything that comes along and must pick up quite a bit of dough from day to day," the anonymous investigator writes. Then: "I think a lot of his vaporings are just drug-born phantasies that disappear along with the rest of the effects." The memo also contains an accusation that the *Mirror* prepared an investigative feature on Davenport that would have exposed his bribe taking and his general corruption but that the story was buried on the specific orders of Norman Chandler himself.

Regardless of his motivations, Davenport was now leading the charge against housing, perhaps with the protection of Norman Chandler. On the day after Christmas, 1951, the council voted to cancel the housing deal. It then voted early in 1952 to turn the housing issue over to voters in the form of a referendum: the fate of the ten thousand units would be determined by a popular vote. However, Bowron and the housing authority argued that neither the council vote nor the referendum could be legally binding. The city had already entered into a housing contract with the federal government.

The courts agreed with Bowron. The council vote was meaningless. The referendum was legally meaningless. But the ruling came too late, and the vote was held anyway.

The campaign was brutal, and it was long. The election would be held on June 3, but CASH started distributing campaign material in January. It ran newspaper ads decrying crime in public-housing projects based on the false report from the LAPD. The *Times* ran story after story about the ills of public housing. All the combined powers of the Times-Mirror Company, of Fritz Burns, of Baus & Ross, of Ed Davenport and his anti-housing colleagues came to bear. Frank Wilkinson, Fletcher Bowron, and the ten thousand units of public housing were soundly, if only symbolically, defeated.

After the referendum, the housing authority pressed on. Howard Holtzendorff was not the kind of man to let the will of the people stand in his way. Under Holtzendorff's guidance, the agency personally sued the anti-housing council members for failing to meet the city's contract with the federal government. It also continued the condemnation proceedings unabated.

However, Mayor Bowron conceded that although the city did indeed have a binding legal contract, it would be nearly impossible to implement such an ambitious program after such a thorough public beating at the polls. In August he and Holtzendorff flew to Washington to renegotiate the city's housing contract personally with President Truman. The renegotiated deal would reduce the number of new units from ten thousand to seven thousand and eliminate the unpopular thirteen-story towers from the Elysian Park Heights project.

Richard Neutra and Robert Alexander's acropolis was not meant to be. But for the opponents of public housing in Los Angeles, this would not be enough. "If the public housing program is wrong, as a majority of the citizens of Los Angeles and of the City Councilmen believe, then it is as wrong at 7,000 units as it is at 10,000," wrote the *Los Angeles Times*.

The billion-dollar blackjack had landed a blow in the referendum, but housing was not dead yet. In a year, Bowron would be up for reelection. For Norman Chandler, Fritz Burns, and their allies, the only smart thing to do would be to keep swinging, no matter who might be part of the collateral damage.

# 50.

THERE WERE DOGS IN PALO VERDE. THERE WAS ONE HOUSE IN PAR-
ticular, on Reposa Street, right near where the bus would drop you
off. The lady who lived there was called Juana la Perrera: Juana the
Dog Lady. Her dogs didn't mess around. They weren't beholden to
fences, leashes, or discipline. If you wanted to pass her house, you
knew that you had better get to where you were going before the
dogs could catch you. On the way back it was the same thing. Big
old dogs running, barking, and kicking up dirt on the quiet streets.

Abrana and Manuel kept Chihuahuas. They had lots of them
over the years. When the eviction notice came, she had one called
Silverio. He followed her everywhere. He would curl up in her lap
on the couch. Manuel had a girl dog named Suzie. He would give
her treats like he did with his grandchildren.

There was one remarkable dog on Paducah Street near the
church. He was a medium-size dog with short hair. He was not
very handsome. Some nights, this dog would howl at the moon like
a wolf or like the packs of coyotes that used to live in Elysian Park.
It wasn't like the normal barking or like the dogs from Juana la Perrera's house. It was a real baying sound. Everybody could hear it.

Gradually, the neighbors noticed something. When this dog
howled, it meant that somebody was dying. It came to be so that
if the families on Paducah Street heard him at night, they would
wake up and start talking. They would look around the house. In
the morning they would go outside and ask the neighbors. The dog
was howling. Who died last night?

# 51.

On Friday morning, August 29, 1952, Frank Wilkinson would have woken early. He had before him a grueling and repetitive day of testimony in a condemnation suit at the Elysian Park Heights site. The suit had been playing out in the background even as the fate of the housing program hung in the balance, even as Ed Davenport screamed and yelled about Communist infiltration in the housing authority, and even as the *Los Angeles Times* and the *Mirror* continued to bash public housing.

If Frank read the *Times* that morning, he would have learned of a major US air raid in Pyongyang, North Korea. He would have read that members of the city council had hired a powerful local attorney to defend them against the charges being brought by the housing authority for their refusal to meet the terms of the city's contract with the federal government.

This would be Frank's third day of testimony in the hearing. On mornings like this, he tended to be serious and introspective. Decades afterward, in his eulogy for his father, Frank's middle child, Tony, would recall his process as he prepared for public appearances: "Emerging from his shower, he had gone from a naked man, layer by layer, starched white shirt—cufflinks, suit and tie, tight shiny shoes till he disappeared behind his clothes. This funny, silly, loving, deaf man, my father was ready for a battle."

On that particular August day, Frank put on a tan suit with wide lapels and a white shirt. His tie had diagonal stripes. It had been raining all week, but now the skies were clear. Jean and the kids were out of town, and after work, Frank was going to drive over to Glendale, where his sister Hildegarde and his brother, Budge, both lived, for dinner.

He understood that the situation for public housing remained perilous, and he understood that his dreams of ten thousand units

*Frank Wilkinson*

were dead, but seven thousand units were not nothing. He was expecting to testify about slum conditions and rat infestations. It was important that he be sharp. The star witness on behalf of the defense—expected to argue that the communities of Palo Verde, La Loma, and Bishop were in fact salvageable—was none other than Fritz Burns.

"Driving to a meeting where he was going to speak he became grim—silent," Tony recalled. Frank drove downtown from the family home in Los Feliz. The hearing began promptly at 9 a.m., and Frank was called up to the witness stand for cross-examination. He took his seat behind the wooden banister, Judge Otto J. Emme sitting on a riser to his left, and an American flag resting limp on a pole beside his right shoulder. He was wearing glasses, the wire from his hearing aid running down into his pocket.

At about five minutes after nine, just as the day's hearing was beginning, Frank watched as one of the attorneys for the defense removed a sheath of paper from his briefcase. Frank could not see what was written on the documents. He could not have known that those pages represented the end of his life as he knew it.

Frank was prepared to defend his agency's decision to clear out the communities and to talk about rodents in more detail than anybody wanted to hear. He was not prepared for what happened next. Felix H. McGiness, the attorney for the defense, consulted the documents and abruptly asked Frank to please list all of the organizations, political or otherwise, that he had belonged to since his freshman year at UCLA.

The subtext of this question was clear to Frank and to everybody in the courthouse. McGiness was hunting for links to Communism. In Los Angeles, opponents of public housing had spent years trying to tie the projects to Communism. Now Frank Wilkinson was being asked the question. The courtroom was silent.

Frank waited for one of the attorneys representing the housing authority to object. He thought that if an objection came, the judge might sustain it, and the question would be withdrawn. After all, Judge Otto Emme had been a friend to organized labor. He was a decent and thoughtful man. And this question was surely beyond the purview of the hearing. Frank waited and waited, but no objection came.

So he began to answer. He began to list the clubs he had joined and the schools he had attended. He had belonged to Sigma Alpha Epsilon fraternity. He had belonged to the interfaith coalition.

When he finished, McGiness pressed him. It was as if the attorney knew Frank was leaving something out. As if he already knew Frank's political associations, as if he already knew Frank's entire biography. Finally, Frank had enough. He turned to the judge, but really he was speaking to the entire courtroom. He knew that what he said would not only be transcribed by the court reporter but also reproduced in newspapers that evening and the following morning:

> I believe that I shall be compelled by matters of personal conscience to refuse to answer the question, and state that I am doing so because of personal conscience, and I'd like to assure you that there is nothing that I have belonged to that I am not completely proud of and that my personal record wouldn't make me proud to state, but

I do not want to answer this question, and if necessary I would hold that to answer this question might in some way incriminate me.

===

THE JUDGE SUSPENDED the hearing and advised Frank to go get an attorney. Almost immediately after the news leaked out of the courtroom, Ed Davenport seized the floor in the council chambers to propose a resolution asking the House Un-American Activities Committee to investigate Frank and the general Communist infiltration of the housing authority. As Frank wandered to the housing authority offices to meet with Holtzendorff, this resolution was passed unanimously.

In a single morning, Frank had gone from expert witness for the housing authority in a case that might determine the fate of the most ambitious and important project of his career to an instrument of that very project's destruction. In his office, Holtzendorff apologized to Frank and then suspended him indefinitely. Later that afternoon, Holtzendorff would be called as a witness in Judge Emme's courtroom and reveal Frank's suspension.

Frank spent the rest of the day scrambling to find an attorney. Monsignor O'Dwyer tried to set him up with a Catholic lawyer, but the attorney said no. Frank looked up an old friend from his UCLA days who was practicing law downtown, but the friend insisted on asking Frank if he really was a Communist, a question that Frank again refused to answer. Finally, Frank wandered into the office of Robert Kenny, a progressive lawyer who had been the attorney general of California. Kenny was well-regarded, but he was also an activist who was known to defend Communists. Frank had resisted coming to see him on advice from Holtzendorff. But he was desperate. When Frank finally walked in, Kenny and his partners were already preparing a brief on his behalf. "What took you so long?" they asked.

By the time he was through with Kenny, Frank was totally wrecked. In the course of a single day, his entire career had come unmoored. It was painful, and it was confusing. What was that piece of paper the attorney had taken out of his briefcase? Why had he been singled out, and why now? The answers to those questions were big and messy and would change the course of the city. But he didn't know that yet. Now he could only cry. He cried as he got into his car and left downtown.

Without thinking about it, still crying, Frank drove to the Forest Lawn Memorial Park in the hills overlooking Glendale. This was where his mother and father were buried. Forest Lawn was a peaceful and serene place. Hubert Eaton, the visionary behind it, had single-handedly transformed the industry of death and grief in America from something dark and mysterious into a pastel-colored, tranquil canvas: "I shall endeavor to build Forest Lawn as something different," he wrote, "as unlike other cemeteries as sunshine is to darkness, as eternal life is unlike eternal death."

But when Frank reached the cemetery, the ornate wrought-iron gates were locked. It was after five p.m. Forest Lawn was closed for the evening. So Frank drove on down the hill to dinner. When he reached the driveway in Glendale, he collapsed onto the dashboard of his car. He couldn't even bring himself to go inside. Hildegarde and Budge, both physicians like their father before them, injected him with morphine. They carried their younger brother into the house and put him to bed.

═══

THE NEXT MORNING, Frank was on the front page of the papers. He remained there, even after he lost his job. Holtzendorff, who had relied on Frank's organizing skills to carry the housing authority for the previous decade, quickly turned on him. Frank had been worth the trouble when he was working twelve-hour days, but now the best thing for housing—and for Holtzendorff himself—was to cut ties. Holtzendorff made a public show of requesting that the California Senate Factfinding Subcommittee on Un-American Activities, also known as Little HUAC, investigate Frank.

Life for the family instantly turned into a surreal nightmare. Jean would be fired from her job at East Los Angeles Girls Vocational High School because she refused to testify against Frank. When the couple got an outpouring of community support, the letters were held up as supposedly being part of an organized Communist plot on their behalf. They had three children and suddenly no income. In late September, Frank went into Good Samaritan Hospital for knee surgery. When he awoke, he found a subpoena from Little HUAC pinned to his hospital gown.

The committee, which had risen to power under Jack Tenney during the 1940s, was taken over in 1949 by a jovial mortician named Hugh M. Burns. In his later years, Frank said that he believed

Holtzendorff had always been suspicious of Frank's nearness to the Communist Party but that he had intentionally chosen to keep himself ignorant of Frank's politics. The less he knew the better. However, Holtzendorff was also too smart to take anything for granted. As Frank described it, Holtzendorff made generous campaign contributions to politicians who presented a potential risk to public housing. These included Ed Davenport in the city council and Hugh Burns in the state senate. In Burns's case the contributions came with an implicit understanding that Little HUAC would not look too closely at the goings on in the housing authority.

Now Holtzendorff cashed in on all those contributions by having Burns do just the opposite: take a very close and very public look at the housing authority. Frank was called to testify before Little HUAC on October 28, two months after the ambush at the condemnation hearing. This time, Frank was represented by a group of attorneys led by Kenny. And this time, using Fifth Amendment grounds, he declined to answer nearly every question put to him. After Frank, Jean was called, and she also declined to cooperate. The following witness was a young man named Patrick Burns. Patrick was the only son of Fritz Burns. He testified that while studying at USC, Frank had been a guest lecturer in one of his courses and had taken the class on a slum tour in a rented bus. He accused Frank of misrepresenting the elder Burns and of using the guest lecture as a platform to recruit for the Communist Party.

After the hearing, Frank was summarily fired by Holtzendorff. Or as Carlton Williams put it in the next day's *Los Angeles Times*, "Frank Wilkinson, top-bracket official of the City Housing Authority and chief propagandist for the city's unwanted $110,000,000 Federal public housing scheme was fired from his job yesterday."

After his testimony and his firing, Frank put out a lengthy statement. The statement is a remarkable summation of his life and his worldview in this fragile moment:

> I believe that it is my right to think what I want, read what I choose and associate with whomever I please. All of these things belong to me; they are my rights as an American citizen; no one has the privilege to subject me in any manner to compulsory and improper invasion of matters of private conscience.
>
> The greatest threat to our country today is fear. The hysteria that grips the land has frequently resulted in recent years in

headlong flight from the constitutional principles upon which our government was founded. The voluntary abandonment of our cherished freedoms of speech, thought, and assembly, must stop before democracy is destroyed.

As a child, I received everything that could be desired to encourage within me the fullest development of such natural talents as were bestowed upon me. I received economic security, sincere spiritual guidance, and most wonderful of all, the all-encompassing wholesome affection of family living. Later, I learned that my good fortune was not the lot of countless numbers of people in this country and in the world. I became aware of the shocking discrepancy between what we as a people *do* and what we *say*. Above all, I came to despise hypocrisy. I determined then that I would have to abandon my religious ideals and patriotism unless I strove to do all that I could to build a better life for all people on earth. This is the life to which I have aspired.

I admit many shortcomings; I have made many mistakes. However, in concert with others, I have tried, during the past fifteen years, to do what I could to rid my own city of slums and to see that decent homes were provided without discrimination to those in need. It has been an almost unbelievably difficult struggle. Now, at the moment when it appears that major steps forward are at last to be achieved, I have become a personal target of attack by the anti-housing lobby.

To bow to expediency and answer the questions that have been put to me in court and by the Senate Committee on Un-American Activities would be a deliberate violation of the very constitutional principles on which I believe a better world of tomorrow can *only* be built. Therefore, I will never under compulsion, affirm or deny, directly or indirectly, my religious or political affiliations. Those are matters of personal privilege to be disclosed to whom I choose, at such time as I deem appropriate and at such a place as I see fit. These are rights which cannot be taken from me. These are the cardinal principles of our American heritage. I cannot in conscience violate principle in order to achieve the expediency of the moment.

In this time of mounting hysteria, no one can safely affirm or deny either past or present associations. This frightening trend must be stopped. Each of us, in our turn, must oppose each encroachment upon our constitutional rights. If we do not stand up now, history will find us guilty of contributing to the destruction of our democracy.

If I have belonged, or if I may now belong, to any religious, political, or other organizations, it has been completely consistent with my desire to achieve through the use of democratic processes the ultimate attainment of a nation and a world wherein all people shall walk with dignity, develop their maximum capabilities and share fully in the abundance of the earth.

The principles I have stated have long been known to the Housing Authority. In the immediate controversy, I feel that my constitutional rights should have been upheld by the Housing Authority, its attorneys, its Executive Director and its commissioners. Their failure to do so has in no way softened the savagery of the anti-housing opposition's attack. On the contrary, it has opened yet wider flood-gates for more serious assault.

No progressive social reform ever can be achieved and sustained at the sacrifice of our basic constitutional principles.

This was Frank Wilkinson down to his (long-winded) essence. It had everything: the religious overtones, the martyrdom, the radical confessional honesty. Frank had the capacity to contextualize himself and his activism in the grand sweep of history. He thought of the world in moral terms, and that gave his politics the urgency of the faith he had been raised in. He not only hated hypocrisy; he was incapable of it.

But the statement couldn't alter the reality of Frank's new life. He was fired. Monsignor O'Dwyer was quickly transferred away from Los Angeles. The housing movement would have to go on without them. Frank and Jean became personae non grata in polite society. Hildegarde and Budge were asked by medical colleagues in conservative Glendale to disown him. Even Frank's sister Betty, in Berkeley, was cornered and asked by the members of her women's club to sign a document denying that she was a Communist. Betty, like the rest of the Wilkinsons, was a conservative: the furthest thing from a Communist. But she refused to sign and was forced to relinquish her membership.

The family receded into itself and into the small community of activists that it had belonged to even before the nightmare began. It had been a strange childhood for Frank and Jean's kids, and now it was even stranger. They had, up until 1952, lived a life surrounded by big ideas, but those big ideas had always felt distant and theoretical. Now they were urgent.

For the first years of the children's lives, Frank had never been home, but all of a sudden he was around the house. The naked emotion that made him such a potent political activist made Frank volatile as a parent and husband. When he was working a lot, he would come home with his big personality and his warm sense of humor and take over the room. He called himself Popsiedoodle. His children had discovered that when Frank was fibbing, his hearing aid would make a squealing sound. He knew how to have fun, and he loved to be loved. But it could also be exhausting to be around a person like that, even if that person is your father. He brooded. He had to be the center of attention. He expected his children to reflect well on him, and when they didn't, he withheld affection.

Frank did not handle conflict well inside the home or like to acknowledge that things were difficult, even when they very clearly were. Frank and Jean did not fight often, but when they did, they shouted. When Jean was angry at him, Frank would act as if her anger was not allowed or acceptable. "Now Jean's very upset, so we must all be very quiet," he would say. "We must all be nice to her. She's having certain emotional issues." It seemed like he was always performing, always in character. And Frank wanted his family to be that way too. The family was part of his superhero persona.

To get by, the Wilkinsons turned to the generosity of their extended family and their friends in the party and in the movement. They lived almost rent free thanks to the kindness of an elderly woman named Martha Criley, who Frank had met in his housing work and who used to drive past their house in an old limousine to check up on things. Jean and Frank's lawyers were all pro bono.

Frank retreated into his domestic life. He was wrecked, destroyed. He threw himself into housework, the same way he had when he was a boy in Beverly Hills, obsessing over the edges of his family's lawn. He ironed Jo's little dresses and did the grocery shopping. Then, in the afternoon, he read.

Frank was once again finding the basis for his ethics. During this quiet moment, he came to believe that the questioning he was submitted to in court and in front of Little HUAC was not only immoral but also illegal under the First Amendment of the Constitution. By compelling people like Frank to talk about their political beliefs, the government was violating their right to free speech. This epiphany would set the stage for his next great fight.

# 52.

ABRANA AND MANUEL HAD TO BEGIN ADJUSTING TO LIFE IN A NEIGH-
borhood that was diminishing. They had no choice. Now that the
housing authority could legally demolish houses and begin the massive project of grading for the new construction, the neighborhood
took on an eerie quality of being both desolate and busy. Families
were leaving every day, but they were being replaced by earthmovers. Lines of dump trucks came to transport dirt down into the city.
In Don Normark's *Chavez Ravine: 1949*, a resident named Rudy
Flores described the scene:

> People would take everything, the lighting, the doors, and bricks
> by the truck loads. They had those auctions every Saturday. First
> they knocked the houses down. Then they moved all the dirt, start-
> ing from Effie. Only two streets in or out of that neighborhood.
> They go to work every morning and come home every afternoon
> and you see them. "Here comes Lalo, here comes Tule." They'd all
> stop in the store before they get home and have a beer and talk
> about their jobs and what's going on with their kids and all that.
> Bulldozers came in the night. Huge dump trucks to pick up the dirt.
> Three of them at one time knocking down the hill and flattening it.
> They came down Bishops Road to Broadway, and they had some
> guy down there with flags and lights to stop the traffic. They went
> from nine o'clock at night until four in the morning. And them
> trucks worked like a merry-go-round. When they'd be coming up
> it was so steep that they'd use two tractors. Truck'd go like the bat
> out of hell.

Leaving was not necessarily easy. Abrana and Manuel's nephew
Gene Cabral recalled home shopping in Downey with his wife in
the early 1950s after his brother sold the family house on Malvina.

*Abrana Aréchiga*

This was after the *Shelley v. Kramer* case had made restrictive housing covenants technically illegal. They walked into a model home only to be told that as a matter of fact there were no houses currently for sale. Féliz and Camilo Arévalo picked Lincoln Heights because it was the community that most resembled Palo Verde, high up in the hills. But it wasn't the same.

"I didn't realize the impact of it until I had to move away, until my parents took me away and all of a sudden I'm in a new neighborhood with no friends," said Al Zepeda, who was a teenager when his family moved to Cypress Park. The Zepedas had been living on Paducah Street, right near the Palo Verde School and the Santo Niño church: what Al called the "civic center" of Palo Verde. Al's mother had lived life in Palo Verde, La Loma, and Bishop ever since traveling alone from Mexico to Los Angeles as a teenage girl. She was used to watering her plants in the front yard and talking to her neighbors in the streets in the evenings. She spoke Spanish. She was happy there. But in Cypress Park she had neighbors who didn't speak Spanish and who were afraid of Mexicans. She was lonely. Palo Verde was a hard place to leave behind. Even the residents who left would come back often, just to see what was happening or to catch up with their friends and relatives who were still there. "We'd get the bus and still come back to the neighborhood on Friday nights. For a long time, we did that."

In August 1951 the *Los Angeles Times* published a front-page story titled "Settlement Losing Battle for Its Life." In addition to mislabeling a well-established neighborhood in the middle of Los Angeles as a "settlement," the story paints a bleak picture of life in Palo Verde. A housing official speaks cheerily about how resettlement is ahead of schedule, while remaining residents state that they are fearful to leave because of how their former neighbors have been treated on the outside. Marshall Stimson, the landowner who sold many of the initial lots to families now being forced out, is quoted reminiscing longingly about how he used to wander into Palo Verde "just to sit on somebody's porch and listen to the guitars at night."

For the families who remained, the fight to keep their homes may have felt urgent, but it was in fact muddled: the mechanism by which the city was confiscating homes could be stopped only through the courts. This was a playing field that inherently favored the government. After all, government bureaucrats and lawyers were experienced with eminent domain. The families whose homes were at stake were not. Plus, many of the families did not speak English; some could not read or write in any language. Abrana and Manuel relied on their children to translate and interpret for them. But their children had their own lives and, in many cases, their own children to take care of.

In early 1952 the Aréchigas missed out on filing an appeal in court when the city sued to condemn their property. A judge ordered the $10,050 that was their property's declared value, minus $11 of back taxes, deposited into a holding account with the county clerk's office. Nothing seemed to happen in the aftermath of the condemnation. The city made no move to evict the family, and the family made no move to collect the money. Their daily life did not change, but the condemnation would set the Aréchigas on a separate legal path from many of their neighbors who did file appeals. Carmen Acosta was one of those neighbors. Her family lived across the street on Malvina. Carmen counted Abrana and Manuel as her godparents. They had held her at her baptism at the Santo Niño church. They had helped look after her when her father died young. Carmen's family were holdouts too. She believes that the reason Abrana and Manuel failed to appeal the city's condemnation suit and allowed their house to be condemned was probably something relatively simple. They weren't home at the right time. Or their children were not home to help translate. The consequences of that simple lapse would be enormous. But they would take years to play out.

In the moment, Abrana remained unmovable. She could only watch her neighborhood disappear. She was one of the residents featured in the *Los Angeles Times* article. Along with Agnes Cerda and another neighbor named Angie Villa, Abrana is described wandering through the eerie streets:

> They see the houses of wood and stone and plaster that cling to the hillsides above the streets, that climb the mountains like vines, with rooms added as more and more children arrive.
>
> Many of the houses are empty now and bear signs that say "No Trespassing," or "For Sale—To Be Moved." And the silent women look hard at their village. And see its end. They see the passage of Chavez Ravine.

# 53.

After months isolated in the family home, Frank was finally able to get a job as a night janitor at a department store in Pasadena. The job was given to him by an elderly sympathetic Quaker. He earned a dollar per hour, and he had to make sure that nobody saw him entering or exiting the store.

The family was constantly reminded of its own second-class status. The boys were denied entry into a YMCA camp, then were finally admitted as long as Frank and Jean weren't seen picking them up or dropping them off. Jean found work as a private tutor. In some ways things were not that different. They ate dinners of frozen hamburger patties and frozen vegetables just like before; even in the best of times, neither Frank nor Jean was much of a cook. Jean's mother came to live with them for stretches to help around the house. So did Frank's sister Betty. Frank's sister Hildegarde and her partner, Margarethe Peterson, dropped off groceries every week.

Once, Frank had the kids over to the department store in the middle of the night and served them ice cream at the soda fountain. It was magical. They had all the ice cream they could eat, and they had the whole store to themselves. They had, in that moment, their father all to themselves.

The repercussions of Frank's testimony in Otto Emme's courtroom weren't just limited to the Wilkinson family. The entire city government was sent into a fit of paranoia and madness. Jean was one of about a dozen Los Angeles teachers fired for suspicions of Communist ties. The city council devolved into a pro-wrestling–style melodrama loaded with insults, passive-aggressive threats, false accusations, and some old-fashioned Ed Davenport racism directed at Edward Roybal.

Meanwhile, the eminent domain proceedings continued. Mayor Fletcher Bowron was subpoenaed to appear before Judge Emme. One day, as he was exiting the courtroom, he was approached by a man named John Hogya. Hogya was thirty-nine years old, six foot three, and two hundred pounds. He towered over the paunchy Bowron, who had just turned sixty-five and looked even older. Hogya was a member of an anti–public-housing group called the Small Property Owners League. He stepped in the mayor's path and loudly and repeatedly asked Bowron if he remembered the advice that Hogya had given him about Frank Wilkinson.

"I don't remember," said Bowron, "and I don't remember you."

"Yes, you do. You remember me warning you about Wilkinson."

"The mayor," according to the *Los Angeles Times*, "shook his head and smiled."

"If you're going to give us low-cost housing, I'd like also to have the low-cost martinis that you drink at the Jonathan Club," said Hogya, referring to an exclusive social club downtown. "I like martinis myself, but I can't afford them."

Bowron was a former judge and a man used to being respected. He was well-mannered, and even when he was on the wrong side of an issue—which he was many times in his career, especially on the subject of Japanese internment—resented the notion that people might think of him as dishonest or corrupt in any way.

"Just who are you, coming around here trying to insult me? Whom do you represent?"

"Well, I don't represent Communists," said Hogya.

"Do you represent Joe Stalin?" Bowron retorted.

"No," said Hogya. "You represent Joe Stalin."

Then, without warning, Bowron reared back and slugged Hogya. The blow glanced off the big man's shoulder, and an aide jumped between them before Hogya could swing back. According to the *Times* report, the aide also helpfully told Hogya that the mayor, in fact, was not a fan of martinis.

Afterward, Hogya ridiculed Bowron, and so did the newspapers. The Red-baiting anti-housing campaign had clearly rattled the buttoned-down mayor.

=

BY LATE 1952, the opponents of public housing had, in Frank Wilkinson, an individual they could point to as "proof" of Communist infiltration of the project. And in Bowron they had a mayor who was reeling. But Bowron was still in office. Holtzendorff was still running the housing authority. And despite the efforts of Ed Davenport and company, the city still had its contract with the federal government. If public housing was going to truly be defeated, it would take a regime change in the mayor's office.

Just before Christmas, a group of Los Angeles business leaders convened in a boardroom in the *Los Angeles Times* building. They had been called there by Norman Chandler for the express purpose of selecting a candidate to run for mayor against Bowron. Whoever they picked would have the financial backing of the business community and the benefit of the newspaper as a mouthpiece. The group had a list of more than thirty potential names and finally arrived at a little-known Republican congressman: Norris Poulson. This would be their man. Poulson was perfect. He was a blank slate. With him as a candidate, his backers could make the campaign a referendum on public housing.

On the day after Christmas, Chandler sent Poulson a letter laying it all out. "Dear Norrie," he began, before offering Poulson the deal of a lifetime. He offered a bottomless well of campaign funds. He offered to make sure that the mayor's salary would be raised soon after Poulson took office. He offered the use of a chauffeured Cadillac "to strut around in." In his later years, Poulson told the historian Robert Gottlieb that when a man like Norman Chandler made an offer like the one in that letter, there was no choice but to accept it. This sounds like something out of the movies: a cabal of millionaires pulling the strings to determine the fate of a city. But it really happened. Poulson's campaign was placed in the hands of the public-relations firm of Baus & Ross, which had handled the housing referendum, and more importantly he was placed under the tutelage of *Los Angeles Times* City Hall reporter Carlton Williams: "I know Williams told council members how to vote, even doing so in council chambers," Poulson later told Gottlieb, "and he was constantly telling me what I should do as well."

On December 31, 1952, the Poulson campaign began in earnest with a front-page story in the *Los Angeles Times* written by Williams. Despite the fact that Poulson was unknown to most of LA, Williams wrote that he was already "viewed as a major contender." Williams didn't have to say who it was that viewed him that way. The answer was the paper itself.

═══

IN JULY 1952, the month before Wilkinson's fateful testimony, Republican delegates nominated Dwight D. Eisenhower as their presidential candidate. Eisenhower was totally inexperienced in politics, but he was a war hero. The man he bested at the convention was a seasoned Ohio senator named Robert Taft. Taft, whose father was President William Howard Taft, was generally thought to be a reliable small-government conservative. But there had been one notable exception in his career: he had been one of the key sponsors of the 1949 housing bill that had started all this madness in Los Angeles.

For a running mate, Eisenhower did not choose his rival, Taft, but a man who was, essentially, Taft's opposite: California Senator Richard M. Nixon. Nixon had some Ed Davenport to him. He was not especially ideological, but he was a fierce foe of public housing and a gleeful anti-Communist who had risen to prominence in Congress as a member of HUAC. Where Taft was an old-money politician from a storied eastern family, Nixon was a scheming upstart from Orange County, California. Shortly before he won the vice-presidential nomination in 1952, Nixon and his fellow California senator, William Knowland, had even tried unsuccessfully to sneak a provision into a budget bill that would have killed the housing program in Los Angeles once and for all.

During the general election, Nixon pounded Eisenhower's opponent, Adlai Stevenson, for being soft on Communism. A few years earlier, Stevenson had testified as a character witness for a State Department employee named Alger Hiss, who stood accused of spying for the Soviet Union. The Hiss case had been a national sensation, in which all the grand ideals and base fears of the McCarthy era played out each day on radio broadcasts and in the papers. It was in some ways a bigger and more dramatic precursor to what Frank Wilkinson would go through. Nixon made his career on it, and McCarthy himself used it to justify his own outrageous anti-Communist tactics. Ultimately, Hiss was convicted of perjury—but not espionage, because the statute of limitations had run out.

The week after Frank Wilkinson was fired, Eisenhower beat Stevenson in a landslide and became the first Republican president since Herbert Hoover. As the calendar turned from 1952 to 1953, the aftershocks of Wilkinson's firing and Eisenhower's election were still rattling Los Angeles. There had been a major referendum on housing in June, a dramatic turn in the housing debate in August with Wilkinson's demise, and then a presidential election in November. The city's voters barely had a chance to take a breath before the campaign for mayor began.

=

"It was a bloody and bitter campaign," remembered Herbert Baus of Baus & Ross. "Recriminations flew thick and fast. We attacked Bowron bitterly." Poulson and his allies spent the months leading up to the April 1953 primary pounding Bowron on housing. It was the same script that had played out in the referendum the year before and the same one Nixon had used to rise from the House of Representatives to the Senate and then the vice presidency. The insinuation was simple and emotional. Public housing was a Communist plot, and Fletcher Bowron supported public housing. Voters could do the math. They had read Frank Wilkinson's testimony in the newspapers.

Poulson defeated the incumbent Bowron in the primary but did not reach the majority he needed to avoid a runoff. It was in the runoff that the campaign truly began. Bowron felt besieged. He had served the city for fifteen years and, in his eyes, done so honorably, rooting out corruption and seeking consensus where he could find it. He had made wide-ranging alliances across the political spectrum that had evolved over the course of his time in office. Just four years earlier, he had even been endorsed by Chandler's *Los Angeles Times*.

But now he saw voters getting worked into a rabid state of anti-Communist fervor by that same paper. He had men like John Hogya shouting him down as he went about his business. He had watched Frank Wilkinson, whose father had been a good friend from the old anti-vice crusades, ruined. At one point during the primary, somebody had placed a grenade in the backseat of Bowron's car while he was delivering a speech. It was not armed, but the message was sent.

On May 5, 1953, three weeks before the general election, Bowron went on the radio and gave the first in a series of speeches that laid bare all the machinations he believed were behind the campaign to oust him. Instead of attacking Poulson himself, Bowron went after Chandler and his media empire. Bowron's speeches were an attempt to turn himself, the incumbent of fifteen years, into an underdog.

The Poulson campaign, Bowron said, was in fact being run "by a small, immensely wealthy, incredibly powerful group to force you to elect as your mayor a man who will represent them—not you—a man who will do their bidding, not yours."

"The *Los Angeles Times* is the mouthpiece of a small group of people who control a vast commercial, financial, agricultural, and industrial empire. Norman Chandler should run for mayor himself."

Then, for good measure, he accused the *Times* of lying in its coverage of the housing issue.

Bowron was angry and defiant, and his attacks appeared to be working. His base was rallying, and victory seemed to be within his grasp. His campaign distributed a cartoon showing Norman Chandler as a literal puppet master controlling the bespectacled Norris Poulson. But even Bowron, a well-established political power in Los Angeles, was subject to schemes beyond his control. His attacks on Chandler drew the attention of Chandler's allies in City Hall.

Back in March, during the primary campaign, a city councilman named George Cronk had written to an anti-Communist congressman named Clare Hoffman of Michigan, requesting that Hoffman's committee come to Los Angeles to investigate the housing authority. Hoffman's House Special Subcommittee on Government Operations was technically meant to oversee governance, but in Hoffman's hands it had become a HUAC-style weapon to attack enemies and investigate allegations of Communist infiltration. This was the spirit in which the committee had been invited to Los Angeles. After Bowron's attacks on the *Times* began, Ed Davenport repeated the invitation.

Hoffman, Poulson's colleague in the Republican caucus and a fearmonger of even greater temerity than Davenport, scheduled his committee to open hearings in Los Angeles on May 18, just eight days before the election. This was, for the Poulson campaign, a rather remarkable stroke of luck. There would be a highly publicized congressional hearing into the biggest campaign weakness of Poulson's opponent just days before the election. And to make matters even better for Poulson, the hearings would be led by Hoffman, who was more shameless and more ghoulish and more willing to pander to humankind's worst instincts than any politician on the scene in LA.

Hoffman was a fascist sympathizer who had tried to start a movement to get Franklin Roosevelt impeached for entering World War II *after* Pearl Harbor. He spoke at America First rallies and spread conspiracy theories alleging that fluoridated water, polio vaccines, and the mental health movement of the 1950s were elements of a grand Communist plot against America.

Democratic members of the committee boycotted the hearings in protest of their timing ahead of the election. Bowron called them "political hatchet work." Even Norris Poulson requested that the hearings be delayed because they gave the impression that he was resorting to dirty tricks. But Hoffman pressed on, even without the support of the mayor, his opponent, or the Democrats on his committee.

All the big names in local politics were going to testify, and all on live television. Howard Holtzendorff was subpoenaed. Bowron was subpoenaed. So was Police Chief William Parker. Just before the hearings were to begin, Frank Wilkinson was sitting at home with his family when the phone rang. On the line was his former colleague Ignacio López. López, who still worked for the housing authority, was calling to warn Frank that process servers were on their way. "Soon after he called there was a knock on my door and I thought it was committee staffers coming to issue the subpoena," Frank later said. "So I dashed out the back door, climbed over a fence to another street and met Nacho."

López drove Frank to a Russian bath in the Boyle Heights neighborhood. There, of all places, they figured, nobody would come looking for him. But they didn't think about the fact that the Russian bath was just down the street from the LAPD's Hollenbeck Station and was a favorite hangout of officers there. Frank was known around Hollenbeck—he had managed the Ramona Gardens projects and lived in the nearby Estrada Courts projects. His picture had been all over the papers for almost a year.

As they walked through the bathhouse in only their towels, with subpoena bearers still scrambling around the city trying to find Frank, one of the cops turned and said, "Hey, there goes Wilkinson." After that, he and López quickly dressed and fled. They drove out to Sherman Oaks, to the home of a couple Frank knew named Robert and Ann Richards. He was a screenwriter, and she had been an employee of the Writer's Guild; both had been blacklisted from Hollywood after pleading the Fifth in front of HUAC.

While the hearings got under way, Frank stayed indoors and out of sight. "I drank homemade corn whiskey and watched the hearings on television," he recalled. The hearings were a spectacle. Hoffman yelled and banged on tables. Frank watched with particular interest when LAPD Chief William Parker took the stand.

Frank had always been suspicious of Parker, especially after Parker had provided doctored crime statistics to Fritz Burns the year before. He knew Parker was on the opposite side of the housing issue. But he was not prepared for the testimony that followed.

As Frank watched, Parker produced a sheath of papers. This was, he quickly realized, the same document that the attorney at the eminent domain hearings had been referring to on that fateful day in court the previous August. The document that had signaled Frank's downfall. The dossier, Frank later learned, had been circulating among anti-housing forces since January 1952. It supposedly contained incontrovertible evidence that Frank Wilkinson was a Communist. On television, Frank watched as Parker testified that early in 1952 he had presented this dossier to Mayor Bowron, as well as dossiers on nine other housing authority employees. Parker said he tried to convince Bowron that it would be politically expedient to remove Frank. But Bowron simply threw the dossier in the trash and said, "I trust that boy."

Parker was then asked by the committee to read the dossier on Frank Wilkinson out loud, as long as he could do so in a way that did not compromise any ongoing police work. Parker said that he could read the entire file. "This information came to me through official channels," he said.

Later, Frank would learn that the official channel that Parker was referring to was the FBI, which had begun surveilling Frank a decade earlier. But as he watched Parker on television, he just knew that somebody had been watching him and that this somebody had passed on this "official report" to the anti-housing attorneys.

It dawned on Frank that he had been the victim of what was essentially a conspiracy. He had been spied on by law-enforcement officials who compiled a dossier on his private life. The dossier, which contained nothing illegal, was then passed to persons outside of the law-enforcement community who used it as part of a campaign of character assassination that they hoped would advance their own business interests. They were able to do this because of a climate of fear that they and their allies stoked as owners of influential media outlets. Now the dossier was once again being used as a prop by law enforcement and anti-housing elected officials in what was essentially a show hearing meant to strike fear into voters and advance a candidate who had been hand-selected by those same private interests.

It was dizzying to think about. On one hand, it must have been heartbreaking. All of Frank's work in housing had been taken from him, and he himself had become a scapegoat. Even though he was indeed a Communist, to write off Frank's work in housing as "communistic" was an insult not just to Frank but also to the work itself. To him, housing and slum clearance weren't ideological issues; they were moral ones. They were the path to a better world, to the Heaven on Earth that his father had been trying to make before him. On the other hand, Frank Wilkinson was at the center of the biggest story in Los Angeles, a martyr to a cause he believed in. He had been so effective at his job that men like Norman Chandler and William Parker felt the need to destroy him. His vision for a slum-free Los Angeles was crumbling, but at least this was a sign that he had been doing something right.

Parker began to read. He had a way of sounding both casual and patronizing when he spoke about people he didn't respect: "The report on Wilkinson, dated January 31, 1952, is entitled: Wilkinson, Frank B. Wife: Jean Benson Wilkinson. 2019 Rodney Drive, Los Angeles, California." Parker went on to list previous addresses and run down the basics of Frank's biography from Michigan to Beverly Hills High School. The dossier contained a great deal of insinuation and circumstantial evidence. Mostly, it consisted of Frank attending meetings, sometimes speaking at them. Finally, toward the conclusion, Parker declared, "Subject has been an active member of the Communist Party, Los Angeles County section, for many years."

Parker did not offer specifics or accuse Frank of any crimes. But it didn't matter. Frank had now been declared, on live television, by the chief of police, to be a Communist. In the days that followed, the *Times* ran story after story tying Bowron to the Communist Frank Wilkinson and to the Communist housing project.

The damage was too much for Bowron to overcome. Norris Poulson won the election, and Norman Chandler and his allies had themselves a new mayor. Poulson's first order of business was to unmake the Elysian Park Heights project. He negotiated a deal with the federal government, which technically held the deed to the land purchased for the project, to buy it all back. The only provision was that the city had to use the land for a public purpose.

This was the end of Frank Wilkinson's dream and would essentially mean the end of new public housing in Los Angeles. All those hours of organizing, of slum tours, and of drumbeating had been for nothing. All the work of Neutra and Alexander would be remanded to waste bins and archives.

It meant that the people of Palo Verde, La Loma, and Bishop had been evicted and watched their community dismembered for nothing. But for Abrana and Manuel Aréchiga, who remained on Malvina Avenue, this also meant something else: a chance. After all, now that the government wasn't going to do what it had tried to kick them out for—now that there wasn't going to be a public-housing project—how could it make them leave?

## Part V

---

# MANIFEST DESTINY

# 54.

Rosalind Wyman grew up on progressive politics and Pacific Coast League baseball: Franklin Delano Roosevelt and the Hollywood Stars. She was ambitious, and she was earnest. Her parents ran a drugstore in the middle of Los Angeles, and in 1932 they turned it into a working campaign office for Roosevelt. While a teenage Frank Wilkinson and his father handed out buttons on behalf of Herbert Hoover in Beverly Hills, the young Roz Wyman stared up at posters of FDR from her crib. She went to Los Angeles High School and then to the University of Southern California. In 1950 she went to work for the actress-turned-congresswoman Helen Gahagan Douglas in her losing US Senate race against Richard Nixon. She saw what a determined woman could do on the campaign trail and the way that a woman could make people believe. Douglas was an inspirational candidate, but Nixon was a ruthless one. He did what came naturally: he called Douglas a Communist. Douglas was "pink right down to her underwear," he said.

Then, in 1952, Roz Wyman put off law school to go to work for Adlai Stevenson. Douglas and Stevenson both lost, but Roz Wyman was hooked on the fight, hooked on the idea that you could do something. When her city councilman opted not to run for reelection in 1953, Wyman decided to run herself. She gathered the signatures and got onto the ballot. Nobody thought much of her. After all, she was twenty-two years old, and there hadn't been a woman elected to the council since 1915.

While Norris Poulson hammered Fletcher Bowron on housing and tied him to Communism, Roz Wyman ran a campaign on the possible. She enlisted her USC classmates and the Young Democrats and her mother's friends. She went door-to-door right after *I Love Lucy* aired because she knew that her neighbors would be home. She boiled her platform down to bullet points and printed them on tens of thousands of 3 × 5 index cards. She was in favor of housing, unions, and integration. She wanted more funding for the arts. She wanted, as much as anything else, for Los Angeles to be a world-class city.

And she wanted to do it through baseball. One of the bullet points on those index cards was a pledge to make Los Angeles a major-league city.

In this effort she was not alone. There had been talk about big-league baseball in Southern California going back decades. In the early 1930s a newspaper editor named Mark Kelly began making noise about bringing the big leagues west. But there was always a reason it couldn't happen: Los Angeles was simply too *far*; Los Angeles did not have the right kind of stadium; even as the Angels and Stars outdrew major-league teams in attendance and the population grew, Los Angeles was not a big-league town.

The St. Louis Browns nearly moved to LA in late 1941, but they were thwarted by the onset of World War II. Then, after the war, the Pacific Coast League made a bid to become a third major league, joining the American and National Leagues, but the owners on the East Coast dismissed the idea. In baseball as in everything else, the conquest of the Pacific would have to happen on the Atlantic's terms.

The most relentless of the LA baseball boosters was himself a transplant, a sportswriter named Vincent X. Flaherty. Flaherty had come out from Washington, DC, and immediately taken up the cause in the pages of the *Los Angeles Examiner*. He was a stereotype of a stereotype. He wore a fedora and breathed in gossip like it was oxygen, then breathed it out into pattering, innuendo-laden prose. In *Forever Blue*, his biography of Walter O'Malley, the writer Michael D'Antonio paints Flaherty as unceasing in his schmoozing and seduction: "In 1948, he accompanied former county supervisor Leonard Roach to the American League's annual meeting at Chicago's Palmer House hotel, where they promoted the city. In 1950 he contacted every single club, including the Dodgers, attempting to sell them on moving west. He was focused most intently on faltering clubs in cities with two big-league teams, especially the Braves of Boston and the St. Louis Browns."

It got to be that for Flaherty and people like him, the quest to bring big-league baseball to Los Angeles was as much about personal pride as civic pride, as much about being the person who made LA a big-league city as about LA in fact becoming one. The cause gave Flaherty something to write about, and it gave him the chance to hobnob with the rich and powerful. In 1946 he had even represented Louie B. Mayer, the head of MGM Studios, in a bid to buy the St. Louis Cardinals.

Civic boosterism had never been fully altruistic in Los Angeles; there was always money to be made in making LA a bigger and shinier and more desirable place. There was always something to be sold, status to be claimed, and power to be gained. For the businessmen of Los Angeles, just as it had been for Jorge Pasquel, baseball could be a means to an end.

But there was also the reality that by 1950, Los Angeles was a big-league city by any conceivable definition and that baseball needed LA as badly as LA needed baseball. The pro football Rams had arrived in 1949 and become an instant success. In 1950 there were two million people in Los Angeles—more than double the populations of Boston and St. Louis, both of which had two major-league clubs. LA had glamour and cachet, and people across the country were pulling up stakes to go live there.

The fact that big-league baseball hadn't already reached the West Coast was a character flaw, a result of baseball, almost by its very nature, being resistant to change and obsessed with its own past. Even in the 1950s, the fact of baseball and the mythology of baseball were inseparable. It was already a sport that froze its greatest moments into historical time even as they were occurring. The batter steps out of the box. The pitcher wipes his nose. The organist bleats something. Each moment like a scene on ancient Greek urn.

In its exclusionary hardheadedness and its preference for soothing mythology over uncomfortable truth, baseball was not unlike the country that made it. Some of the literal writers of the American myth—Walt Whitman and Mark Twain—had been baseball advocates. Vincent X. Flaherty and Roz Wyman could not have been more different, but they agreed on one thing: if the big leagues weren't going to go west on their own volition, they would need to be dragged across the continent.

"I didn't understand how we could be a great city without having a major league baseball team," Wyman later said. But just as good a question would have been whether big-league baseball could really claim to be the national pastime without a team in Los Angeles or, for that matter, San Francisco.

In April 1953, Wyman stunned the city by winning her primary. Then on May 26, 1953, the same day that the city voted Norris Poulson into office, effectively killing any chance that Elysian Park Heights would ever be constructed, Wyman became the youngest council member in the history of Los Angeles. She also became the council's only woman, only Jewish member, and biggest baseball fan. The headline in the *Mirror News* said, simply, "It's a Girl." The *Times* story about her victory gave a preview of what was to be in store for Wyman and for other women in politics: "An attractive brunette with fine clear skin, she was dressed simply on her victory day in a plain white blouse and royal blue skirt and plain suede pumps—answering phone calls in crisp, decisive terms as though she welcomed the hubbub and fully enjoyed it."

The confluence of events on May 26 would prove to be crucial in determining the fate of both baseball and the city of Los Angeles. In his scholarship on mid-century Los Angeles, the historian Don Parson wrote about a shift from "community modernism" toward "corporate modernism," from top-down planning meant to lift up the floor for the city's poor and working classes toward top-down planning meant to elevate the ceilings for its wealthy elite. "Corporate modernism" meant favoring business-friendly infrastructure and redevelopment, including the "construction of prestige sports facilities."

Parsons argued that the election of 1953 was the tipping point. The defeat of public housing, the banishment of Frank Wilkinson, and the ushering in of a mayoral regime that would primarily serve the needs of its corporate backers meant the end of "community modernism."

But it's not clear that community modernism and corporate modernism were inherently mutually exclusive. After all, Roz Wyman supported "community modernist" products such as housing *and* the arrival of big-league baseball. She fervently believed that baseball could be a uniting civic force. And in this belief, she was joined by some of the city's most progressive politicians, including Edward Roybal and Kenneth Hahn, the ambitious pro-housing councilman who had recently left City Hall for a position on the powerful Los Angeles County Board of Supervisors.

The first piece of legislation that Wyman proposed after taking office called for testing out the Los Angeles Memorial Coliseum as a baseball venue. She immediately became the engine of a well-organized and coordinated effort to bring big-league baseball to Los Angeles. And she was savvy enough to make room in this effort for her ostensible political opponents. The baseball advocates included the new mayor, Norris Poulson, the reclusive aerospace industrialist Howard Hughes, MGM boss Mayer, and the hotel baron Conrad Hilton. With all these people lining up in support of bringing a team in, it seemed like just a matter of time.

The Braves and Browns flirted with Los Angeles before moving to Milwaukee and Baltimore, respectively. The hapless Washington Senators (a team so bad they inspired the Broadway musical *Damn Yankees*) thought about it too. In October 1953, Vincent X. Flaherty wrote a letter to the owner of the Brooklyn Dodgers, Walter O'Malley, reminding him what a great baseball town Los Angeles could be. "Let me remind you that it never rains in Los Angeles during the baseball season," he said.

The one thing that LA needed was a big-league stadium. In October 1954, Flaherty lent his column space to Kenneth Hahn, who wrote an emotional plea for the city to purchase and then upgrade Wrigley Field. With the promise of a truly big-league ballpark, Hahn wrote, the city could draw the Philadelphia Athletics to Los Angeles as soon as the following season: "If we really want major league baseball in Los Angeles, we can't procrastinate any longer. No time is left to talk about building a new stadium or locating a site on which to build. The red tape involved in that kind of thing could take years."

Hahn was right about the red tape—it would indeed take years to build a new stadium—but he was wrong about the Athletics. They were bound for Kansas City. Despite the best efforts of Hahn and his pro-housing allies in the preceding years, the future site of the city's new stadium was already being emptied. In the aftermath of Norris Poulson's election and amid protracted legal battles, the city had entertained a long list of possible uses for the land that had once been slated for Elysian Park Heights.

There could have been a zoo, an airport, a county jail, a music center, a convention center, a college campus, a golf course, a world's fair, office buildings, an auditorium, a series of playgrounds, a parking lot, or any imaginable combination thereof. But the hills from which the bricks that built early Los Angeles had been formed and on which Abrana and Manuel Aréchiga had built their house and their life, the hills on which the communities of Palo Verde, La Loma, and Bishop had grown from the dirt and then been swept away in the name of progress, were destined for something else: baseball.

# 55.

IN THE EARLY 1950S, ABRANA AND MANUEL'S SON JUAN, HIS WIFE Nellie, and their older daughter, Helen, drove down to Mexico with their friends Feliz and Camilo Arevalo. They all piled in the car and drove from LA to Zacatecas. Then they rode in the hired truck up to Monte Escobedo, where Abrana and Manuel came from and where there were still aunts and uncles. Juan got a vision of what life might have been like if his parents hadn't left their hometown. What it might have been like to grow up far away from the movie theaters, the police academy swimming pool, the streetcars, and the dances: what life was like up there among the rocks.

Then they drove down to Mexico City and stood before the altar at the Basilica of Guadalupe, the holiest Catholic site in the New World, situated at the base of the hill where the Virgin Mary appeared on a tapestry before a poor Aztec named Juan Diego. They stared up at the hillside where the miracle happened and then stared up at the tapestry inside the church. This very site was in many ways the nexus of their culture. It was their origin story: indigenous, Spanish, Mexican, American. Their parents had fled Mexico forty years earlier, and here they were in Mexico's heart.

This was the land conquered by Cortés and the Spaniards and then conquered again by Winfield Scott and the Americans. This was where Juan Escutia fell to his death from the Chapultepec Castle clutching Mexico's tricolor flag. And now Mexico City was blossoming. The foreign economists called it a miracle. The Mexican Miracle. The miracle of modernization. In America in the 1950s, they were talking about slum clearance and revitalization. They were talking about blight; Juan and Nellie heard it every day. They heard it when Frank Wilkinson came knocking on their door and as they watched Palo Verde clear out, house by house. And here they were in Mexico, where they were talking about it too. Not far from La Basilica de Guadalupe, the Mexican government was setting out to build a housing project that Frank Wilkinson could only have dreamed about.

It was going to be located right on the site where the final Aztec warriors had fallen to Cortés's army, and it was going eclipse Elysian Park Heights in both size and ambition. They would call it the Conjunto Urbano Nonalco Tlatelolco. Tlatelolco would be a modern, planned community for fifty thousand people. It would have room for the poor and the middle class and the rich, all together in one place with landscaped gardens and tall towers. The same forces that drove Richard Neutra and Robert Alexander drove Tlatelolco architect Mario Paní. Paní was a visionary, but he was afflicted by his own visions. He saw the world from ten thousand feet, which meant that sometimes he didn't see the people living in it. "We still need to regenerate over half of Mexico City, which is full of awful neighborhoods," Paní once said. "The one advantage is that most of these neighborhoods are so awful that they are just waiting to be regenerated, to be torn down and re-built properly."

In the middle of it all, beside recently unearthed Aztec ruins and a sixteenth-century Spanish church, would be an open plaza: the Plaza de Las Tres Culturas, celebrating the three cultures that made the country what it was: Aztec, Spanish, and finally Mexican. This is where, in 1968, Tlatelolco would become infamous for the first time, as the site of a government massacre against student protesters. Hidden machine guns perched on rooftops rained bullets down on students, who were lured into the square and then trapped by strategically placed troops and vehicles. In 1985 Tlatelolco would become infamous once again, as buildings throughout the complex crumbled in the devastating Mexico City earthquake. But unlike Palo Verde, which was destroyed, and unlike Elysian Park Heights, which was never constructed, Tlatelolco still stands. It is undernourished and underserved, but it is still there: a vision of modernism left in the past.

# 56.

IN SEPTEMBER 1955, ROZ WYMAN AND ED ROYBAL FLEW TO NEW York City on a mission to bring home a ball club. But not just any ball club. Los Angeles was done flirting with bottom-feeding, historically marginal teams like the St. Louis Browns and Washington Senators. Instead, it was courting a franchise to match its growing place in the national imagination and the global economy, a franchise that would live up to its own sense of self-worth as a destination city: the Brooklyn Dodgers.

The Dodgers were baseball's most forward-thinking club and also its most glorious, triumphant losers. They were the team of Jackie Robinson, Roy Campanella, and Duke Snider, yet they were also the team fated to be crushed in the World Series by the Yankees over and over again. The Bums. The spirit of an entire borough embodied in a glorious spunky and ill-fated roster. Many books have been written on their legend. Many tears have been spilled over their fate.

The Dodgers were coveted long before they actually left Brooklyn. In the fall of 1953 the comedians Abbott and Costello, creators of the beloved "Who's on First?" sketch, appeared before the Los Angeles City Council to receive an official commendation for their work advocating big-league baseball in LA. They handed out pins reading "Let's go Big League Los Angeles" and talked up the virtues of the national pastime as a wholesome outlet for the city's delinquent youths.

Children "look to baseball players as idols and children's conduct is directed into constructive avenues instead of juvenile delinquency when they have as their heroes such fine examples of good sportsmanship and Americanism," said Lou Costello.

Costello, a man whose career had begun on the burlesque circuit, knew firsthand the temptations of celebrity that big-league

*Walter O'Malley*

players encountered. But here he was, yet another American bending baseball players into something more than mere mortals, and willfully propagating the notion that a made-up game played with a bat and ball could somehow reveal the highest spirit and ideals of a nation. The myth of baseball, like the myth of Los Angeles, required constant upkeep.

Costello also took the time to note that attendance was down in Brooklyn, that three teams in New York were too many for one city, and that if LA was really invested in the idea of becoming a big-league town, well, the Dodgers were ripe for the picking.

It would be silly to say that Lou Costello, of all people, predicted the future of Dodger baseball. But he did have a point. There were good reasons to think that the Dodgers would never leave Brooklyn. At the time that Roybal and Wyman landed in New York, the Dodgers were in the midst of their best season ever, in the process of running away with their third National League pennant in four years. On September 7, 1955, O'Malley wrote to Wyman telling her that he would be too busy to meet with them, "as we will all be preoccupied in concluding this year's pennant race, and preparing for the World Series."

The Dodgers would open the World Series by losing two straight games at Yankee Stadium: the same old story. But what followed would be the greatest triumph that Ebbets Field had ever seen. When the Series got back to Brooklyn, the Dodgers won three in a row behind Snider, who hit two home runs each in games four and five. After the Yankees won game six, Dodgers starter Johnny Podres threw a shutout in game seven to give the franchise its first-ever championship.

But even as his team finally triumphed in the World Series, O'Malley was fretting about finding them a new home. O'Malley's solution was to propose a new ballpark not too far away from Ebbets Field, at the intersection of Atlantic and Flatbush Avenues. O'Malley didn't want to just build any stadium either. The many faults of Ebbets Field—broken sight lines, steep stairways, claustrophobic tunnels—had led him to think deeply about what a ballpark could be, with the application of some imagination and with the spectator experience kept squarely in mind. O'Malley was not afraid to challenge conventional thinking. At one point he consulted with the futurist architect R. Buckminster Fuller to design a park enclosed by a clear geodesic dome. It would seat 52,000 people and feature parking for anybody who needed it.

But to build any kind of new park, O'Malley first needed to assemble the property at his desired site. And to do so, he would need the help of Robert Moses, the all-powerful bureaucrat who held the key to New York City land use. O'Malley and Moses corresponded frequently throughout the 1950s, but they were at odds in temperament and in ambition. O'Malley hoped that Moses could employ Title I of the 1949 Housing Act—the same bill that had led to the destruction of Palo Verde, La Loma, and Bishop in Los Angeles—to help condemn land for a new Brooklyn stadium. Unfortunately for

O'Malley, Moses hated baseball and refused to entertain the notion that a privately owned stadium would meet the "public-purpose" requirements to enact urban renewal under the law.

Moses had another idea: he wanted to build a publicly owned ballpark in Queens, at the site of the World's Fair. The Dodgers could move from Brooklyn and rent the stadium from the city. This was as untenable to O'Malley as the notion of donating public land for a private enterprise had been to Moses. O'Malley wanted to build the stadium the way he wanted to build it. He wanted to be owner, not tenant. The result was a classic standoff. Two powerful, egotistical, and cunning men with competing goals, competing styles, and competing visions for their city.

Roz Wyman and Ed Roybal left New York empty-handed in 1955, but the future of the Dodgers in Brooklyn was already in doubt. LA's pursuit of big-league baseball was in full swing, and O'Malley, in his letter to Wyman, had left the door open: "At a later date perhaps there might be a time when a meeting would be appropriate."

THE FOLLOWING SEASON, after yet another World Series appearance (this time nature corrected itself, and Brooklyn again lost to the Yankees), the Dodgers set off on a goodwill tour of Japan. The tour was a mid-century update on the barnstorming tours taken by early pro clubs up and down the East Coast, and by Albert Spalding and his globe-trotting team of baseball evangelists back in 1888.

On their way to Japan, the Dodgers stopped for one night in Los Angeles. There O'Malley sat down with Kenneth Hahn, who wanted to pitch him on a potential site for a new ballpark. Years later, Hahn would claim that over coffee at the Statler Hotel, O'Malley made an oral promise to move the Dodgers to Los Angeles. But Kenneth Hahn said a lot of things.

O'Malley certainly understood that meeting with Hahn could only help his negotiating position in Brooklyn, but there is no solid evidence that he was ready to move yet. What O'Malley did do was listen as Hahn sold him on the benefits of a potential stadium site, land that, unlike his desired Brooklyn site, had already been almost completely cleared.

The land that Hahn was pushing was the abandoned Elysian Park Heights site. Immediately after Poulson was elected mayor in 1953, he began to talk about the possibility of building a ballpark there. Later, Hollywood Stars owner Bob Cobb told the *Los Angeles Times* that he had been thinking about baseball in the hills as far back as 1950, when he visited the police academy to help set up kitchen facilities there. He even went so far as to hire renowned local architect Stiles O. Clements to draw up a blueprint.

As the Pacific Coast League continued in its effort to become a third major league, Cobb kept returning to the site. "It seemed natural," he said. "There were 250 acres to be developed, four freeways would run into it, and it was ideally central."

The courtship with Los Angeles continued after O'Malley returned from Japan, and it moved quickly. First, O'Malley sold Ebbets Field (with an agreement that the Dodgers could still play there); then he traded his minor-league franchise in Fort Worth to the Chicago Cubs for the Los Angeles Angels and their stadium, Wrigley Field. With that, O'Malley now had a stake in Los Angeles; he owned a franchise in the Pacific Coast League and, more importantly, real estate in the city. Then, during spring training of 1957, O'Malley entertained Hahn and Norris Poulson at Dodgertown in Vero Beach, Florida. By the time the season began, fatalistic Brooklyn fans were already certain that they were watching their beloved club's death march.

In May, O'Malley visited San Diego to buy his team a new airplane: a Convair 440, which could take the club from coast to coast with only a couple of stops. The purchase of the new plane was suspicious in itself, but even more suspicious was the fact that O'Malley also went up to Los Angeles. Hahn arranged for O'Malley to take a ride in a sheriff's department helicopter and get a better sense of the city.

O'Malley, at this point, knew almost nothing about Los Angeles. He knew the city by reputation, by demographic charts and maps, by its long presence in the Pacific Coast League. He had studied it as a businessman. But he had spent almost no time in LA. He had no sense of its civic culture or of its people. He had purchased Wrigley Field without ever laying eyes on it. He was, and always had been, New York through and through.

The helicopter took off from the sheriff's department training center in East Los Angeles, and as he soared up over the infinite city, O'Malley was privileged with a perspective that millions of Angelenos had never had: a bird's-eye view of their city as it stretched from the sea to the horizon. Buildings resplendent, new, and shiny rising up from the Earth like block towers on a child's cluttered bedroom floor. Fresh coats of paint. The freeways twisting and braiding across the landscape. Somehow it all fit together, the old and the new and the seemingly impossible: the finally completed Watts Towers, the new Capitol Records building in Hollywood like a stack of 45 rpm records, and Disneyland all the way down in Orange County. The following year, 1958, the television station KTLA would launch America's first news helicopter, and only then, seeing the footage beamed down into their TV sets, would residents begin to get a sense of their city's scope.

The helicopter was in the air for nearly an hour. The skies were emptier and quieter and clearer then. O'Malley floated over downtown in a glass bubble, over the concrete riverbed and the colossal four-level freeway interchange. He still wore a pin on his lapel that read "Keep the Dodgers in Brooklyn." This was far from Brooklyn, as far as you could get in the realm of American baseball. He hovered over the crevices and cliffs and the springtime flowers at Elysian Park, the earthmoving equipment, and those last, stubborn homes clinging to the dirt in Palo Verde, La Loma, and Bishop. Somewhere down there were Abrana and Manuel Aréchiga.

The following day, O'Malley huddled with Norris Poulson, City Attorney Roger Arnebergh, and other local officials at the Statler Hotel. He was still wearing his button. He was still, by all accounts, trying to make Brooklyn work. But he was also negotiating in earnest. And by the time he flew back to New York in his brand-new Convair 440, O'Malley had hammered out the general parameters of a deal that could—and ultimately would—bring Major League Baseball to the West Coast.

The Dodgers played out their season as ghosts in Brooklyn. In June the city of Los Angeles appointed a businessman named Chad McClellan to negotiate directly with O'Malley. As the Dodgers plodded toward September and the Angels floundered in the Pacific Coast League, O'Malley and McClellan haggled on the finer points of a deal. The Dodgers were far from contention. The stands at Ebbets Field were empty and mournful. But everything was in place. O'Malley would trade the Wrigley Field property to the city in exchange for about three hundred acres of land that had once been Palo Verde, La Loma, and Bishop but had now definitively become Chavez Ravine.

There were only a few minor details standing in the way. First, Walter O'Malley had to make it official. He had to pick up the phone and tell Norris Poulson, Roz Wyman, and Kenneth Hahn that this was happening, that this had not all been some great con, some over-the-top negotiating ploy, a delusion of the type that Los Angeles has always been so good at crafting.

On October 7, as the Braves and Yankees played in the World Series, the city council voted on whether to approve the deal with O'Malley. Even then, despite the frantic efforts of Poulson and Wyman, the Dodgers' owner would not commit. In his book *City of Dreams*, Jerald Podair set the scene of a dramatic council session. As Wyman lobbied hard for the ten votes she needed to solidify the deal, Poulson dragged her off the council floor to speak to O'Malley by phone. With a firm commitment, she told the Dodger owner, she could lock in the votes.

O'Malley waffled and refused to commit. But Wyman got the votes. And the following day, he finally committed. The Dodgers were leaving Brooklyn. The club announced the decision via press release: "In view of the action of the Los Angeles City Council yesterday and in accordance with the resolution of the National League made October first, the stockholders and directors of the Brooklyn Baseball Club have today met and unanimously agreed that the necessary steps be taken to draft the Los Angeles territory."

Now Los Angeles would have to ensure that the land it had promised the Dodgers was really available. Poulson had already moved to strike the public-purpose restriction from the city's deed to the former Elysian Park Heights site. But would doing so be legal? Would it be politically viable to turn a site that had been slated for public housing into a privately owned ballpark?

Then, finally, there was the small matter of the people who still lived there.

# 57.

Juan and Nellie Aréchiga drove to Mexico all the time, just not usually as far as Zacatecas or Mexico City. They would go to Tijuana. They would drive down State Route 99—this was before Interstate 5 was built—all the way to San Diego and line up at the San Ysidro border crossing with the other cars. Juan and Nellie were both American, with birth certificates and driver's licenses to prove it, so even as people were being rounded up and deported in their childhood backyard, Elysian Park, as part of Operation Wetback, they felt OK going down there. Tijuana was charming. The population was still only about sixty thousand people. The crossing itself was quiet and easy. There were chain-link fences and turnstiles, not concrete and barbed wire. The border guards sat in booths like toll collectors.

Sometimes they would go with their kids in the station wagon. Sometimes Féliz and Camilo Arévalo would also come. Juan and Camilo would drop off the wives and kids to shop and wander around and take pictures sitting on the backs of donkeys. Then the men would disappear for a few hours.

Juan would have everything arranged ahead of time. He would take orders around LA, then call ahead to the liquor stores and bars. After he dropped off the wife and kids, Juan would make his rounds, filling up the car with case after case of tequila and mezcal. Camilo went with him only a few times, but he saw enough to know that Juan was an expert.

Before heading back across the border, Juan would go to a ranch owned by a friend of his and slowly take his car apart and begin to pack in the tequila. Juan was in his element here. He was always good with his hands. He was always a craftsman and a creative problem solver. Decades before drug cartels would become famous for building secret compartments in cars and engineering tunnels and catapults and submarines, Juan Aréchiga found a way to smuggle case after case of tequila into Los Angeles.

"They would take out the windows," Camilo said. They would wrap the bottles up in newspaper and set them in carefully so they wouldn't break or rattle. They would hide them in the doors and beneath the upholstery and in the side panels. The entire car would be filled up with booze, but if you didn't know where to look, you would never find it.

Juan would buy a fifth of tequila in Mexico for about fifty cents and sell it for about three dollars in Los Angeles. He used his cousin Gene Cabral's garage as a dropoff point. Once, Juan was caught because a neighbor from Palo Verde ratted him out. The guy was trying to do the same thing: sneak tequila over the border in his car. But he didn't know how to wrap it up in newspaper like Juan did. He didn't know how to hide the tequila in the upholstery and frame. This guy drove up to the border, and the cops could hear the bottles rattling. And the first thing he did when they put the cuffs on him was to give up Juan Aréchiga.

With Juan in and out of jail, Nellie and the girls spent more time with Manuel and Abrana. The neighborhood was fading away, but the Aréchiga compound was still full and loud and busy. Abrana went through her routine, the same way she had been going through it for decades. She fed her goats and her chickens. She grabbed the chickens by the neck and swung them around until they were dead. She plucked them and boiled them. She watered her garden and cleaned the spikes off the cactus paddles before she chopped them up. She made fresh tortillas, the echo of her hands clapping bouncing off the hills and lingering in the empty streets.

She fed her grandchildren. She made menudo on the weekends. She dried her clothes on the lines in the back just so. There weren't so many neighbors passing by to yell at anymore. The stores had closed. The police cars still came cruising up and down Malvina Avenue, to and from the police academy. Abrana taught Nellie her secrets. She looked at her daughter-in-law with sad eyes and said, "You're going to live the same life I did."

But that would have been impossible. Despite her best efforts, the life she had was almost gone. The city was still insisting that the Aréchigas leave their properties and pick up the $10,039 sitting in escrow, and the Aréchigas were still insisting that they had no interest in doing so. There were a dozen or so other property owners still resisting eviction, but the Aréchiga family's failure to appeal that initial condemnation suit had forced them to make an independent and more aggressive legal challenge. In 1953, after the housing project was canceled, the Aréchigas sued the housing authority to reverse the condemnation of their home. After all, what did the government need it for now?

"In view of the fact that the Housing Authority has decided to abandon the project, the Aréchigas say they see no reason for giving up their home," the *Los Angeles Times* wrote. The suit set off a years-long legal battle. And as their case wound through the courts, the family continued to make the best of things.

Sometimes, Manuel would take Nellie and the girls to visit Juan in jail. Manuel was gray-haired by then, his face lined. But his hair was still thick. And his eyes still had that sparkle to them. He would not say much, but he would see everything. He watched people. He understood them. On the way home, he would stop at the store with the girls and buy them a treat: a soda or a candy or a piece of cake. Just a little something special. Papa Comida.

Finally, Juan and Nellie left Palo Verde for good, or at least left what remained of it. They used a loan from Nellie's parents to buy a house on Riverside Drive, just down the hill from the old neighborhood along the Los Angeles River.

Then, a few years later, Juan and Nellie got a letter not unlike the one Manuel and Abrana had received in July 1950: they were going to have to sell their home to make way for the new Glendale Freeway. Eminent domain. They moved to Echo Park.

# 58.

JO WILKINSON REMEMBERS THE FIRST TIME SHE HEARD HER FATHER talking about jail. It was 1957, and she was still a child—eight or nine years old—and even at that age Frank used to talk baby talk to her. She was shy, she was his youngest, and she wanted him to love her and shower her with attention and be Popsiedoodle all the time, so she responded the same way, and that's how their relationship was.

She was hiding behind her mother's skirt while the grown-ups talked. It was Frank, Jean, and a man named Carl Braden and his wife, Anne. They were talking and talking and talking. Jo did not pick up everything. It was adult stuff. But there were always a lot of adults and a lot of adult talk in the Wilkinson house. Children really are sponges. The grown-ups were talking about jail and about the First Amendment. And Carl had already been to jail once. Carl was loud, he had a big round belly and round frames on his glasses, and he liked to eat ice cream by the pint. Anne had a pinched-in face, and she seemed quieter at first, but she spoke in long sentences that cascaded one after the other.

Frank was gone a lot in those days. His housing career was over, but in late 1953, after his blacklisting, after Elysian Park Heights was killed and the city's eyes turned elsewhere, Frank was offered a job with a group called the Committee to Preserve American Freedoms. The committee's express purpose was to fight HUAC, and its slogan was "Courage Is Contagious." Frank had been a martyr to the cause of public housing, and now he turned his attention to the systems that had destroyed him and the program he loved: it was a natural progression. It was also a national job, and Frank's life became even busier and more hectic than it had been when he was working at the housing authority.

Frank's main task was to organize in communities where HUAC and HUAC-style hearings were being held. When the committee issued subpoenas in some city near or far, Frank would drop everything to fly in and help. He would wrangle coordinated legal assistance and try to build a united front. In the 1950s a subpoena from HUAC was itself a weapon. Merely being called before the committee could ruin a person's life and reputation. One could escape legal trouble by pleading the Fifth Amendment, which protected witnesses from self-incrimination, but as Frank and Jean had learned, pleading the Fifth was essentially a guilty plea in the court of public opinion.

In 1957 a Stanford scientist named William K. Sherwood swallowed a fatal dose of poison rather than be forced to testify and plead the Fifth on television. Sherwood was a father of four and a biochemist doing cancer research. "The committee's trail is strewn with blasted lives and the wreckage of youthful careers," Sherwood wrote before his death.

During his work organizing against HUAC, Frank was slowly coming to a moral realization of the kind that had typified his life. His values and his circumstances were coalescing just as they had when he saw the poverty in Bethlehem and swore off God, just as they had when Monsignor O'Dwyer first introduced him to the slums of Los Angeles. Back then it had been simple: the poor needed homes. Now Frank was older. He had recently turned forty. But he was still the same strident and guileless idealist. He was still the boy who reached out for the coyote in the street in Douglas, Arizona.

Frank believed that the very existence of HUAC violated the free-speech rights of all Americans. Very few people had refused to answer HUAC's questions on First Amendment grounds since the Hollywood Ten. One of them, in 1955, had been the musician Pete Seeger. But Seeger had not been cited for contempt or sent to jail. "We will not save free speech if we are not prepared to go to jail in its defense," Frank used to say. "I am prepared to pay that price."

Frank wanted to coax HUAC into arresting him for contempt and then take the challenge to the US Supreme Court, where, as he put it in his oral history, the court "would either have to send me to jail, or declare that the First Amendment was violated by the Un-American Activities Committee." This was no small thing for a father of three. Frank had already lost one good-paying career.

To go to jail would mean not only leaving the family in a financial bind but also leaving the family, period. Just as it had with housing, Frank's single-mindedness was what allowed him to take bold stands and do meaningful work as an activist. But it also led him to willfully ignore the obvious consequences of his actions. Previously, those consequences were felt by the residents of Palo Verde, La Loma, and Bishop who had lost their homes and communities for the sake of an outsider's grand, unrealized dream. Now they could be felt by his children.

Frank became something almost unrecognizable to them. He was still Popsiedoodle sometimes, silly and fun and the world's greatest father when you had his attention, but they so rarely had it. Jo remembers that she used to think of Frank, coming home all charged up on injustice and lifting her into his arms, as her very own Atticus Finch. But then she worked up the courage to crawl into Frank's lap and ask him if it was true—if he really was a Communist. "He got this cloak over him. He just changed. And he said, 'Until such time as a Communist can answer that question'—and he gave me the speech. I'm eight or nine. At that moment, I knew I wasn't special."

# 59.

WALTER O'MALLEY LANDED IN CALIFORNIA A HERO. HE HAD DONE IT. Major League Baseball in Los Angeles. He had pushed the sport and the city to their destinies. He had allowed himself to be seduced by the sunshine, the smell of citrus, and the views from his helicopter. And for good measure, he had brought the New York Giants with him to play in San Francisco. (Horace Stoneham, the Giants owner, had been plotting a move to Minnesota, but O'Malley convinced him to look into San Francisco so that the clubs could continue their rivalry.)

As the Dodgers airliner flew west, radio announcers in LA tracked its progress, mile by mile. Five decades on, the city was a long way from the hot-air balloons meandering over Chutes Park. Now it had a baseball team to match its growing size and status: the Brooklyn Dodgers, the franchise of Duke Snider and Jackie Robinson, had, like so many millions of people, including Duke and Jackie's own parents, come west in search of vines and fig trees. The words "Los Angeles Dodgers" were painted on the plane. There were brass bands and cheerleaders and thousands of fans waiting on the tarmac.

"Some of the spectators claimed they saw Sputnik crossing the horizon as they awaited the coming of the Dodgers," wrote Paul Zimmerman in the *Los Angeles Times*. "If that was the Soviet satellite, it thoughtfully passed beyond the horizon well before the big celebration."

O'Malley emerged from the plane in a fedora. He greeted Rosalind Wyman and Kenneth Hahn. They donned blue baseball caps with the letters *L* and *A* emblazoned on the front. O'Malley addressed the waiting fans through a public-address system and promised them greatness. In return, they cheered him and covered him with flower petals. The crowd pushed closer and closer to O'Malley, the bringer of baseball. Duke Snider fought his way through the masses of people to join the dignitaries. One other man made it to the front. He shoved a sheath of paper into O'Malley's hands. "Greetings from the City of Los Angeles," the stranger said. "We're glad to have you here. Here's a summons from the people of Chavez Ravine."

He was a process server.

———

THE SUBPOENA WAS the gift of a group called the Citizens Committee to Save Chavez Ravine for the People. The Citizens Committee didn't have a great deal to do with the actual residents of Palo Verde, La Loma, and Bishop, but its presence is a good reminder that in Los Angeles, politics are always fractured, and common interests can lead to unexpected alliances.

At the heart of the committee was a union between small-government politicians led by Councilman John Holland, who had previously been a vocal opponent of public housing, and business interests opposed to Major League Baseball in Los Angeles, led by John Arnholt Smith, the owner of the Pacific Coast League's San Diego Padres, a man more commonly known, appropriately enough, as Blackjack.

In a sense the formation of the committee echoed the previous fight against public housing. It was political conservatives and business executives uniting with a small group of home owners that they would normally have had little interest in. But this time it was different. There were only a couple dozen families left in the communities. And the consensus of the city's broader business class had shifted.

In 1953 it had taken the full weight of Norman Chandler's influence, the pocketbooks of his allies, and the confluence of a national anti-Communist scaremongering campaign to boot Fletcher Bowron from office and kill the housing initiative. This time the downtown interests led by Chandler were all behind O'Malley and his ballpark. The Dodger deal was a victory for exactly the kind of boosterism that had made LA what it was and had made the Chandlers and their allies among the city's richest and most powerful men.

However, the Citizens Committee to Save Chavez Ravine had something else in their pocket: a convincing argument. The committee's case was simple and intuitive. The problem wasn't baseball. The problem was a sweetheart deal for a New York businessman at the expense of the LA taxpayer. The committee argued that the city was relying on property assessments that inflated the value of the ten-acre Wrigley Field site to make it seem comparable to the three-hundred-acre Chavez Ravine site. On that note, the Chavez Ravine site was excessively large, so what did O'Malley need so much land for? Finally, why was the city committing millions of tax dollars for land improvements that would benefit only a single private business?

The debate over Dodger Stadium presaged similar conversations that would soon play out in cities across the country. Are pro sports teams really a public good? Do their economic and cultural benefits really merit public investment? The committee argued that Los Angeles should consider building a publicly owned ballpark and then renting it out, like what San Francisco was doing for the Giants—this was the kind of big-government spending John Holland hated, but at least it made business sense to him—or else it should consider keeping the parking lots as municipal property and trading O'Malley a smaller piece of the three hundred acres for the stadium itself. There was also a spat over oil rights.

"LET'S KEEP CHAVEZ RAVINE FOR THE PEOPLE!" said the campaign literature. "Look at the possibilities if this great 300-acre block of land were exploited for public use in the same way a faction of the City Council wants to prepare and improve it for a privately-owned ball club and individual."

The committee was not particularly interested in the rights of holdout residents such as the Aréchiga family, whose property was part of the three-hundred-acre block of land that it sought to exploit for public use. They may have been called the Committee to Save Chavez Ravine for the People, but the people they were saving Chavez Ravine for were not the ones who lived there.

Nor did the committee particularly care about the costs O'Malley was incurring or the risks he was taking. His proposed stadium would be expensive and heavily financed. It would require earthmoving on a massive scale. This was not compelling to them. Nor was the fact that as a single owner building a stadium with a single purpose, O'Malley had more freedom to be architecturally daring than the builders of the multipurpose municipal park in San Francisco. To John Holland's constituents, mainly white, working-class home owners, it didn't matter what O'Malley was building: it mattered how he was paying for it.

Before the Dodgers even announced the move west, the committee began collecting signatures to challenge the proposed stadium deal in a referendum vote. Not long after O'Malley's arrival, they had gathered enough to secure a place on the ballot. In April the Dodgers would play their first game in Los Angeles, in the Memorial Coliseum with its hundred thousand seats and its oblong, decidedly un-baseball shape. Then in June the city's voters would go to the polls to decide whether they wanted to grant the team a permanent home.

=====

ON OPENING DAY, 1958, the Dodgers rode in a parade of convertibles through a cloud of confetti from downtown to the Coliseum. Vin Scully, the not-yet-legendary announcer who followed the team from Brooklyn, set up shop for the first time in Los Angeles. And O'Malley, ever conscious of growing his customer base, began the first regular Spanish-language radio broadcasts of major-league games. The Dodgers had broadcast a few games in Spanish back in Brooklyn, but now they would be on the airwaves, on America's first ever all-Spanish frequency, KWKW, for the entire season.

That first year, the main Spanish play-by-play man was a veteran announcer named René Cárdenas. Waiting in the wings was a young newscaster from Ecuador named Jaime Jarrín. Jarrín spent the 1958 season listening to Cárdenas in Spanish and Scully in English, reading every book he could find about baseball and preparing to begin broadcasting a sport that, growing up, he had been completely unfamiliar with. Soon, Jarrín would become a fixture in the city, reading promos for Farmer John hot dogs and Union Oil in Spanish as Scully did in English; later still, he would be the guide and interpreter for a young phenom from Mexico named Fernando Valenzuela.

In the beginning, Jarrín and Cárdenas re-created road games from a studio in Los Angeles. Scully would call from the visiting press box before the first pitch and give them the lineups and whatever atmospherics might be necessary. O'Malley and the Dodgers front office were aware of the enormous potential of the Spanish-speaking market. Jarrín recalled that decades before Valenzuela, O'Malley used to ask him when he would help the team sign a

Mexican Sandy Koufax. In 1960, when the Dodgers called up pitcher Phil Ortega, the boss insisted that Jarrín take every opportunity to remind his audience that Ortega was Mexican American. That went over fine until Ortega told Jarrín that he did not consider himself Mexican American at all. He identified as Yaqui Indian.

The Dodgers, with the Jewish Koufax but no Mexican Koufax, struggled in those first weeks in LA. The Coliseum was full of fans and movie stars, but the strange playing dimensions, especially the 240-foot left-field fence topped by a massive 40-foot screen, made it disorienting. Cheap pop flies lingered in midair and then became home runs. Duke Snider, not awed at all by the deep center-field fence, told shortstop Don Zimmer that he could heave a baseball over it from home plate. He couldn't. But he did dislocate his elbow trying.

Meanwhile, the stadium vote loomed. The pro-Dodgers faction hired the familiar campaign team of Baus & Ross to make their case. "Vote B for Baseball," they said. The campaign material was crisp and white and featured a soaring image of the downtown skyline and a vague threat that if the deal was rejected, the Dodgers might leave town just as quickly as they had come. But overall, in traditional Los Angeles fashion, the material was optimistic to the point of self-delusion: "Freeway congestion caused by Dodger games in Chavez Ravine is almost 99% myth!"

The opposition tried to frame the deal as a referendum on civic sovereignty. This was our town, they argued. Not Walter O'Malley's, not Norris Poulson's, and not Norman Chandler's.

Holland was relentless. Along with his council colleague Patrick McGee, he argued that the Statler Hotel meeting that O'Malley had held with Poulson and City Attorney Roger Arnebergh the previous May had in fact been the beginning of a conspiracy. He wrote to members of Congress, including US Senator Estes Kefauver, who had made his name taking down the Mob, hoping to spur an investigation. In one campaign memo the committee played up the existence of a letter that Poulson had written O'Malley following the Statler Hotel meeting. This, they argued, was evidence of wrongdoing. They called it, ominously, the "Dear Walter letter." The committee's memo concludes with the following paragraph: "Finally Mr. Mayor, what other letters written in 'riddles,' what other secret memorandums and documents are in your files or the files of other City officials. The People of Los Angeles who are going to vote on the Dodgers-Chavez Ravine contract when it appears on the June 3rd ballot, have a right to know what Supervisor John Anson Ford has so properly termed the 'half hidden fast moves that resulted in this deal.'"

The pro-Dodgers forces relied on the credibility of a realtor named Charles Detoy, who had appraised the value of three hundred undeveloped acres at Chavez Ravine as comparable to the ten-acre Wrigley Field, an assessment that was generous to O'Malley. A month before the election, Blackjack Smith wrote Detoy a lampooning letter, ending with a series of belligerent questions about his methods and reasoning. He included a stamped, self-addressed envelope.

Blackjack Smith may have been working with only his own private interests in mind, but he was hitting a nerve. The same swath of the city that had been terrified of public housing was equally suspicious of the stadium deal's "half hidden fast moves." They were suspicious of the rich and powerful men who seemed to always be deciding what was best for them.

The answer on the part of the pro-Dodger forces was not a logical appeal; it was an emotional one. National League President Warren Giles threatened that the league would pull the franchise from Los Angeles without a yes vote. Then O'Malley, who had been sitting out the campaign, walked Giles's threat back, but not far enough to fully remove the fear from voters.

Finally, on Sunday, June 1, two days before the election, while the Dodgers played the Cubs in Chicago, all the forces working on their behalf in LA coalesced to create the perfect and perfectly Hollywood campaign event: a five-hour, star-studded telethon. The Dodgerthon was aired on KTTV, which was owned by the Chandler family and which hoped to air future Dodger games. Celebrities paraded across the screen and made their pleas: Dean Martin, Jerry Lewis, Debbie Reynolds, George Burns, Jack Benny, and even a very somber Ronald Reagan. Jackie Robinson prerecorded a video message to his hometown fans on behalf of his old club.

O'Malley himself appeared at a wooden prop desk holding his usual cigar. He took questions from callers concerned about the deal and gave witty, charming answers. "He gave viewers warmth and dignity, and using a blackboard and pointer, he gave them O'Malley style facts," wrote *Sports Illustrated*. O'Malley, who could seem imperious behind his jowls and fine suits, "created an image of a gentle, kindly, fatherly type, who wanted nothing in this world (at this moment) but 300 acres of city property to build happiness and parking spaces for all."

The telethon concluded with a live feed of the Dodgers plane landing triumphantly in Los Angeles, returned victorious from Chicago. There to greet it were thousands of baseball fans who had heeded the show's advice and gone down to the airport to show their support.

But it remained to be seen whether this would actually work. As the campaign played out on the front page and the Dodgers' struggles played out in the sports pages, the team continued to face legal challenges from activist attorneys. One suit was filed by a lawyer named Julius Ruben and the other by a lawyer named Phill Silver on behalf of a taxpayer named Louis Kirschbaum. Soon the cases would be consolidated, and soon they would cause a lot of trouble for Walter O'Malley.

On Tuesday, June 3, the polls opened to great turnout—especially for a nonpresidential year. Nearly two-thirds of voters came to cast their ballots in the gubernatorial and senatorial primaries—and, of course, on the question of B for Baseball. Polls in the days leading up to the vote anticipated a close finish. It was indeed close. O'Malley waited in his owner's box at the Coliseum as the tally came in. By the time the game ended, it was clear that his stadium dreams had survived intact.

Prop B passed by about 25,000 votes, 52 percent to 48 percent. The difference had been a massive pro-baseball margin in the city's urban working-class areas. Nearly 70 percent of voters in Ed Roybal's heavily Mexican American district had elected to uphold the deal. So had 65 percent of voters in South Central Los Angeles, which by 1958 was largely African American. Combined, the margins in these districts added up to about 25,000 votes: enough to overcome the opposition in the San Fernando Valley and John Holland's Eagle Rock district.

The celebration was short-lived. Two weeks later, the Ruben and Silver lawsuit went to trial in superior court in downtown Los Angeles. And on July 14, Judge Arnold Praeger issued a decision: the entire Dodgers contract was illegal. The city council did not have the right to change the public-purpose clause in the deed to the Elysian Park Heights site, and neither did voters. "The City Council has no right or power to give a private organization carte blanche with respect to the spending of public money," Judge Praeger wrote.

The city and the Dodgers, now codefendants in addition to everything else, would appeal to the California Supreme Court after yet another suit was brought by Silver. "I remain an optimist," O'Malley said.

# 60.

After her husband, Pio Vargas, died, Abrana and Manuel's daughter Lola married a man named Elias Colón. Elias was a neighborhood guy, just like Pio had been. That's the way relationships were in Palo Verde. Everything was connected. In 1942, just before he enlisted, Pio had been a witness at the wedding of Elias Colón's brother Louie. And now Pio was dead, and Elias was married to his widow.

Elias had been in the navy. He was drawn to the water. He and Lola had two girls, Dolores and Rachel. He used to take them out to lakes on the outskirts of town. With Lola and Elias working full-time, the girls lived most of the time at their grandparents' house on Malvina. They were still toddlers when Frank Wilkinson came knocking on the door, and they were still little girls when most of the neighbors sold and left.

To Dolores, the empty streets and the construction crews around Palo Verde weren't weird or eerie; they were just normal. They were what she was used to. The whole neighborhood became a playground for her and her cousins and the few friends who were still around. Empty lots and dirt backyards and trees and plants. It was all hers.

Abrana and Manuel took good care of Dolores and Rachel. They spoiled them as they did all their grandchildren. There was always Mexican music playing in the house, and Dolores remembers Abrana's sense of humor. Abrana still didn't speak English, but she used to laugh and say her name was "Abrahama Lincoln." The only chore the girls had to do was to wash the dishes after dinner.

Manuel would take them out with him in his old Model T and drive around the city looking for glass bottles that he could turn in for cash. His car had a rumble seat and a horn that went *aroooga*.

It was all a great adventure. He used to call it *rastreando*. Tracking down. Hunting. Searching. Every bottle added up.

Otherwise, they were free to play and free to explore. The Palo Verde school had been closed in 1955, so after that the girls had to take a bus down the hill and out of the neighborhood. They would come home each day to find Palo Verde slightly different: a tree uprooted, a hill graded, a house that had been there in the morning suddenly gone by the afternoon. "I remember them taking the houses out," Dolores said, "rolling the houses out, because they didn't knock them down. They rolled them out. I guess they put them somewhere else—I don't know where."

The workers would run two parallel steel beams under a house, then jack the beams up onto dollies. Once the house was up on the dollies, the crews would hitch it to the back of a semitruck. Then, very slowly, they would tow the houses down the hill and out into the city.

The houses went to other parts of LA. They went to scrap yards. They rolled down the hill and out of sight forever. They were absorbed by the city, the same way that the residents of Palo Verde were absorbed after they left. Los Angeles is always repurposing itself. Destroying its own history and straining toward the future. Eating its old and worshipping its young. Some of the houses went to Universal Studios, where they became part of movie sets. The fictional town of Maycomb, Alabama, where Gregory Peck's version of Atticus Finch lived in the film version of *To Kill a Mockingbird*, was supposedly constructed partially from Palo Verde homes.

When Dolores was eleven years old, her father died. Elias Colón had been a drinker, but that was not what killed him, at least not directly. As Dolores told it, police saw him sick on a highway. Figuring he was drunk, they hauled him in. They thought he would sober up in a holding cell. However, it turned out that Elias had double pneumonia. He died in police custody. Lola Vargas was not even forty, and she had already been widowed twice. After Elias died, she met a man named David Fernandez. He was a good guy, said Dolores. He had been in the air force. Lola liked to tell jokes about that. She had three husbands, she would say, one for each branch of the military: Pio in the army, Elias in the navy, and finally David in the air force.

One afternoon, Dolores and Rachel came home to see a crew of workers standing before their childhood home. The girls watched as a group of strange men dug the house out from its foundation. They stood in the street as the men lifted the house onto a trailer. They waved good-bye to their windows, their doors, and their childhood rooms as a truck pulled their house down the street, dust from the construction kicking up under the tires and the sun setting behind the mountains. They watched the house roll down Malvina to what was left of Effie Street and out of sight forever.

"Bye, casa mia," Dolores said.

# 61.

IN THE SUMMER OF 1957, JUST AS THE DODGERS WERE PREPARING TO move from Brooklyn to Los Angeles, Frank Wilkinson did the opposite, moving from Los Angeles to New York. The idea was to bring his organizing against HUAC to a national audience: the committee was more active on the East Coast, and he would be closer to Washington, DC. That summer, the Wilkinson family drove across the country, stopping off to visit activists in cities along the way. They carried with them suitcases and a petition calling for the abolition of HUAC. On their first day in New York, they parked their car and went upstairs to a friend's apartment in Harlem. By the time they came down, the car's windows were broken and their suitcases were gone.

Frank organized rallies at Carnegie Hall. Jean and the kids grew to love the city life. But Frank found himself bogged down by the competing agendas of various progressive organizations. The infighting frustrated him. So did the moderate tendencies of some of his colleagues. At his behest the family planned to return the following summer to Los Angeles. But before they did, Frank got a call from Carl and Anne Braden. HUAC had begun issuing subpoenas in Atlanta.

The Bradens were civil rights activists with their own deep history, especially in Kentucky. In 1954 they had purchased a house in a white neighborhood in Louisville on behalf of a local black family, the Wades. The Wades had been searching for a home in a quiet residential neighborhood but were unable to buy one because of segregated housing practices. This was well after the US Supreme Court had banned redlining and restrictive covenants, but the individual racism of white residents and the institutional racism of banks and insurance companies in the housing industry made it so that there was still de facto segregation.

The problems began immediately after the Wades moved in. The house was shot at. A brick was heaved through their window. White neighbors burned a cross on their lawn and phoned in threats. The Wades enlisted round-the-clock armed defense from the local activist community. Then, a few months after they moved in, the house was bombed with dynamite and destroyed. Somehow, there were no injuries.

In a twist of justice fitting of the era, after months of "investigation" the suspects arrested for the bombing were not Klansmen or bitter neighbors. They were none other than Carl and Anne Braden, who had purchased the house in the first place, and three other activists. The Bradens were accused of buying the house, selling it over to the Wades, and then blowing it up with dynamite, all as part of an intricate Communist plot to discredit and destroy the Commonwealth of Kentucky. Carl Braden was convicted of sedition: plotting to overthrow the government. He served eight months before the US Supreme Court ruled in a separate case that sedition could be only a federal crime, not a statewide one.

These were the people who called Frank Wilkinson to Atlanta. In July 1958, Frank arrived and checked into the Biltmore Hotel. Shortly thereafter, a US marshal knocked on his door and handed him a subpoena. Frank hadn't even begun organizing in Atlanta, and he was already being summoned. He was stunned. The marshal told Frank that he had received a call from Washington the day before informing him that Wilkinson would be checking in and that he would need to be served. To Frank, this was proof positive that he and his allies had either been infiltrated by the FBI or had had their phones tapped.

But this was also an opportunity to test the legality of HUAC. Frank had already appeared before the committee one time, in December 1956. It had been a raucous hearing. At one point a committee member came down off the dais to examine Frank's hearing aids because he was sure Frank did not hear him yelling. After Frank refused to answer any questions on First Amendment grounds, the committee cited him for contempt. However, Congress had to uphold the citation if he wanted his case to go to trial. For some reason it didn't, so Frank's legal challenge would have to wait.

This time, if he was cited, Frank felt he would have a better chance at winning and striking that fatal blow against the committee. The year before, the US Supreme Court had limited some of the committee's investigating powers in another case, *Watkins v. United States.* "Who can define the meaning of un-American?" wrote Chief Justice Earl Warren in his majority opinion.

The Atlanta hearings were melodramatic. Richard Arens, HUAC's council and interrogator, spoke in long paragraphs, detailing Frank's alleged crimes and misdeeds against the government. He referred at length to Frank's testimony in Los Angeles from late 1956. He grandstanded. He found props. He waved Frank's hotel phone records from the day before in front of the committee. The long-distance telephone calls that Frank made from Atlanta must surely have been evidence that he was part of a Communist conspiracy, Arens argued.

But each time Arens asked a question, Frank declined to answer. He offered his name and nothing more—not even his address: "As a matter of conscience and personal responsibility, I refuse to answer any questions of this committee."

There were television cameras on and a room full of people and a bunch of dour congressmen sitting before him, but Frank maintained his calm. This was his purpose in life now. This moment.

"I challenge, in the most fundamental sense, the legality of the House Committee on Un-American Activities," he finally said, inviting a contempt charge. "It is my opinion that this committee stands in direct violation by its mandate and by its practices of the first amendment to the United States Constitution. It is my belief that Congress had no authority to establish this committee in the first instance, nor to instruct it with the mandate which it has."

# 62.

WHEN WILLIE DAVIS WAS A BOY, HE WOULD TIE A BASEBALL TO A piece of string and loop it onto the clothesline behind his family's apartment. They lived in Estrada Courts, a public-housing project in Boyle Heights. Every unit had a little lawn, a little concrete path leading up to the door, and a little set of clotheslines in the back. Willie would string the ball up there, then take an easy right-handed swing and watch it zoom down to the other end of the line. Then he would pull the ball back to where he started. He would look around to make sure there were no neighbors passing by. Then he would do it again.

One of Willie's neighbors in those days was Frank Wilkinson. In the late 1940s, when Frank was still working for the housing authority, the Wilkinsons lived in Estrada Courts. Frank's son Jeffry, who was about the same age as Willie, remembered it as a great place to grow up, vibrant and diverse. It was the kind of place that Frank dreamed a public-housing project could be.

"We weren't poor, but we certainly weren't rich," Willie said later. "I really remember the people and how they took care of each other. They really didn't have much, but what they did have they shared."

Willie and his brother ran around East Los Angeles. They played every sport, but especially baseball. Willie's mom said that he would keep a bat behind the front door and come get it every day after school. That's how she knew he was home. He had a paper route, and he was late for school all the time at Roosevelt High.

The Davis family came out to Los Angeles from a tiny town in rural Arkansas called Mineral Springs when Willie was just a toddler. It was 1942, and there were wartime jobs in LA. Willie later said he remembered staring out the window back in Mineral Springs and watching the trains go by. Soon he would be on a train himself. Soon he would be growing up into a tall and lean young man with a deep voice and a way of carrying himself like he was always standing at a bar, waiting for a drink, not in any particular hurry, watching the trains go by.

The vibe that Willie Davis exuded was never quite a match for what he was feeling. He was a hard competitor and a thoughtful, philosophical soul. He was, like Abner Doubleday and Juan Aréchiga, a seeker. At Roosevelt High School he set a national record in the long jump. He ran track and played basketball and baseball. Three sports. The number three would come to mean everything to Willie. It would be his number on the Dodgers, be part of his nickname, 3-Dog, and be his philosophy in life. There were three Willie Davises, he would say later: "Willie Davis has been a lot of things in the past. But Willie Davis now is the things that he's been in the past, and the things that he will do in the future. So now is actually the past. It's now and the future all soaked up into one body."

The varsity sweater he wore to class dangled over his thin frame. When he graduated, he had a full athletic scholarship waiting for him at UCLA. But he also had an offer from a man named Kenny Myers. Myers was an ex-ballplayer and a common sight around the LA sandlots. He was short and fat and a perpetual cigar smoker. In his own playing days, he had a beautiful swing, but he couldn't keep the weight off. Now he was a scout for the Dodgers and a baseball teacher with funny ideas about the sport. He was always tinkering, always inventing new training devices: a contraption that launched the ball straight up from home plate, a bat with a ball already attached to it, a bat with a butterfly net on the end.

Kenny Myers was a good fit for Willie because Kenny was also a seeker. They called him Monk. He was seeking some kind of truth in baseball. He told Willie he couldn't sign him yet, but he could help. If Willie wanted to be a ballplayer, really truly wanted it, then he could skip UCLA and go to work with Kenny. There would be hours upon hours of miserable labor, and there would be no guarantees. But this was the path to the big leagues. Willie said yes. He wanted it.

The first thing Kenny did was turn Willie around and teach him to bat left-handed. For some reason, even though Willie was a natural lefty, he had always hit righty. Willie swung until his hands bled. He used all the strange devices Myers put in front of him. His swing from the left side would never be beautiful, but it would work. Then Kenny taught him how to play center field. Willie had been a pitcher in high school, but he was too fast to be anything but a center fielder.

Willie graduated from Roosevelt in 1958, that first year of Dodger baseball in LA. Sometimes Kenny would take Willie up to the press box in the Coliseum, and they'd sit with the sportswriters and watch the games together. They'd watch the great outfielders. Duke Snider, Willie Mays. "It was like starting school," Willie said. Sometimes they would walk all the way back to Estrada Courts just talking baseball. Six miles of baseball. Then one day Kenny brought Willie and his mother into the Dodger offices. It was time to sign his first contract.

They sent him to Reno, where he was the best hitter in Class C. Then the next year they sent him to Spokane, Washington, where the Angels had moved after the Dodgers came to town. Willie was the best hitter in the Pacific Coast League. He stole thirty-seven bases, and in September the Dodgers called him up to the majors. The first time Willie Davis got to play in the Coliseum, he hit a home run off Juan Marichal. The opposing center fielder was Willie Mays. He was twenty years old, and Duke Snider, watching from the bench, was thirty-four.

Duke must have known that his time was coming. He must have known that Willie was coming. He must have smelled the avocado trees. The next year, Willie Davis was placed next to Duke in the locker room at spring training. Willie wore number 3. The 3-Dog. Duke wore number 4 like Gehrig had. That year, Willie was the subject of a documentary film called *Biography of a Rookie: The Willie Davis Story*. It was hosted by Mike Wallace before his *60 Minutes* days and directed by Mel Stuart, who would go on to direct *Willy Wonka and the Chocolate Factory*.

They hit together, Willie and Duke, baseballs firing toward them one after another from the brand-new pitching machines that the team had installed. Fourteen years, the difference in their ages, was not such a long time. Neither was the distance between Compton and Boyle Heights so great. But there was a clear sense of the past and the future. Duke was no longer the Duke. And Willie was just becoming himself. "I am Hall of Fame material. And I continue to be until I die," he said. He was all possibility. All tools and talent. Willie Davis was Hall of Fame material nurtured under the auspices of the Housing Authority of the City of Los Angeles.

# 63.

AT THE START OF THE 1959 BASEBALL SEASON, THE ARÉCHIGA FAMILY
journeyed down to City Hall, which back then was still the tallest
building in Los Angeles and which was still visible from the hill
in their backyard. There, Mayor Norris Poulson was hosting the
Dodgers for a ceremony to launch the new season, a meaningless
official gesture. He planned to proclaim the week of April 12–18
"Good Luck to the Dodgers Week." But as the Dodger players
descended from their charter bus and up the marble steps of City
Hall, nine members of the Aréchiga family and one neighbor,
Glen Walters, interrupted the proceedings. Walters, a tall blonde
screen actress deep into middle age, stood out in any crowd and
especially among the Aréchiga family. They held aloft picket
signs:

"We are being forced out so the Dodgers can move in"

"Mr. O'Malley, if you want our property, pay for it."

"Go back to Brooklyn, O'Malley"

Poulson put his arm around Dodger Manager Walter Alston. He
made a joke or two and tried to laugh the whole thing off. But as
the Dodgers lined up on the steps for a portrait with Poulson, Walters began to yell and push forward. Walters was a regal-looking
woman with an air of an earlier time in the way she carried herself, shoulders back. She had appeared in more than fifty movies,
usually as an uncredited extra. She had a presence and a voice and
knew how to use them. According to one newspaper report, she
hugged Manuel Aréchiga, her longtime neighbor. "This man is 72
years old," she said, her voice rising. "He has worked every day of
his life. And what does he get? You take away his home."

She pushed closer and closer to the team. "Thieves!" she yelled.
"Bandits." When one player, who was never identified, began to

laugh, Walters, who was taller than him by a good measure, turned, leaned over him, and called him a "pipsqueak."

Finally, Walters was escorted away from the scene by plain-clothes police officers. She hurled a picket sign at the mayor. The protest was over. City Hall and the Dodgers remained unmoved. And the Aréchigas remained unmoving.

# 64.

On May 7, 1959, Los Angeles turned its eyes back to Brooklyn, back to a time before the Dodgers had come west and before the telethons, the ballot measures, and the will-they-won't-they. A few months earlier, the California Supreme Court had ruled in the team's favor, which meant that for now the stadium deal was still on. Despite on-field struggles and off-field challenges, the Dodgers had been a success in Los Angeles. They drew nearly twice as many fans as they had in their final year in Brooklyn and more than any Dodgers team since 1947, the year Robinson broke the color barrier.

It was a Thursday night, and nearly 100,000 men, women, boys, and girls filled Memorial Coliseum to watch an exhibition game between the Dodgers and their former crosstown rivals the New York Yankees. This was, the papers said, the largest crowd to ever watch a baseball game. Thousands more were turned away at the gates. The occasion for all this was a fund-raiser for Roy Campanella, the former Dodgers catcher who had never gotten the chance to play in Los Angeles. In January 1958, a few months after the team announced the move, Campanella crashed his car on an icy road. He was paralyzed from the waist down.

The game was a big deal, a logistical feat and a first-order spectacle of the kind that O'Malley prided himself on. The Yankees flew into town after a series in Kansas City, which was as far west as any American League team on the map back then. Revenues from the game were to be split between a fund for Campanella's medical bills and charities of the Yankees' choosing. The decision to honor Campanella in a city where he never played was a reminder that O'Malley had not fully let Brooklyn go. He was in LA now, but he was still New York born and bred, and moving west had not done anything to change the Dodger organization's internal composition or erase its history.

In decades to come, when sports franchises moved, they would rebrand, rename themselves, and make a point to erase their pasts. But Campanella was a Dodger—period. The size of the crowd was a testament to the fact that Angelenos had embraced not just the team in its present state but also all of its history. Los Angeles is always rewriting its past in the hope that doing so might brighten its future. The Dodgers celebrate their Brooklyn achievements to this day. For O'Malley the Campanella game was badly needed reassurance that Southern California was the right home for his team.

Campanella may never have played in Los Angeles, but he was a beloved baseball figure whose appeal transcended race and geography. His father was Italian and his mother African American. He had grown up in Philadelphia and had become a star in the Negro Leagues and a star in Jorge Pasquel's Mexican League. For a decade, he was arguably the best catcher in baseball and the best player on a Dodgers team stacked with future Hall of Famers. He won three Most Valuable Player awards and carried the franchise to its first and only World Series victory in 1955.

Campy, as he was known, had signed with Brooklyn only a few weeks after Jackie Robinson and had come up from the minors in 1948, the sixth black player in Major League Baseball. They were often seen as complements: Robinson, brooding and determined, the fire, and Campanella, easygoing and quick to laugh, the water. On the field, Campy was as tough as anybody. Off it, he seemed to float above hard times. At least until the accident.

The crowd outside nearly overwhelmed the gates of the Coliseum. A cavalry of motorcycle cops had to be called in to put things in order. But inside, it was all splendid baseball magic. Before the first pitch was thrown by Sandy Koufax, Campanella was honored with a tribute recounting the glories of his career. Then, during a short break between the fifth and sixth innings, the stadium lights were turned out, and the 93,000 people in attendance all struck matches simultaneously, lighting up the darkened stadium like a night sky brimming with stars. Vin Scully asked the fans listening at home to say a prayer for the catcher. It was surreal. In his autobiography, Campanella likened the gesture to watching the Coliseum transform into a massive birthday cake.

# 65.

THREE MILES AWAY, ABRANA AND MANUEL ARÉCHIGA SAT IN THEIR home. The streets of Palo Verde were quiet, as they always were in 1959, but the homes on the Aréchiga property were still full of life. The house at 1771 Malvina almost certainly smelled of dinner, and the air was probably filled with music, though not from the city's only all-Spanish radio station, KWKW, which would have been broadcasting Jaime Jarrín and René Cárdenas's call of the Dodgers-Yankees game at the Coliseum.

The following day would be May 8: the deadline for Abrana and Manuel's eviction order. It had been nearly forty years since they built the house and nearly a decade since that first letter from the housing authority had arrived in their mailbox on the corner of Malvina and Effie Street. That corner was different now. The houses around it were almost all gone, and the ones that remained looked like they were sinking into the dirt. The mailboxes were still there, but now they looked almost like headstones. Little monuments to past lives. The dirt streets were no longer grooved the way they had been from the neighbors' cars. Chaparral grew in places where it didn't before. In one final desperate last gasp, mother nature had taken Palo Verde back. Vines crawled up the remaining walls of crumbling houses, and trees crowded the telephone wires.

By now, Abrana and Manuel had become quite familiar with eviction orders, with sheriff's deputies, and with empty threats. The city had spent nine years making it known to the family that the land they lived on was no longer theirs. And yet they were still there.

Frank Wilkinson's towers had been as good as built, overlooking the downtown skyline—then they weren't.

There was supposed to be a zoo, a convention center, a cemetery.

There were lawsuits, one after another.

There was Walter O'Malley in his helicopter.

The paperwork had been signed; the referendum had passed. Meanwhile, the $10,039 remained untouched in escrow. So far, the Aréchigas had outlasted all of it. Their property was still neatly kept and full of life. There were handwritten protest signs posted in the front yard above the rock retaining wall and below the sweeping branches of the large pine that shaded the house.

The city had tried everything to get them out. If you read through the old newspapers, the various attempts start to feel like a slapstick comedy routine. Once, Abrana reportedly turned her hose on a group of deputies. Another time, the city sent a dogcatcher to round up her Chihuahuas; he did not succeed. Dolores remembers that at some point in the 1950s, her mother Lola got into an argument with a woman deputy on the front porch, and the two ended up rolling around in a brawl. In 1957, according to one newspaper report, the family had even gone so far as to pack their belongings. The city threatened to charge the Aréchigas rent, but that plan never went anywhere because in a typical catch-22, the city had already ruled the home a slum dwelling as an excuse to evict them, so renting the home out would have effectively made the city government a slum lord. The home was perfectly fine. In fact, nobody had even bothered to turn off the Aréchigas' essential services. They still had electricity, still had running water, still had gas.

But this looked like it might actually be it. The legal battle that they had begun in the fall of 1953 was coming to an end. In March 1959 a judge had given them thirty days' notice. Then in April, Councilman Ed Roybal had talked city officials into another thirty. Roybal hoped that in the meantime, the family and the city could reach some sort of settlement. The Aréchigas were now represented by Phill Silver, whose lawsuit against the Dodger deal had been rejected in January by the California Supreme Court. The family wanted to see their own case go all the way to the US Supreme Court. The council deliberated on a proposal to let them stay on Malvina until the Supreme Court had a chance to hear the case—or not hear it, if that was the court's will. This proposal was rejected.

Ed Roybal was a reasonable man who was able to take two conflicting ideas and hold them in his head at the same time, a rare skill among politicians. He understood that Dodger Stadium was inevitable. For as many wrenches as the Aréchigas and activist attorneys like Silver could throw into its legal gears, the program was too big, the momentum too great. Public housing was defeated because there was a coalition of powerful interests working against it. That was not the case with Dodger Stadium. Dodger Stadium was the chosen cause of those interests, the will of the institutional powers of Los Angeles, and in the wake of Proposition B, the proven will of a majority of voters.

But Roybal also understood that the Aréchigas had a point. He understood that they stood for something larger than themselves and that even if they didn't stand for anything, they were human beings who deserved to be heard. As the council's only Mexican American member and as a person who had advocated in favor of both public housing and the Dodgers' move west, Roybal felt a certain amount of responsibility for the Aréchigas' predicament. After all, in the context of everything that had happened—lives ruined, megaprojects canceled, utopian dreams shattered, city elections swung and then swung again, multimillion-dollar stadiums proposed, historically significant baseball teams moved—in the context of remaking the physical and civic landscape of a major American city, the demands of Abrana and Manuel Aréchiga did not amount to much.

Their grievance was reasonable, and it was minor. Numerically speaking, it came down to the difference between the $10,050 a judge had set as the property value of their lots and the $17,500 valuation that had been offered by a city appraiser and then over-ruled by the aforementioned judge. This was it: $7,450. What was $7,450 when set against the huge deal that the city had made with Walter O'Malley? Against the millions of taxpayer dollars and tens of millions more private dollars that would be spent on this project? Against the grand scale of the stadium that was going to be built in these hills? Abrana and Manuel Aréchiga wanted to be paid a fair price, and they wanted the dignity that the fair price represented.

The surreal nature of their plight was thrown into sharper relief by the fact that there remained a dozen or so property owners in the community who were not facing eviction that morning. These were the families who, years earlier, had filed the appeal in court that the Aréchigas had, for some reason, missed out on, hence set-ting themselves on a separate legal path. These were families whose homes had not been officially condemned. And perhaps more im-portantly, these were families who had held out quietly, who had not picketed City Hall, and who had not spoken to the papers.

Because of the Aréchigas' legal actions and because of their fear-lessness, they had become the public faces of resistance in Palo Verde, La Loma, and Bishop, even if all they wanted was a fair deal.

But city governments aren't built to meet regular people half-way. And in this case, they didn't have an incentive to. Perhaps the city could have had the property reassessed; perhaps the city could have just swallowed it and paid the Aréchigas the full $17,500. The trouble of evicting them might end up costing more than that any-way. But doing so would have required a flexibility and sensitivity that the relevant Los Angeles politicians simply did not possess.

Sometimes I think that Walter O'Malley himself should have simply cut a check. Had he known how poorly his partners in local government would handle things, perhaps he might have gotten more involved. At one point, the Aréchigas essentially asked him for that check. On May 6, two days before the eviction order, the *Los Angeles Mirror-News* published a letter from Manuel Aréchiga. "I haven't anything against the Dodgers," he wrote, "but if they want my land let them pay a reasonable price for it, not take it away."

I am almost certain that O'Malley read this letter because there is a copy of it in his old files, guarded lovingly in the family office in downtown Los Angeles. I wonder what he would have thought when he did. Would he have been defensive? After all, the people taking Manuel Aréchiga's land were not Dodger executives but the same government officials who had been trying to take it for a de-cade. Would O'Malley have thought Manuel to be misguided? Or would he have thought that this was an intentional strategy? Trying to subtly shift the blame to O'Malley, who might be an easier target than the faceless bureaucrats at City Hall? After all, despite what he wrote, Manuel and his family had protested the ceremony with Poulson, so it was clear that they held some antipathy toward the Dodgers, even if it was performative.

I do not believe that the Aréchigas were misguided or disingen-uously blaming the wrong person for their problems. I believe they were simply following the money to the end of its course. The fam-ily had been helpless while their land was confiscated by the hous-ing authority with eminent domain; had been helpless when, after the demise of public housing in Los Angeles, that land had been transferred back to the city; and now remained helpless as their property was transferred to a rich and powerful stranger. This had all been the result of an ongoing systemic failure. And because of the trade that he had worked out for Wrigley Field, that stranger, Walter O'Malley, would be the ultimate beneficiary of that systemic failure. When he acquired the land, O'Malley also acquired moral responsibility for what was left of the communities. If justice was going to be done, it would need to be by his hand.

This was Abrana and Manuel's truth. Needless to say, O'Malley himself saw things differently. O'Malley's truth was that he had made a fair deal with the city. It was a legal deal. He acquired land to build a ballpark that would serve millions of fans and enrich the community at large. He did not move his franchise across the country expecting to inherit responsibility for an ongoing civic tragedy. He did not move his franchise across the country expecting to find families living on the site of his new stadium. In his eyes the city was responsible for taking care of its own end of the bargain and delivering the land that it had sold him unoccupied. He had been patient. He had been accommodating. He had taken a great personal risk and been rewarded by a lawsuit and a referendum election. The methods the city used to clear the land—well, those were not Walter O'Malley's concern.

So now here the Aréchigas were. Waiting. Watching the clock. Maybe singing. Maybe praying. While the city celebrated the Dodgers and Roy Campanella and lit their matches in tribute, Abrana and Manuel could only wonder what the morning would bring. Legally, they were at their end. It was likely, they knew, that men in uniforms would come to take them away from their home. It was likely, they knew, that politicians would strut and squawk. But they could not know how the following hours, days, and weeks would shape up. They just knew that something was coming.

# 66.

When Roz Wyman was running for city council, she used index cards to tell the voters in her district that she wanted to bring big-league baseball to Los Angeles. Five years later, Walter O'Malley used index cards to plot out what that big-league future would look like. Each card was neatly typed with a thought, an idea, a lark relating to the new stadium he would build in his new hometown.

There were dozens upon dozens of cards. Taken together, they captured the scope of O'Malley's vision and the minute, detailed focus of his attention. Some featured a sentence or two of explanation, others just a single word or phrase.

One card said: Bowling Alley.

Another said: Drainage.

O'Malley was a perfectionist afflicted with both grandiosity of vision and the inability to let even the smallest details go. He was a man who dreamed of installing a multitrack monorail system in the parking lot of his hypothetical ballpark and who simultaneously obsessed over the coarseness of the gravel to be used in said parking lot. He was, very clearly, a micromanager. He could not help himself.

As an undergraduate at the University of Pennsylvania, O'Malley had studied engineering. He never lost interest in the subject. (O'Malley collected interests and hobbies like a person with way more free time than he actually had. He loved, among other things, raising exotic orchids, baking sourdough bread, and deep-sea fishing.) When O'Malley began to consider upgrading or replacing Ebbets Field in 1946, he struck up a friendship with the best engineer he could find: Captain Emil Praeger. Praeger (no relation to Arnold Praeger, the judge who ruled against the Dodgers in superior court) had worked on park and highway projects in New York. Then during World War II, working for the navy, he had designed a

247

floating breakwater that Allied forces used in their landing at Normandy. He was known, especially, for his creative use of poured concrete.

O'Malley and Praeger collaborated on stadium ideas for Brooklyn throughout the next decade. Praeger also designed the Dodgers' spring training stadium in Vero Beach, Florida. The work continued in Los Angeles, where Praeger had helped O'Malley figure out how to fit a baseball diamond into the oval-shaped Coliseum. Dodger Stadium would be the culmination of their partnership.

For O'Malley it would also be the culmination of a career spent thinking and rethinking the desires of baseball fans and how the in-person experience of the sport could be amplified by its built environment. The many plans taken up and abandoned in Brooklyn, including the never-built Buckminster Fuller dome, were all steps on the long road to Dodger Stadium. In a letter to season-ticket holders after the 1958 season, O'Malley's general manager, Buzzie Bavasi, wrote that the upcoming stadium would be "another monument added to the many scenic beauties of Southern California." He promised greatness: "The Dodgers' organization has had drawings, blueprints, and engineering studies of the ideal ballpark under consideration for more than a decade. Now all of this zealous, painstaking planning is about to bear fruit."

O'Malley was so committed to building a stadium that suited his personal aesthetic and moral sensibilities that he was willing to ditch New York for the freedom to do so. This was his cause: he believed in the creation of a complete fan experience. He wanted to build a stadium that was a destination in and of itself. Whereas pro baseball had begun in Los Angeles with a ballpark inside a larger amusement park, O'Malley wanted the ballpark to *be* the amusement park, to be all things to all people. This was, after all, the promise of ballparks and of baseball. Baseball was the man maker, the god maker, the kingdom maker. If Walter O'Malley built a castle, a kingdom would surely follow.

In the late 1970s, Joan Didion would write that freeway driving was the only secular communion that the people of Los Angeles had. But O'Malley already knew better. The appeal of sports might be arbitrary, and their institutions might occasionally be self-serving, immoral, and exploitative, but the power of them, especially of baseball in mid-century America and in a city built on mythology, was undeniable. Through smart design, creativity, and high-quality customer service, O'Malley could elevate the national pastime into something even more sacred than it already was, and simultaneously elevate the fan's stature in it. Walter O'Malley, the Catholic, would honor this secular communion.

Decades before ball clubs put playgrounds, batting cages, and virtual-reality experiences into their stadiums, O'Malley envisioned a milk and ice cream bar for kids. He envisioned dancing, lighted fountains like something out of the future Las Vegas. He had his executives tour Disneyland for inspiration. In turning baseball into the national pastime, Albert Spalding had sold America on the myth of Abner Doubleday. In turning the national pastime into a consumer product of the highest order, O'Malley sketched out plans for a Doubleday Lounge on the club level of his stadium.

This cause—the fan experience—was more important to him than which particular fans he was delivering that experience to. Moving to Los Angeles, as crazy as it may have been, was a necessary precondition for building the stadium of his dreams and thus fulfilling baseball's high purpose and his own legacy. The truth is, no city was better suited for O'Malley's ambitions. O'Malley's own writing at the time confirms this. The index cards confirm it. And in Roger Kahn's legendary book, *The Boys of Summer*, O'Malley went so far as to say it: "They called me a carpetbagger. One man wrote I left because I believed the colored, Puerto Ricans, and Jews were taking over Brooklyn. Lies, pejorative lies. My son, Peter, came home from Penn and said 'Dad, what are we going to do? The things in the papers are terrible.' They are Peter, but they will pass and the great ballpark I'm going to build in California will stand. That will be remembered—a monument to the O'Malleys." He was right.

Together, O'Malley and Praeger surveyed and resurveyed the landscape that the Dodgers had acquired. The hills had been carved, flattened, burned, logged, and built upon for hundreds of years, going back to before Norris Poulson or Frank Wilkinson or Abrana Aréchiga were born; to before the time when Santa Anna mistakenly gave America bubble gum; to before America took the majority of his country, including these very hills, from him in 1847; to before the time when Cabrillo sailed up the coast; to back when the Tongva people, who were the city's original inhabitants, climbed them unmolested. And for everything that had happened in their gullies and on their plateaus, these hills remained totally unsuitable for baseball. Walt Disney himself had considered this site for his new amusement park, but the flat citrus fields of Orange County were more amenable to his vision.

Building a ballpark here would be harder than building one on a level city street or in the middle of an orchard. But the hills also had advantages. If you had the money and the will, you could make the hills move. They could be sculpted. What O'Malley and Praeger realized was that instead of building on top of the hills, as Neutra and Alexander had planned to do with Elysian Park Heights, they could save themselves a lot of trouble by simply surrendering to them: by building down instead of up. This would ultimately be the genius of Dodger Stadium. They modeled their design on ancient Greek and Roman amphitheaters and on their first collaboration, Holman Stadium in Vero Beach. The landscape could serve the stadium, and vice versa.

The second great notion of O'Malley and Praeger was to build a stadium with perfect sight lines. This was of particular concern because Ebbets Field had been notorious for its obstructed views. Here the entire stadium would be designed with the viewing experience in mind. That meant, instead of using support columns for the various grandstands, they would be carved into the hillside and jut out using what O'Malley called the "cantilever theory" of stadium construction: each level anchored into the Earth and floating seemingly unsupported over the level beneath.

With this settled, O'Malley and Praeger began to consider the various trappings of the park. Among other things, O'Malley wanted to include a subterranean level behind home plate. These seats would be like a third dugout, allowing a view unlike anything fans were accustomed to. He had seen a similar setup after the 1956 season when the Dodgers played at Korakuen Stadium in Tokyo, and he took to calling them the Japanese boxes.

There were index cards for everything. He wanted the home bullpen at the same elevation and compass direction as the pitcher's mound. He wanted to ensure that the umpires would have "easy access to and from playing field NOT via route to be used by players." He wanted pumped air to keep the American flag waving beyond center field, even on windless days. And on windy days, he wanted to defend the park from the cold blasts with a "movable louvered design." He wanted to beam infrared heat to the seats so that fans accustomed to mild Southern California weather didn't skip chilly night games.

But above all, what Walter O'Malley wanted was parking. In Brooklyn there hadn't been any. In Los Angeles there would be a great sea of parking filled by great rivers of cars streaming in via the freeways. This was the great tragic joke of the whole story. Palo Verde, La Loma, and Bishop would not remain as they were in the hills above downtown. Nor would they be the site of a public-housing project. They would not even be the site of a ballpark. They would be, in the end, the site of a parking lot.

O'Malley and Praeger designed the stadium so that the various parking lots were on tiers corresponding to the elevation of the seating levels. Instead of dealing with ramps or stairs inside the stadium, you could simply park on the level of your ticket and walk through a turnstile without having to trek uphill or downhill. But you wouldn't have to walk from your car anyway because there would be a little tram or a great speeding monorail to take you from the outer reaches of the parking lot to the stadium entrance.

# 67.

In his book *Chavez Ravine: 1949*, the photographer Don Normark recalled the first time he encountered the three communities. He was looking for a place to take a panoramic shot of the city up in the hills:

> I didn't find the view, but when I looked over the other side of the hill I was standing on, I saw a village I never knew was there.
>
> Hiking down into it, I began to think I had found a poor man's Shangri-La.

Normark thought that he had found a little slice of heaven. Something mystical. The phrase "a poor man's Shangri-La" has lived on. The guitarist and songwriter Ry Cooder used it for the opening song on his Chavez Ravine concept album. "Palo Verde girls never let you down," he sang.

There was always supposed to be a better world in those hills, a better life. Abrana and Manuel had been looking for that life in 1922. Palo Verde wasn't perfect; it wasn't really Shangri-la. But it was theirs.

There was supposed to be utopia here. Wasn't that what Frank Wilkinson had been trying to build before the trap was set?

Wasn't that what Walter O'Malley was trying to build too? A place where everything else disappears? A place where the city and its troubles fade away? An alternate universe where everybody gets along and the complications of real life give way to the simple facts of green grass and brown dirt and painted white foul lines?

"The paradox of Dodger Stadium is the paradox of Los Angeles," wrote Christopher Hawthorne in the *Los Angeles Times*. "It's a ballpark where we find a much-needed civic communion in the middle of the city by leaving the city behind."

This was the dream. This was what these hills had always been for, even as every iteration of home in them had been built over and erased. A new history. A new Los Angeles to momentarily leave behind in the ecstasy of baseball. But in 1958 that dream was still a stack of index cards. It was still crammed into filing cabinets. The last roots of Palo Verde were unbroken. Palo Verde girls never let you down. The dream would have to wait.

# Part VI

---

# *RASTREANDO*

# 68.

THE SUNSETS AT DODGER STADIUM LINGER. THE SKY BEHIND THE outfield pavilions slowly darkens, and the clouds turn pink and gold. The mountains and palm trees behind the stadium fade into silhouettes, and as the sun descends behind the stadium on the third-base side, the shadows slowly swallow up the entire playing field. Vin Scully, who was known to go on about "cotton candy" skies, once admitted that the sunsets could be distracting even as he broadcast games. Millions of people have watched the sunsets over Dodger Stadium. But few people are ever there in the mornings to see what the sunrise looks like, coming up on the other side of the stadium from behind the hills of Elysian Park.

On the morning of May 8, 1959, the sun came up over Palo Verde two minutes before six, peeking over those hills and filtering through the trees. If Abrana and Manuel Aréchiga had been able to sleep, they would be rising soon. The morning would be filled with that heavy quiet of knowing that something is going to happen but not knowing what. There were a thousand small decisions to make. What would they do with their valuables? Abrana's saints and the framed photos of relatives? Their furniture? The still in the basement where Manuel made his moonshine? Their goats and turkeys and chickens?

It was a Friday, a weekday, which meant that the kids would have school. Lola's daughter Dolores took the bus to Nightingale Junior High. Her younger daughter, Rachel, and Tolina's two older kids, Ivy and Ida, went to Solano Avenue Elementary, which was not as far away but still farther than the empty Palo Verde school. Tolina's husband, Mike Angustain, took off early for his job in the city parks department.

Left in the house were Abrana and Manuel and two of their daughters, Lola and Tolina. Tolina also had her youngest child

home: a nine-month-old baby named Ira. Juan and Nellie's youngest daughter, Jeannie, was there too with her grandparents while
her parents worked and her sisters were at school. Eventually, the
phone rang, and Tolina picked up. The person on the other end was
Alice Martin, a neighbor who was also facing eviction. Martin later
told a newspaper that she asked Tolina what the family planned to
do when the sheriffs came. The answer came: we are going to lock
the doors.

The sheriff's deputies assigned with carrying out the eviction
gathered that morning at the naval armory. This was the same place
the marauding sailors had been stationed in 1943 before they took
their caravan of taxis down from the hills and into the city streets
in what would become the Zoot Suit Riots. In addition to deputies
there would need to be movers and construction crews and public
health officials. There would need to be heavy machinery.

When it seemed clear that there would be problems, somebody
from the family went down to the elementary school and picked up
Rachel, Ivy, and Ida. There was not enough time to grab the older
kids. They remained at school as the rest of the family watched
Malvina Avenue fill up, not with law-enforcement officials but with
journalists. Somebody had tipped off the papers and the television
stations. Carloads full of press came up toward the house from
downtown. They filmed and took still photos of the peaceful final
moments of the Aréchiga property. Then they too waited.

Later, there would be a lot of conspiratorial whispering about
how the media knew what was going to happen ahead of time.
There would be accusations that the Aréchiga family and Alice Martin were being coached all along by sympathetic reporters looking
to get a big story or by shadowy special interests looking to undermine Walter O'Malley, that everything was staged. The city council
even took up a special investigation. But the story had been in the
papers for weeks. The Aréchigas had been public figures for years.
The deadline on their pending eviction notice was no great secret.

However, there was certainly some level of cooperation between
the resisting families and the press. In one of his reports after the
evictions, a newspaperman named Ridgely Cummings described
climbing through a window into Alice Martin's home to wait with
her inside as deputies broke down her door. Cummings, who wrote
for the syndicated Civic Center News Agency, had been a fervent
advocate for the residents in his writing. In her home, Martin had a

list of names that read like a who's who of the Citizens Committee to Save Chavez Ravine, including Blackjack Smith.

The press scurried into position as the squad cars came gliding up the hill, single file, at about 11 a.m. Behind them were cherry pickers, moving vans, and bulldozers. The sun was rising in the sky. The deputy in charge of the eviction was a captain named Joseph Brady. He had a potbelly that stretched against his uniform and a too-short tie. He had the look of a man who would vastly prefer to be somewhere else. There remains at least one silent newsreel clip of the ensuing events. The clip is just over two minutes long, frantically cutting from one scene to another. But between the footage, the memories of witnesses, contemporaneous newspaper reports, and the still photographs taken at the scene, it is possible to piece together a narrative of what happened.

By the time the deputies came up into Palo Verde, the Aréchiga family had gathered in the house at 1771 Malvina. This was the wood-frame house with the handwritten protest signs out front. This was the house that Abrana had insisted would have venetian blinds on the windows. It had the smells of her cooking baked into its walls, and the decades of footfalls had left the wooden floors dull and smooth. The porch had been Abrana's domain for thirty-seven years. This was the house where everything would end. Before the deputies arrived, the family nailed the front door shut from the inside.

The newsreel footage cuts from the squad cars to a line of deputies walking up the wooden steps to Abrana's porch. There are already photographers on the porch waiting for them. There is a bull's head mounted on the facade overhanging the steps. We don't hear it, but once the deputies reach the front door, there is an exchange between a Spanish-speaking deputy and the family inside the house. The deputies try to convince Abrana and Manuel to leave peacefully. They plead. Finally, a deputy is called upon to kick the door in. He raises his boot, placing his hand on a companion's shoulder for balance. Slowly, he breaks the lock and the nails with his heel so that the door cracks open. However, it is also clear that the door is barricaded from the inside by something heavy. The deputies squeeze through a narrow opening into the crowded front room of the house.

Abrana Aréchiga stands before Captain Brady, this sheriff's deputy who has become the living embodiment of every uncaring official, manipulative lawyer, opportunistic businessman, and patronizing politician that she has dealt with over the years. In a threadbare black sweater and long skirt, she stalks the room as reporters and cameramen creep closer and closer. Flashbulbs illuminate the room one after another after another. She lays into Brady, who stands and takes it, looking down at her through his eyeglasses, his hands resting on his hips in a resigned sort of way. The newsreel footage has the quality of a silent film, and not just because it is silent. Abrana's gestures are sweeping, dramatic. The entire breadth and depth of her emotions seem to be contained in the simple flick of a wrist. You don't need to hear her to understand her. Manuel looks on, wearing a fedora and a striped short-sleeve shirt, and it almost seems like he is somewhere else. Tolina stands beside her mother, iron-faced, holding Ira, her nine-month-old. The wallpaper is decorated with flowers.

Outside, utility workers climb the telephone poles running up Malvina and cut the lines. Movers emerge from their vans and work their way into the house, wearing matching white shirts. They begin to carry furniture down the stairs, one item after another: bed frames, cabinets, chairs, as fast as they can. A deputy rips out the front window so the movers can pass the furniture outside more quickly. They take a refrigerator that is filled with bottles of milk meant for baby Ira. All of these possessions are bound for a storage facility somewhere else, somewhere not here. Then everything changes.

Tolina conducts a television interview; afterward, three women deputies refuse to let her reenter the house, even as movers continue to climb in and out, even as her relatives remain inside. In the news footage we suddenly see Tolina holding tightly to baby Ira as a woman in uniform tries to wrestle him away from her. It is the judgment of Solomon playing out in Palo Verde. A crowd gathers around them. The footage is silent, but you can see the screams filling the air. Tolina's daughter, Ida, just a little girl herself, tries to intercede. Then the footage cuts again to Tolina on the ground, kneeling, crying, as deputies restrain her arms, which are now empty.

So much is happening at once. There are photographers and cameramen everywhere, each capturing their own version of the scene. Politicians stand back and take it all in. There are voices we can't hear. The family is scattered over the property. Turkeys and chickens roam about.

Tolina falls to the ground crying. Her older sister Lola cries too. She is being carried down the steps by four deputies, her shoes off, her body writhing, her face contorted, her limbs splayed out, fingers pressing into her skin. This is the image that will stay with people: the thirty-eight-year-old war widow and mother of two being hauled by four men down the stairs of her childhood home. She is wearing all white. A simple blouse and pants with flowers on them. Aurora Vargas, who had been born in Morenci, Arizona, and carried on her mother's lap to California in 1922, who became Lola because it rhymes with Bola and her older sister thought she looked like a ball.

Now Lola is being carried, not by her mother or her sister but by these four men in uniform across the street to an open field, where, standing in the scrub growth, she is cuffed with her hands behind her back. From there she is carried again to a squad car and shoved in the backseat. The *Los Angeles Times* reported that one of the deputies assigned to the eviction was the same woman that Lola had brawled with previously and that her presence was what had made Lola refuse to cooperate.

Years later, Jeannie Aréchiga would remember being placed in the car with her aunt Lola and driven by a deputy to wait out the storm in a quiet part of Elysian Park. She was given a sack lunch. But before she could take a bite, Lola told her, "Don't eat their food." So Jeannie threw the whole lunch out the window and down the hill. After that, they were separated.

In the footage, before Lola can be driven away, Abrana emerges. She walks down the stairs holding a little Chihuahua. She will not go easily, but neither will she give these men the pleasure of touching her. At the bottom of the steps, in her front yard, Abrana puts down the dog and scoops up a rock. She raises it as if to throw. But she looks around. She hesitates. What's the point? There are not enough rocks in these hills. In some accounts of the evictions, Abrana is heaving rocks one after another at passing deputies. In others she is hurling dirt and swearing in Spanish.

Finally, the family gathers, without Lola, on the curb across the street. Tolina has baby Ira in her arms again, and Abrana reaches to take something out of the boy's mouth. They sit under one of the phone poles, which is no longer in service. Abrana cries into her handkerchief. She has a dog in her lap.

They watch as a bulldozer creeps up the road, its wide blade glinting in the midday sun, and slowly nudges their home off of its foundation. It's as if the house itself is nothing: a child's toy made of leftover cardboard. One of the play forts the boys and girls used to build among the eucalyptus trees in Elysian Park. It's as if the very notion of permanence was always a joke, has been for forty years, and they are just finding out now. The front stairs fall to the ground in one piece. The bulldozer backs up, turns around. Slowly, and methodically, it does its job. The roof comes down. Abrana and Manuel watch as the City of Los Angeles renders 1771 Malvina into rubble. The whole thing takes ten minutes.

# 69.

As the reports went out on radio and on television, the entire city seemed to stop what it was doing and turn its attention to Palo Verde. All of a sudden, the remains of the house on Malvina developed a sort of gravity. More politicians came up from City Hall. Onlookers drawn to the possibility of spectacle made their way into the neighborhood simply to see what had happened. Old neighbors came rushing back up over the hills. Some others were already there, bearing witness. The children and grandchildren, the nephews and nieces, the cousins and cousins' cousins of Abrana and Manuel, this family that had spread out across the city in the previous decade returned to the place where it had all begun.

Mike Angustain was on the job when it happened. "I didn't believe the fellows at work when they told me about my house going down," he told a reporter afterward. "They'd been kidding me about getting kicked out, so I thought the news was another of their jokes. But when I drove up the street and looked—my house was gone." Mike and Tolina had been living in the stucco house next door. That home was also demolished.

Dolores heard about it on the school bus. When the bus parked to drop her off, somebody told her they were knocking down the house. She sprinted all the way up the hill to Malvina. "It was already gone," she said. "It was already flat."

This was not like watching the other houses that had rolled away. It was not like watching her own house go either. Those homes had left in one piece. They had rolled out of sight and into some other happy afterlife. But her grandparents' house could have no afterlife. It lay in a million pieces on the dirt. It was gone but not all the way gone. The only thing that was all the way gone was Dolores's mother. After everything, Lola had been hauled to jail. So had the Aréchigas' old neighbor, the actress Glen Walters.

*Aurora "Lola" Vargas*

# 70.

THE CAMERAS DID NOT GO AWAY. CITY COUNCIL MEMBERS ED Roybal and John Holland, unlikely allies, railed against the unjust and brutal evictions. By the time the evening news aired and the following morning's papers were printed, the Aréchiga family had become folk heroes. They would be written into myth in the broadest strokes: at once brave paragons of resistance and poor, desolate people with nowhere to go.

There was power in the simplicity of this portrayal. A helpless family is displaced by a cruel city government in order to seal a contract with a big-business baseball team. How could you not feel for them? Soon the Aréchiga family plight would be more than just front-page news in the local papers. It would be a national story. Letters from across the country came into the offices of Los Angeles politicians. Rarely is abuse of governmental power so neatly packaged for the television news. Rarely are the failings of our democracy and our economic system so neatly distilled for a mass audience.

By nightfall, the Aréchiga story was already written. The vision of Abrana furious and hopeless. The sight of Lola being dragged down the stairs. Manuel in a state of mourning under the brim of his hat, his dark eyes almost hidden from view. But without knowing it, the press was already printing the legend at the expense of the fact. These poor people, everybody assumed, had nowhere to go. Why else would they have stayed this long? Why else would they have put themselves through this suffering?

The truth, as it tends to be, was more complicated. The family picked through the wreckage of their property. It looked as if a very powerful but very self-contained tornado had come through the neighborhood. There was rubble everywhere. Many of their chickens had been crushed to death under the house. Like anybody who has become uprooted, the Aréchiga family was faced with the question of what to do next—where to go? "We'll have to sleep in the street," Tolina told *La Opinión* the day of the evictions. "We have nowhere to go."

In fact, they actually did have somewhere to go. The Aréchigas, between Manuel, Abrana, and their children, owned eleven properties in the Los Angeles area. All that scrimping and saving over the years, all that work work work, the summer trips to the fields and the foundry jobs and the bottle collecting had actually been paying off. The properties weren't just sitting empty. They were either owned and occupied by Aréchiga children or rented out to other relatives. While nobody outside the family knew this at the time, if the family wanted to leave Palo Verde, they could have at least found a couch to sleep on.

In fact, they almost did leave. According to Ridgely Cummings, Roybal secured them temporary housing shortly after the eviction. Tolina and Mike—despite her comments to *La Opinión*—were ready to go. But Abrana, who had left her home in Mexico and then left her home in Arizona, was not willing to leave this home. "They will have to carry us off the land as they carried us out of our homes," she said. She would not leave her remaining animals unattended. Abrana and Manuel Aréchiga had come to Los Angeles in 1922 and set up camp on Malvina Avenue while they built their house. Now it was 1959, and the house was gone. But they were still here.

"We started in a tent then," Abrana reportedly told Roybal. "And maybe we'll end in a tent."

# 71.

THAT FIRST NIGHT, THEY WERE JOINED BY ABOUT FORTY FRIENDS AND relatives. While the Dodgers played in San Francisco, the Aréchigas built a fire and sang campfire songs. They cooked on the open flames and ate tacos. Manuel guarded their belongings with a shotgun. Tolina gathered signatures for a petition to the city. Well-wishers, many under the impression that the Aréchigas were destitute, sent supplies up their way, including a trailer for them to live in, which the family accepted.

The encampment grew into a living protest. Sunday would be Mother's Day, and Abrana tacked to a tree the cards she had received from her kids and grandkids. Cruz Cabral, the nephew who had been repeatedly injured while serving in the Pacific and who had been essentially raised by his aunt and uncle, hung his marine dress uniform adorned with medals outside the tent with a hand-written sign that said, "THIS IS WHAT WE FOUGHT FOR." The newspapers ran a photo of Cruz, stocky and sharply dressed, and Abrana. Beyond them lay the sign, the uniform, and the wreckage of the house on Malvina.

On Sunday, Howard Holtzendorff phoned the family and offered residence in three apartments in Ramona Gardens as a temporary home. Had they accepted, the Aréchigas would have finally ended up in one of the promised public-housing units. Tolina answered the phone. She later recounted the conversation to the *Mirror-News.* "I don't want anything to do with public housing," Tolina said she told Holtzendorff. "That's what started this whole thing. My family likes it here."

Then, Tolina told the newspaper, Holtzendorff's tone shifted: "Don't get smart with me, young lady. I'm being nice. If I want to, I'll clear you and your mother and that tent out of there right now."

# 72.

ON MONDAY MORNING, MAY 11, TOLINA AND FAMILY ATTORNEY PHILL
Silver went to municipal court to plead for a delay on the charges
relating to Lola and Glen Walters, both of whom remained locked
up in the Lincoln Heights Jail. Lola was facing one count of dis-
turbing the peace and three charges for use of force on the arresting deputies. After the delay was granted, Tolina led her sister and
Walters down the street to City Hall.

That morning, the council was holding hearings on the evictions. The chambers were filled with hundreds of Aréchiga supporters, chanting and waving signs. The entire family was there, and the
crowd welcomed Lola and Walters as conquering heroes. The hearings were broadcast across the city and covered by every paper. The
proceedings began with council members taking up a collection on
their behalf. The assumption among the council members was still
that the family was poor. One of the officials who contributed to
the Aréchiga collection was Roz Wyman.

Wyman, however, became a singular target for the family and
their allies. Somebody in the audience carried a sign that said,
"WYMAN WHERE IS YOUR HEART?" As a young mother herself, Wyman made a natural foil for Tolina and Lola. In addition
to being the leading booster of the Dodger Stadium deal, Wyman
had recently cast a vote against allowing the family to stay in their
home until after their US Supreme Court appeal could be decided.

During her testimony, Tolina sobbed and blamed Wyman for
that vote and for the movers who hauled her diapers and baby bottles away. "I blame nobody but her, and she's a mother too," she
said. She sat next to her father, Manuel, with baby Ira in her lap.

Later, Wyman would recall this as among the most difficult
points of her career. Police officers were assigned to guard her in
City Hall. She received threatening phone calls. It's hard to imagine

that tensions would have risen to the point where a physical attack against Wyman was likely, but then again, this was the same city where, not long before, a respected mayor had punched a man in the face for calling him a socialist.

When the council members tried to adjourn for lunch at noon, Tolina urged them to continue, and she offered to buy them sandwiches if they would skip the break. The audience was constantly interrupting, and Council President John Gibson struggled to quiet them. Council members piled on. Roybal compared the evictions to a "Roman festival." Another witness compared the Aréchigas to the heroes at Valley Forge. Mayor Poulson was in Santa Barbara for the day and drove back to LA to avoid a subpoena to appear. He then hid in his office with the intention of submitting a written statement, until the council finally pressured him to come to the chambers. The hearing went on for nearly eight hours.

Throughout the hearing, the Aréchiga family maintained the position that they simply wanted to be compensated fairly. They wanted the $17,500 they believed their property to be worth. In his own testimony, City Attorney Roger Arnebergh acknowledged that the $17,500 assessment had been made, then ran down, step by step, the reasons why the eviction had been legal and why the $10,050 price was not negotiable. Arnebergh made a pleading case for the rule of law. If a city does not execute orders like the one to evict the Aréchigas, he said, then "our entire constitutional government will fall and anarchy will result."

One witness was Henry López, an attorney in Los Angeles and, at the time, a candidate for secretary of state in California. His testimony hit at the underlying tragedy of the events and at why Arnebergh's explanation was so insufficient. Just because something is legally right doesn't make it morally right: "It seems to me that Council has been too concerned with the technical legalities involved rather than the equities of the matter. To my way of thinking, after the public housing deal fell through in Los Angeles, the whole situation should have been negotiated in such a way that these people should have gotten fair prices for their home, and fairer treatment. Then this horrible thing which happened last Friday would not have taken place."

# 73.

In December 1958, Frank Wilkinson's citation for contempt of Congress was upheld by a unanimous vote of the House of Representatives. Soon afterward, he was convicted in federal court and sentenced to one year in prison. He appealed, knowing that his case would eventually head to the US Supreme Court, just as he had hoped for all along.

Meanwhile, the Wilkinsons moved back to Los Angeles. Frank reopened his office with the Citizens Committee to Preserve American Freedoms. He worked closely with the American Civil Liberties Union. In 1960 Frank was in San Francisco when a near-riot broke out at a HUAC hearing. Afterward, he found himself featured in an anti-Communist propaganda film called *Operation Abolition*.

Frank was used to being a target. Throughout the 1950s his offices were broken into all the time. This happened in Los Angeles, and it happened in New York. In the fall of 1960, Frank's Los Angeles office was set ablaze in the middle of the night. Then, on the night after Christmas in 1960, his youngest daughter, Jo, saw a strange object on the landing of the stairs in front of their home. The Wilkinsons lived on the upper floor of a duplex. The object was a sort of flat glass bottle, and she thought it must be some kind of anti-insect device. It was one of those moments where you see something strange and justify it to yourself with whatever easy explanation comes to mind. Frank was out of town, and Jean was out for the evening, so Jo just forgot all about it. It was probably nothing. She went on up and to bed. Her older brother Tony was in the living room reading. Before she fell asleep, Jo heard a bang.

Then all of a sudden there was a crackling sound, and Jo heard neighbors screaming from outside. Flash, the family dog, started barking. They opened the front door and saw flames rising up into the night sky. The house was on fire. Jo and Tony scooped up Flash and escaped down the back stairs. Afterward, Jo sat in the back of a police car as firefighters put out the flames. She tried to tell the police about the bottle she saw; it must have been an incendiary device, and the person lighting it must have hidden in the bushes when they saw her coming.

A few days later, a swastika was painted onto the Wilkinsons' wall. In the weeks that followed, members of the progressive community stood armed guard at the house. Frank came back from out of town. But they never talked about it. Nobody ever talked about it. "Everything is going to be OK," Jean said. They sent Jo off to a folk music camp for the rest of winter break.

Two months after the fire, Frank returned to Washington to hear the Supreme Court's decision in his case. At one time he was sure that he and Carl Braden would lose. He was sure that they would go to jail. But on February 27, 1961, as Frank sat in the gallery, he had hope.

That hope was quickly extinguished. Justice Potter Stewart rose to declare that by a 5–4 vote, the court had ruled against Frank. The court also ruled against Braden by the same margin. This meant that Frank Wilkinson, the man whose Communist Party friends used to call him J. C. behind his back, had succeeded in making himself a martyr. He was going to prison.

Frank would later say that "like Pontius Pilate," the Roman prefect who absolved himself of responsibility for the original J. C. before his crucifixion, Justice Stewart had "washed his hands."

=

FRANK DID NOT spend the months prior to his prison term savoring the last moments of peaceful domestic tranquility. Instead, he spent them barnstorming across the country and giving speeches. He was ordered to surrender in Atlanta, and he wound his way there slowly. On the night before Frank and Carl Braden turned themselves in, Martin Luther King Jr. hosted a reception in their honor at Morehouse College. Afterward, Martin Luther and Coretta Scott King hosted Frank and Carl for a farewell dinner.

The next morning, May 1, 1961, they self-surrendered at the Fulton County Jail. The steel doors closed behind them. Less than two weeks later, Frank and Carl were transferred. They were handcuffed and chained by their feet and chained around their waists. They were on their way to a federal prison in Greenville, South

Carolina. When they stopped for gas, the guards wouldn't uncuff Frank, so he had to get their help to use the bathroom. At Greenville, their mail came late because it was always routed through Atlanta, where the FBI could screen it. The hacks—that's what the inmates called guards—were always tossing Frank's bunk, looking for contraband or Communist propaganda.

Frank and Carl made friends by writing letters home for the inmates who couldn't read or write. Most of the other prisoners were bootleggers. They asked Frank and Carl to run the prison's Alcoholics Anonymous group. Frank was no longer the teetotaling Methodist, but he did it anyway. Running the AA group gave the men a chance to talk freely away from the hacks, and it gave Frank a better understanding of society's problems. After the meetings, Frank would write long letters home. Frank shared mundane details and begged for affirmation. He was reading Winston Churchill's history of World War II. The lights went out early. The cell was cold, and Frank lined his bed with newspapers for insulation.

That summer, Jean and a friend drove Jo and Tony across the country to South Carolina to visit. Jeffry, the oldest, stayed behind: he wasn't speaking to Frank. Their relationship had always been rough, and it always would be. The family members were allowed to visit on weekends and bring in picnic lunches. They saw a Frank Wilkinson who was the same, but different. He was losing weight fast, his mannerisms were toned down, and he was even quicker to cry than usual.

It was a weird way to spend a summer, driving across the country to visit your political-prisoner father. Jo remembers that after Frank had made his choice to challenge HUAC, she was taken aside by a man at a party. The man was Alger Hiss, who was out after nearly four years in prison. Hiss told her that he understood how hard it would be if Frank went to prison; it had been hard for his own son. He said if there was anything she needed, she could call him. He said he could be her godfather. And even though they didn't believe in God, he really was a godfather to her.

While Frank learned how to survive in prison, his allies were working to advance his cause on the outside. Frank applied for clemency from the Kennedy administration. Religious and civil rights leaders across the country signed petitions on Frank and Carl's behalf. Among them were King, Ralph Abernathy, and a very old W. E. B. Du Bois. Jean even met with Robert Kennedy, then the attorney general, to plead their case. But no clemency was coming. In fact, in November 1961 Frank and Carl were suddenly transferred without explanation. They spent a week in solitary confinement in Lewisburg, Pennsylvania, then were sent to another nearby prison in Allenwood. Frank had no chance to gather his books or belongings, not even his hearing-aid batteries.

Allenwood was more sedate. Frank's sister Hildegarde and her partner, Margarethe Peterson, came for Thanksgiving dinner. At Christmas, Frank was overwhelmed with greeting cards. Then, suddenly, it was 1962.

In January Frank got a letter from Jean. Congress had appropriated HUAC its largest budget ever for the coming year. Frank's Supreme Court challenge had been futile, and the committee seemed to only be growing stronger. If all went according to plan, Frank would be getting out soon for good behavior. "Everybody's asking," Jean wrote. "Where do we go from here?"

On February 1, Frank and Carl Braden were released. They boarded a bus to New York, where Pete Seeger was throwing a welcome-back rally and concert. Two days earlier, among his final correspondence from prison, Frank had written back to Jean: "After we abolish HUAC, next we must abolish prisons."

# 74.

Back on Malvina, the family moved into the donated trailer. There was no sense yet of how long this would last. But the evictions were taking a toll. The family members were living without most of their belongings. They were still tending to their animals, but they were forced to stare all day at the ruins of their own lives. The ghost of the house that had once stood at 1771 Malvina. At one point, Lola had a nervous breakdown, screaming out over and over, "They are going to kill my children! They are going to kill my children!" Neighbors calmed her and put her to rest on a camping cot. She refused to visit a hospital.

Soon after the hearing, Roz Wyman received an anonymous postcard suggesting that she ought to check the property records for the Aréchiga family. She later told interviewers that she passed the tip along to a friendly reporter at the *Mirror-News*. On May 13 the results of that tip came to fruition: a front-page story about the Aréchigas' vast property holdings.

The family did not exactly own an empire. But the fact that they owned anything at all—the fact that they were not destitute—was enough to turn public opinion against them. And it gave their political opponents a pretext to unload. Mayor Poulson released a scathing, over-the-top statement that clocked in at nearly a thousand words, including these: "The Aréchiga family is a victim of its own eagerness to extract from the taxpayers more than it was granted by court decisions. The family used its own children as pawns, to gain sympathy. It is perfectly plain now that the family needs no sympathy. It was obviously, plainly, publicly, shamelessly flouting the law."

To people like Norris Poulson, the Aréchiga family could be sympathetic only if they were poor. It made sense to people that a bunch of stubborn, uneducated Mexicans would hold out forever

*Victoria "Tolina" Angustain*

because they had nowhere to go. But what if this stubborn family was actually holding out because they believed—accurately—that they had been screwed over by a rigged and broken system, and they wanted to make a point?

In the aftermath of the evictions and Poulson's statement, Juan Aréchiga wrote a blistering letter to Poulson and members of the council. The letter could have come only from Juan, who was self-educated and fearless, who was smart enough to know back in 1941 what the white establishment thought of him and his family.

In just over three pages, he laid out the truth from the family's perspective, repeatedly calling out Poulson, Wyman, and Council President John Gibson by name. He told the story of how their parents had accumulated their land over the decades and of how they had now lost it:

> My father had a Model-T Ford. On that truck we went to Fresno and picked fruit. We did this for about 8 or 9 years. It used to take us about a week to get there. So the people themselves, can see that my parents made quite a sacrifice to have what they had—2 houses and a lot in Chavez Ravine. The first step in taking possession of their land was for a housing project. That was abandoned. So now does the Housing Authority have the right to sell our land to the city and they in return to sell it to Mr. O'Malley for a private ballpark?

And there it was. Nearly four decades boiled down to a few sentences. The letter continued:

> We are not opposing the park. It is the principle of the thing. It's the manner in which they took possession of the land. I still can't believe that's the right process of law and justice. Mr. Poulson, when you speak of taxpayers, the Arechigas are just that. America is still the land of the brave and the home of the free. Is it? It's an honor to know that we have honorable Councilmen with dignity that believe in protecting the people's rights. So that we all can appreciate our more free and better America, regardless of color or race. And so for you, Mrs. Wyman, why are you so concerned that we run and hide. You must have good reasons. I believe that if my mother was woman enough to give me birth, then I in return should fight with and for her until the end, even if it means going to President Eisenhower for justice.
>
> Mrs. Wyman, you stated that you were surprised to hear that the Arechigas have extensive land holdings. Is it a crime? Because every member of the family is buying a house to live in? Then we should be punished by the law, not by you or Mr. Poulson. Thanks for the arrangements you made for having my parents thrown out on the street like animals. So in return you can expect to be treated the same. (This is not a threat like you lied about before) My parents are old but they still have some pride.

JUAN WENT ON to list the family properties, to excoriate the mayor and the council majority, and to question why, if his family was doing something wrong, the city waited so long to do anything about it. He referenced the Constitution. There was no puppet master pulling the strings of the Aréchiga family's resistance, he wrote. There was only his mother. "You are the selfish, looking for power and prestige, trying to use the Arechigas as a stepping stone," he concluded. "But we won't stand still. We'll fight to the end, the American way, till justice is done."

But the letter was never published in any newspaper or read aloud on any broadcast. In fact, it does not appear to have been read by anybody outside of City Hall. All of Juan's rage and all of his eloquence disappeared into some filing cabinets in a building that did not exist when his parents first moved to Palo Verde. As the media lost interest in the story, the family's platform to tell its side diminished. Slowly, public opinion turned further against them.

The owner of the trailer came to bring it home. The family then moved into a large umbrella tent. One evening, a pair of USC students drove up to Malvina in a sports car to taunt the gathered Aréchigas. The car was decorated with a placard that read "LEAVE, GLORYHOUNDS!" The students had words with family members. When it became clear that the audience was not sympathetic to their arguments, they took off back down the hill.

White Angelenos may have lost their sympathy for the Aréchiga family, but the family itself remained unapologetic. They spoke at length to the media. They maintained that they had never asked for charity (although they had certainly accepted it) and that they had never claimed poverty. "Sure we own property," Abrana told the *Herald-Examiner.* "But Mr. O'Malley owns a lot more."

Lola, whose arm remained in a sling a week after the ordeal, added the following:

> It's true that I own houses. I wish I could own a hundred. I'm within my rights. When they took my husband to the armed forces, where he died fighting in the war, they didn't ask permission to take him. I think I have the right to own my homes. The rest of my family has houses too, but that has nothing to do with the case of my parents. They are defending their legitimate rights, and all of my family is united to defend them. We haven't asked for economic

help from anyone, we don't need it, and we don't want it. We just want justice, and nothing more.

After the family moved into the tent, the city began finding new and clever ways to irritate them into leaving. At one point, the health department claimed that their living conditions were not sanitary. A deputy presented Abrana with an order to get off the property. She promptly ripped it to shreds. Eventually, however, the city found a way to get to them: they threatened to put Lola and Tolina's kids into juvenile detention. This struck a nerve, Tolina said, especially after Poulson had accused them of using the children as pawns.

On May 15, a week after the evictions, Tolina, Mike, and their three children departed the encampment on a flatbed truck. They were bound for a warehouse where their belongings were being stored and after that for a house they owned in Echo Park. Lola would also be leaving soon with her daughters, Dolores and Rachel. She had also convinced Abrana that it was time to go. She used the same leverage that the city had used against her and Tolina: the children. Ultimately, Abrana, who had started this whole thing, decided that being with her grandchildren was more important than anything else.

The only person who remained unconvinced was Manuel. The gentle, steady old man with the thick eyebrows had seemed almost like a spectator throughout the ordeal. He is not seen in the newsreel footage yelling or throwing stones or struggling with officers. He did not testify at City Hall. However, his own life had been given to this place. He had become like one of the trees in Palo Verde. "I won't go," Manuel told the press. "I am going to stay and fight for my land. It is mine. It does not belong to anyone else. I will leave only if they take me to jail. I will go peacefully—but only to jail."

But as the children and grandchildren left and the encampment shrank, it became harder to live in Palo Verde. There was no more Palo Verde. On May 18 Abrana and Manuel received confirmation from City Attorney Arnebergh that by leaving the land, they were not relinquishing their claim to it. Their legal battle would continue. But in the meantime they would live elsewhere.

As friends and family looked on, Abrana and Manuel packed their tent item by item. They were tired. They loaded up their car with the few belongings they had kept with them in the ten days since the bulldozer plowed through their home. They arranged care for their chickens. They scooped up their little dogs. And when everything was packed up and ready to go, the engine in Manuel's jalopy refused to turn over. All those years of staying, and now they couldn't even leave.

A small crowd—including Ed Roybal—gathered behind the car and gave it a push downhill. With a rolling start, the engine caught, and Abrana and Manuel drove off into the rest of their lives. They did so bitterly. Before they left, Abrana joked to a reporter at *La Opinión* that the family had two other properties nobody had written about: *"Dos Lotes en el cementerio de El Calvario. Para mi y para mi marido."* Two plots in the Cavalry cemetery. For me and for my husband.

Abrana would live for the time being with Tolina and Mike. But Manuel refused. He was not ready to concede to the rest of Los Angeles. He would stop over at his children's homes during the day, Tolina said. But he refused to stay the night. Instead, he drove around, searching for something, *rastreando*. A month after the evictions, he was arrested for drunk driving. He found quiet corners. He slept in the jalopy. Palo Verde was gone.

# 75.

When the Dodgers first arrived in Los Angeles, Walter O'Malley envisioned starting construction on his new stadium right away. He was bursting, ready to build: to turn the decade he had spent scheming and dreaming in Brooklyn into something tangible. This was what he had come for. The Coliseum was no place for big-league baseball.

It must have felt like the city was conspiring against him. First there was the subpoena. There was the ballot measure. There was the fact that people still lived on the land he thought would be his. He may not have realized it at first, but when O'Malley acquired the site, he was also acquiring the previous decade of dirty politics and legal warfare and the aftereffects of an essential, almost primordial fight over what it meant to be a city. He was acquiring not just the Los Angeles territory but also the history of those three communities and the weight of the crimes perpetrated against them; he was acquiring the hangover from the war over public housing that had made this land available in the first place. These were stubborn ghosts.

In September 1959, a few months after the evictions, the Dodgers finally held a ceremonial groundbreaking for their new stadium. Five thousand people attended. In October the US Supreme Court declined to hear the taxpayer case against the deal. Then, soon after, the Dodgers unexpectedly won the World Series in just their second year in town.

But construction would still have to wait. Soon after the evictions, the city managed to purchase a condemned tract co-owned by Fritz Burns. However, the city had failed to acquire the final dozen or so properties in the parcel, including a house on Malvina owned by the Acostas, the Aréchigas' former neighbors. In February the Dodgers put up the money and bought the properties themselves. There was only one more piece necessary to begin construction: the abandoned Palo Verde Elementary School building.

The school had shuttered in 1955 and remained vacant as the neighborhood emptied around it and the houses disappeared one by one. It was a Spanish-style building with a tiled roof and a spacious play yard. Once it had sat in the civic center of Palo Verde, beside the church, at the heart of daily life. During the stadium fight the Citizens Committee to Save Chavez Ravine for the People proposed turning it into an office space. Now the city acquired the school for $294,000 from the Board of Education so that it could be handed over as part of the deal with the Dodgers.

With this, the land was finally O'Malley's. But before he could actually build, he would need to remake the entire landscape around the stadium site. O'Malley hired a firm called Vinnell Construction to handle the regrading. Before the project was over, the company would move eight million cubic yards of earth: enough to fill the Empire State Building three times, and then some. Instead of dismantling the Palo Verde school or moving it like so many of the houses that had once surrounded it, the Vinnell workmen took off the roof and simply buried it amid the mountains of dirt. It remains there today, under the parking lots.

Vinnell was a local firm that began in 1931 as an excavation and hauling company and grew in the ensuing decades into something unfamiliar. It worked on the Grand Coulee Dam in Washington and on the Pan-American Highway. It built many of LA's freeways. And while executing projects like the Dodger bid, Vinnell was also slowly morphing from an ambitious Southern California construction outfit into a military contractor and CIA front organization. But that would have nothing to do with baseball. O'Malley so liked Vinnell's performance that once the earthmoving was done, he hired the company to construct the actual stadium, too, insisting that it hire all-union crews.

The construction of the world's first truly modern ballpark would not be cheap. O'Malley would spend more than twenty million dollars, which was far more money than he actually possessed, even after selling Ebbets Field and another stadium in Montreal. He put everything he had, and everything the Dodgers had, on the line. But he was still hard up for a loan. The local banks were scared off by continuing opposition to the stadium by John Holland and the Citizens Committee, by reports that there would be nightmarish traffic on game days, and by the fact that, quite simply, nobody had ever built a stadium on this scale with private money before.

O'Malley was in so much trouble that he thought the entire project might crumble. But help came from an unexpected source. Reese Taylor was the head of Union Oil, which was one of the team's major sponsors. Taylor was also a friend of Norman Chandler, a first-class member of the city's downtown elite; he was part of the clique whose opposition to public housing had helped make Dodger Stadium possible in the first place. Taylor proposed a deal: he would finance the stadium by putting up cash now in exchange for advertising rights in the years to come, thus saving O'Malley from the banks' extortionate interest rates and lifting Union Oil's stature. Union Oil would also get the rights to the gas station being constructed in the center-field parking lot.

The loan from Taylor was a fitting final blow to the people of Palo Verde, La Loma, and Bishop and to the progressive housing advocates who had evicted them in the first place. William Bonelli's *Billion Dollar Blackjack* was published in 1954, just after Poulson was elected and the housing project was killed. In the penultimate chapter, Bonelli predicted that someday "these tracts would end in the hands of the Chandlers or their associates."

It would be unfair to paint mid-century LA politics as totally controlled by a single clique. There were too many competing agendas and too many formidable opponents to the downtown business interests to see it that way. And yet now, with Union Oil and Reese Taylor on board, the tracts had indeed ended up in the hands of Chandler associates.

═══

SLOWLY, THE VINNELL crews carved a deep amphitheater, whose huge shelved steppes would become the foundation for Dodger Stadium's cantilevered grandstands. The actual stadium was built out of thousands of segments of reinforced concrete and steel. The segments, which weighed as much as thirty-seven tons, were cast on-site and then aligned and moved into place like 3-D jigsaw-puzzle pieces with giant cranes. One of these cranes was so heavy that a custom railroad had to be installed to safely transport it across the construction site.

As Emil Praeger and O'Malley's deputy Dick Walsh oversaw the big picture, O'Malley fretted about the details. He ensured that the seats would all be facing slightly inward, toward home plate. He obsessed over their size, material, and paint color. Picture him, nearly sixty years old, rich beyond belief, sitting in sample stadium chairs and contemplating whether they would suit the working-class fans in his adopted city. These were the decisions that fascinated him: the number of restrooms for men and women, the size and brightness of the scoreboards, the width of each aisle, the concessions served on each concourse, the soundproofing of the dugouts. He consulted with local nurseries and garden clubs. He oversaw the raising of the grass that would one day form the Dodgers' playing surface. He worked out complicated drainage issues. "A scientifically designed compost heap would be excellent if it does not violate any city ordinance," he wrote in one memo. "This is important as we have a large landscaping program."

The stadium had to be complete in time for the team's home opener in April 1962, but everything kept going wrong. The stubborn ghosts were at work. Even after grading was complete, a series of political complications held back the start of building until just after Labor Day, 1960. When construction started, tourists streamed in every morning to watch the earthmovers and cranes. Before baseball even began, the stadium and its crew of three hundred construction workers became a destination. Slowly, the stadium began to take shape. Then a crane collapsed, delaying construction. Soon after that, the replacement crane collapsed.

As the fall of 1961 turned to winter, the rains began. Los Angeles was beset by one of the biggest downpours in the city's history. This was the kind of rain that turned the city's hillsides into mudslides, that many years ago had drowned Abrana's chickens. It made construction impossible. It ruined the sod that had been grown so carefully under O'Malley's watchful eye and soaked the new infield dirt. Opening Day was fast approaching, but February 1962 was the rainiest month the city had seen in two decades.

O'Malley blasted air onto the field from a rented Air Force F-84 jet engine mounted on a truck. He used helicopter blades to dry out the sod. He waited for the wet asphalt in the parking lots to dry before repaving it. He took another helicopter ride himself over the site. It was still a site. It was not yet a stadium. He could stand on the flat ground where the hills had once been and look, just like Abrana had, toward City Hall. He had tried his best to deliver Los Angeles what he had promised, tried his best to tame the hills, to turn them into a family-friendly ballpark with clean sight lines, affordable ticket prices, modern conveniences, and ample parking. But Los Angeles still seemed to be fighting him. Even the sky was fighting him.

He began to pay for round-the-clock shifts. Overtime. As the team traveled to Florida for spring training, O'Malley watched his stadium come together little by little. The light towers were tested and then kept on every night until dawn, illuminating the unceasing last-minute preparations. The parking lots were gradually smoothed into shape. The scoreboards were installed, and so was the stadium's Hammond organ.

"We may not have the refinements April 10," O'Malley told the *Herald-Examiner*, "but the roads, seats, diamond, restrooms, and concession stands will be there. So will the parking and the teams."

# 76.

THE EVENING BEFORE HIS MONUMENT OPENED TO THE PUBLIC, WALTER O'Malley hosted a party in the Stadium Club, the private restaurant down the right-field line, where every seat had a view of the field. (The proposed Abner Doubleday Lounge did not materialize.) O'Malley's guests could take in the park as it would look during night games, illuminated by eight spectacular light towers, bright enough to light up the entire city of Seattle. They could see the seats, wide and comfortable, and painted a different color on each level so that, taken together, they mirrored the image of the California beaches from yellow sand to turquoise sea to azure sky.

There was no game going on, but the place was buzzing. Workers were still putting together the wiring on the giant message board over the left-field pavilion. Down in the outfield, the grounds crew was trying to get the grass to look right. The rains had left the sod splotchy and discolored, so O'Malley took the advice of a studio executive and had it dyed dark green. But the green dye wasn't sitting right either. On every level, in every aisle, was a worker.

It was chaos, but it was also the final deep breath for O'Malley before the world would see and judge his creation. He had lived full-time at the Statler Hotel throughout construction, forsaking the family home in Lake Arrowhead. This was the culmination of his dream. In the final weeks he had hardly slept. He would have liked a few more months to get everything in order. To better train his staff (the ushers would at least have their uniforms of gray pants, burgundy coats, and white straw hats) and to better landscape his parking lots. He would have liked the county builders to have finished the off-ramp that was supposed to connect the 110 freeway with the stadium. But the season was starting. This would have to do.

*Dodger Stadium*

That night, April 9, 1962, was the first time an official audience gathered to watch the sun set behind the Dodger Stadium bleachers and see how the park spread its arms to the San Gabriel Mountains to the north and how the palm trees planted carefully in the middle distance framed the view, supplying what the Dodgers' landscape architect called a "skyline and silhouette effect." They were Mexican fan palms, a species native to Sonora and Baja California. So tall and narrow as to be improbable. Some were fifty years old. Most had been rescued from a street-widening project on Pico Boulevard in Santa Monica. Others were taken from the estate of Leslie Coombs Brand, a land tycoon who had developed the suburb of Glendale at the turn of the century. Now they were part of Walter O'Malley's paradise.

=

THE MORNING OF April 10, there were forty police officers and one hundred attendants assigned to direct traffic in the parking lots of Dodger Stadium. There was a helicopter hovering overhead to give orders. There had been warnings about an epic traffic jam, but it never materialized. The lines were long but civilized. The Cincinnati Reds team bus was snarled at one of the entrances, forced to wait its turn among the early-arriving fans and to pay $4 to enter.

This was just as well because to many fans, the game itself was an afterthought. They were there to see the building. They arrived early and watched the ticket takers literally unwrap the brand-new turnstiles. They wandered the grounds and then the concourses and listened to the organ music. They noticed what was missing: public water fountains (not even Walter O'Malley was perfect), a functioning elevator, and ushers with a clear sense of where to guide people. But mostly they saw what was right there in front of them: the unexpected beauty of it.

Before Dodger Stadium, there had been no reason to think of a ballpark as something that could be beautiful. But the design was resonant. There was something inherently pleasing about the slope of the grandstands and about the wavy triangular concrete roofs over the outfield pavilions. Beyond the pavilion roofs were the palms, then the tops of the trees that O'Malley had planted in the parking lot. Beyond the tree line were the hills of Elysian Park, green with the recent rains. Sometimes big puffy white clouds rested atop the hills like pillows. Sometimes you could see straight through to the San Gabriel Mountains. Dodger Stadium felt new but also familiar, modern but also somehow traditional. It was cavernous but not in a way that made you feel small. It was tucked away from the city, but it felt like Los Angeles.

Dignitaries and celebrities were scattered throughout the park. Frank Sinatra got stuck in line waiting for a broken-down elevator. The commissioner of baseball, Ford C. Frick, was there. So was National League President Warren Giles. Norris Poulson and his wife sat in the subterranean dugout club. Roz Wyman, who had been at the previous night's gala, was rewarded for all her hard work with a master key to the stadium. She was only thirty-one years old—younger than many of the players on the field—and she had already changed the course of baseball and LA history.

But O'Malley reserved the honor of throwing out the first pitch for his wife, Kay. Depending who you asked, O'Malley was an ambitious businessman, a cunning negotiator, a callous traitor, or a visionary like no other in the history of baseball. But he had always been a family man. To O'Malley, work and family had always been intertwined, part of a single collective project. Kay had always been by his side and in his ear. Their daughter, Terry, and son, Peter, had always been included in the decision-making process. The success of the Dodgers, the move west, the construction of this stadium: all of it had been a family endeavor. As Walter had told Peter, Dodger Stadium was not just a ballpark or a business triumph but also a "monument to the O'Malleys."

The hot dogs cost a quarter. "The Star-Spangled Banner" was sung by a soprano from Mexico City named Alma Pedroza. The starter for the Dodgers was Johnny Podres, who had been the MVP of the 1955 World Series back in Brooklyn. For the Reds it was Bob Purkey, a knuckleballer who had pitched for the Hollywood Stars back before LA became a big-league town.

WILLIE DAVIS JOGGED out to center field as Podres took the mound. Everything was about to come together for him. Everything was always coming together for Willie, then falling apart and then coming back together again. His cleats sank into the soggy dark turf. The green dye rubbed off on them. He was on his way to the first great season in what would be a long career. In 1962 he would bat .285 with 21 home runs and 32 stolen bases, and make it clear that the era of Duke Snider was over. The position of Dodgers center fielder had been passed from a white man who was raised in segregated Compton and had blossomed in Brooklyn to a black man who was raised in a Boyle Heights housing project and would make his name in a stadium where, for one crucial moment, another housing project was supposed to stand. Brooklyn was over. Los Angeles was forever changed. And Duke Snider, playing right field that day, would be traded in the off-season.

Duke would be going back to New York, which made sense. He could fade away in the city that made him a star and that loved him better than Compton ever could or LA ever could or even Fallbrook, the small town near San Diego where he finally bought his avocado farm, ever could. He would play two more years—one for the Mets, the expansion team tasked with replacing both the Dodgers and Giants in New York—and then briefly in San Francisco for the Giants.

Instead, Walter O'Malley was here, with Willie Davis in center field, with a stadium that should never have existed. It was all a fluke. A historical quirk. The accidental alignment of so many seemingly unrelated events. There was no other way to explain the atmosphere in this place: the way that everything was amplified but also decompressed and the way that the sound of a candy wrapper opening in the seats or a gloved hand thudding against a bag on a close play rang clear and then lingered. Even on that first afternoon among the red, white, and blue bunting, with the sun high in the sky, Dodger Stadium was otherworldly. But that kind of cosmic stuff made sense to Willie. He saw it.

You could have drawn a line from Dodger Stadium to Willie's old neighbor Frank Wilkinson at Estrada Courts, and Willie would have been right there with you. Frank Wilkinson, the man who put it all on the line to build housing projects like the one Willie grew up in. The man who lost everything so that somebody else could come along and build this beautiful ballpark. Frank came home from prison shortly before the stadium opened. He liked baseball well enough, but for years he refused to visit Dodger Stadium. The stadium—its very existence—was an insult to him.

You could have told Willie Davis about Palo Verde, La Loma, and Bishop, and he would have been right there with that too. You could have told him that Abrana and Manuel Aréchiga had moved to City Terrace, to a little house on another high hill. Abrana and Manuel had chickens and dogs in City Terrace, and a little garden; Manuel built a new still in the basement to make his *matagente*. On Sundays they would always have the whole family over for parties. You could have told Willie that they still had not withdrawn the $10,039 waiting for them in escrow. You could have told him that they could see the lights of Dodger Stadium from their window and that every time they did, it broke their hearts all over again. He would have said he knew that feeling. "You're always on your own," Willie said once. "Even when you're on a team, you're on your own."

The first batter of the game, the Reds' Eddie Kasko, hit a double to left field. The second batter, Vada Pinson, singled him home. It took until Duke Snider came up in the bottom of the second for the Dodgers to record their first hit in Dodger Stadium. It took until the bottom of the fourth for the Dodgers to score their first runs, when Snider and Jim Gilliam came around on a Ron Fairly double.

The score was tied at two going into the seventh inning when Podres got in trouble. Pinson doubled with one out, and Podres walked Frank Robinson intentionally. Then Wally Post, a big power-hitting outfielder, crushed a fly ball to dead center, over Willie Davis's head and over the fence behind him.

Nobody ever thought Willie Davis was good enough. Even though he played for two decades and even though he played in one of the toughest eras for hitters of all time. They said he was all tools and no brains. "He can run, hit, throw, and field," they said. "The only thing he's never been able to do is think."

Willie could think fine. His mind just wasn't built the way that some people thought a ballplayer's mind was supposed to be. He did the hard work. He learned to bat left-handed. He put up the numbers year in and year out, some years better than others. But he wanted it so bad, he hated to lose so much, he hated to fail so much, that he could never stay the same. The balance was there if you took the long view, but it was never there day in and day out. He was always changing his stance, tweaking his swing, looking for the right answer. He was a seeker. He wasn't Jackie Robinson, and he wasn't Duke Snider. He was Willie Davis. And as the Dodgers became a dominant club in the 1960s, that was more than good enough.

It was Willie Davis and Tommy Davis, no relation. It was Maury Wills and John Roseboro, the man who inherited the catching role from Roy Campanella. It was Don Drysdale and Sandy Koufax. With this beautiful ballpark and with a younger set of players, the Dodgers stopped being the team that used to play in Brooklyn. They became a product of their new environment. They starred in Hollywood movies and TV shows. They played to the stadium's spacious outfield dimensions, they ran like hell, and they pitched like hell and smothered teams in the oppressive symmetry and deadening air of Chavez Ravine.

The Dodgers lost on Opening Day 6–3. The Wally Post home run was too much to overcome. By the time they came up to bat in the bottom of the ninth, the stadium was three-quarters empty. This would be a recurring condition in Dodger Stadium, and it was one of the few kinks that O'Malley was not able to work out. By the following season, there were drinking fountains, escalators, and even more flowers; the ushers knew where everything was.

There would be no monorail, no dancing fountain, no infrared heating. But there were people, and that was the most important thing. The Dodgers won ball games and set attendance records, and O'Malley kept ticket prices low. The stadium evolved little by little, but it never really changed, even as the city around it did.

As the Dodgers established themselves in their new home in the 1960s, a century of systemic exclusion, dirty politics, and racist policing finally began to boil over in the rest of the city. LA was a fragmented, segregated, and unequal place. Frank Wilkinson believed that these problems were a direct result of the demise of public housing.

Frank Wilkinson never changed. After he got back from prison, he set out once again to defeat HUAC. He met and fell in love with an activist housewife in Ohio named Donna Childers and divorced Jean. Donna and her three children came out to LA and moved with Frank into a house in Windsor Hills, a neighborhood that had been developed by Fritz Burns, of all people. By then, Jeff, Tony, and Jo were living in the Bay Area, and Jean moved up there too, settling in Berkeley and getting back to teaching, the career she had lost in 1952.

Frank continued to lecture and to organize even after HUAC was finally abolished in 1975. But then Frank had another one of those great earth-shifting moments. It was like Bethlehem all over again. It was like sitting in the witness stand in Judge Otto Emme's courtroom and getting asked, for the first time, to recite his political affiliations. Frank learned through Freedom of Information Act requests and an ensuing lawsuit that the FBI had been surveilling him since 1942, when he led that first housing-integration protest with Monsignor O'Dwyer. They had continued to watch him for more than thirty years: before, during, and after his stint in prison. His FBI file ran to 132,000 pages. All of a sudden, everything made sense. Reading the files, it was like looking back on the inexplicable and mysterious events of his life with the benefit of a decoder ring.

They had spied on him constantly and worked to subvert him at every turn. All those resources. All that manpower, just for him. He learned that the witness who testified against him in front of HUAC was considered unreliable by the agency and that J. Edgar Hoover had taken a personal interest in his case; every time he went somewhere to speak, the agency worked to infiltrate his life and undermine him, even going so far as to recruit members of the American Nazi Party as counterdemonstrators. It was all right there in the files. The dossier that William Parker had shown to Fletcher Bowron and then waved in front of the television cameras suddenly had an explanation, too.

But worse was the revelation that in 1964 the FBI had been aware of an assassination attempt to be made on Frank as he spoke at an ACLU meeting and that the agency had done nothing to try and stop it. There was a memo from the day of the meeting sent from the LA field office to Hoover laying out the name of the would-be assassin and the bureau's plan to stake out the house and observe. There was no mention of interceding. There was no mention of warning Frank away. Frank attended the meeting, oblivious to what could have happened. The following day's memo read, simply, "No attempt was made."

Frank lived to be ninety-one years old. Long enough to speak to my high school history class in 2004 and plant the seeds for this book. He outlived Poulson and Parker and Hoover and Burns; he lived long enough to see himself become a mythological figure in the story of Los Angeles and America. Toward the end, he went back to Douglas, Arizona, with Jo and his second wife, Donna. The old house was still there. He remembered the coyote and the smell of leather upholstery.

It did not take long for Frank to start going to Dodger games. He liked baseball, and he liked being among people. But he could never come to the park and not see what he felt was supposed to be there. You could work for a better world, but that did not mean the world was going to comply. "It's absolutely the tragedy of my life," he said. But to Frank the tragedy wasn't just the evictions. The tragedy was that the public housing was never built, that the better world he envisioned never came to be. After the Watts Riots of 1965, Frank wrote as much in a column for *Frontier Magazine:* "Had our plans been allowed to bear fruit, tens of thousands of African-American and Mexican American children would have been lifted out of the stifling pressures of the ghettos, into the good air of integrated, beautifully designed, low rent communities. Year after year, tens of thousands more would have followed, and we could have begun the process of reintegrating the old ghetto areas—areas that burst into flame in the uprising of 1965, and are even more isolated and run-down today."

Frank believed that every child could have grown up to achieve their dreams. They could have grown up like Willie Davis.

In the 1966 World Series, Willie Davis set a painful record. The Dodger pitcher at the time was Sandy Koufax in what would turn out to be his final career start. According to Koufax biographer Jane Leavy, afterward, the pitcher walked over to Davis on the bench. "Koufax draped an arm around Davis' shoulder and said, 'Don't let them get you down.'"

Two years later, Davis had stolen three bases in a single World Series game, equaling a record held by Ty Cobb. The pitcher in that game was also Koufax.

Willie Davis would struggle. He would make tons of money and blow it all right away. He would do time in jail. He would become a Buddhist and chant in the clubhouse and suffer the ridicule of his teammates for practicing what he believed in. He would become a golf instructor and teach the fundamentals like Kenny Myers had taught him baseball. He would always find his way back. Everything coming together again. Past. Present. Future. He would be a father and a grandfather. Three generations. Three errors, three steals, 3-Dog. He would talk slow and cool like he always had and move through life like he was sitting and watching the trains go by.

Willie's final home game at Dodger Stadium came, like his first, against the Cincinnati Reds. It was the closing weeks of the 1973 season. Willie was just thirty-three years old, and he was the only player still on the team from when the stadium opened in 1962. Only the manager, Walter Alston, and the owner, Walter O'Malley, remained. Only the stadium remained.

Willie pinch-hit for catcher Steve Yeager in the bottom of the seventh inning and lined an RBI single to left field. Then, in the ninth, he flied out to right. After the 1973 season, Willie was traded to the Montreal Expos. He would bounce around the game for another decade. He would play a stint in Japan. But he would always be a Dodger. He would always find his way back. Willie Davis believed in reincarnation.

The Dodgers were marching toward future glories not yet imagined. They were marching toward Steve Garvey, Davey Lopes, Bill Russell, and Ron Cey. They were marching toward Fernando Valenzuela, a pitcher who was so much more than the Mexican Sandy Koufax that O'Malley had joked about signing. Valenzuela, a shy and confounding left-hander from a small town in Sonora, did more than anybody else to realize O'Malley's dreams for what his stadium could be: always full and guaranteed to please, no matter what happened on the field, a place for true civic communion. In the 1980s, Dodger Stadium became Valenzuela's stage. He elevated the franchise, the sport, and the city, then transcended them all.

When Valenzuela pitched, his eyes rolling upward toward the heavens, his body easing into that slow and rhythmic delivery, Jaime Jarrín's voice carried all the way from the Dodger Stadium press box to the farthest reaches of the Spanish-speaking world. Jarrín became Valenzuela's interpreter and his confidant. And Valenzuela became something more than a brilliant, charismatic pitcher. He became a phenomenon and then a symbol.

To some people, Fernandomania was the bookend that the story of Palo Verde, La Loma, and Bishop needed. As if because Fernando drew Mexican fans to the ballpark, the scars simply faded away and then disappeared like some trick of magical realism. But they didn't. No matter how much the city loved its baseball team or its ballpark, the scars couldn't disappear. Baseball may have mystical powers, but it cannot erase the past. It cannot redeem us. The beauty of Dodger Stadium is broad; it is collective. It belongs to everybody. But the pain suffered by people of Palo Verde, La Loma, and Bishop was specific. It was theirs.

=

IN AUGUST 1962, a few months after Dodger Stadium opened, Juan Aréchiga was convicted of smuggling. "Defendant knowingly received, concealed, and facilitated the transportation and concealment of 133 bottles of various types of Mexican liquor," said the sentencing document. He got eighteen months. Later on, he would tell his grandkids, "Don't do the crime if you can't do the time."

Juan worked for the Dodgers for a while in the 1970s. He used to clean up the stadium after games. He was right back where he started. Right back where he was born. He could walk out and into the parking lots and picture the land the way it used to be, before the hills were flattened and the earth pushed aside. Before the houses were bulldozed and rolled away, and the trees uprooted. Somewhere underneath it all were the rocks from his parents' retaining wall, the two-by-fours his father had put up to frame that very first house in Palo Verde.

Palo Verde was gone, but it was still there. You could feel it sometimes in the parking lots late at night when there were packs of coyotes wandering through. You could feel it in the way every-body acted when the community got back together at the reunion dances that Gene Cabral would throw, and then at picnics at Ely-sian Park, in front of the rec center they had helped build in that last optimistic moment before the eviction letters came. Everybody bickering and reminiscing and giving each other shit and being happy and sad at the same time. They were all spread out now, but something was still holding them together.

Abrana and Manuel kept on living, kept on surviving after the evictions. Day by day, they managed to adjust. Abrana was fond of roller derby and pro wrestling. She and her daughter Celia would pack tacos and take the kids to the Sports Arena. Abrana was not completely cynical either. She should have hated politics, but even after everything that happened, she still found herself adoring the Kennedys. Once, her granddaughter Helen told me, Abrana touched John Kennedy's foot at a parade in Los Angeles. She was ecstatic.

When Manuel died, in 1971, Abrana was alone for the first time since she lost her first husband in Morenci. But she was not totally alone. She always had a child or a grandchild, a niece or nephew to keep her company. The Aréchigas may have been physically up-rooted, but they were still a family.

Shortly after Manuel's death, a *Los Angeles Times* reporter came to interview Abrana. He described a person who was largely the same as she had been in Palo Verde: pacing her house, roaming "around the vastness of her extreme personal moods." She was still thin, still gray-haired, and still cooked her own dinners and cleaned her own floors. She was still Two Guns Brooks, but now she had no children or neighbors to yell at from her porch. She had no bat-tles left to fight. She got by on Social Security and, as she told the writer, "my tears."

In August 1972, fifty years after she had come to Los Ange-les, but now without her home and without her husband, Abrana Aréchiga died. She was buried next to Manuel. On a hill, of course. They have matching rectangular grave markers etched with the scene of a sunrise coming over tall mountains set among the trees.

Abrana was gone, and Palo Verde was gone, and so was the Santo Niño church where she had prayed for so many years. But the old priest, Father Tomas Matin, was still alive. He had held onto the Santo Niño church registers. When Abrana died, he wrote her name into the book in the same looping cursive he had used for all the baptisms, marriages, and funerals that had marked the passing years in Palo Verde. She was still part of the community.

The church books are still there, sitting on a shelf in the rectory at St. Peter's on Broadway, about halfway between Dodger Stadium and City Hall. The lives of Palo Verde, La Loma, and Bishop scrawled onto the smudged pages. The life and death of Abrana Aréchiga and the people she loved. The writing of the priest, shakier in old age, weaving one last thread back into Abrana's past. There were her parents' names, Vacilla Bañuelos and Juan Cabral. There was her daughter Lola as next of kin. There was her age: seventy-five years of life on Earth. And there was her place of birth, in Mexico, high up among the rocks.

# ACKNOWLEDGMENTS

If you read the preface of this book (prefaces, like acknowledgments, are optional), you may recall that it has its origins in a classroom. Frank Wilkinson visited my US history class at Culver City High School in 2003 at the invitation of a teacher named Andrea Spero (then Andrea McEvoy). I don't remember much of what he actually said that day. But I am certain that this book would not exist in any form if not for that visit—if not for the teacher who made it happen. I am also certain that I would not be the writer or person I am today if not for the many caring, thoughtful, and patient teachers, mentors, coaches, and editors who have helped me along the way.

My first and most important teachers are my mom and dad, Debbie and Neil. Thank you for teaching me to be curious, empathetic, and steadfast. I have tried to be. Thank you for encouraging me to be a writer, even in moments when it has seemed like a silly decision. Thank you for the gift of Spanish. Michael and Evan, thank you for being the best brothers and best friends a person could ask for. Thank you for keeping me honest. I am lucky to have been raised by a village and to remain surrounded by a loving family: Shelly, Janine, Mark, Cindy, and Joel—thank you. Lesley, Danielle, Travis, Jared, Riley, and Ryan—thank you. Cheryl and Mike—thank you.

This book has been percolating in my subconscious for more than a decade. It has gone through many different iterations in numerous abandoned MS Word documents and notebook pages. For years, I worried that the subject matter would be too esoteric, too weird, too Los Angeles. The person who ultimately convinced me otherwise is my agent, David Patterson. I thank him for believing in me as a writer and for supporting my ideas, no matter how seemingly obscure. I hope that I have proven David right: that although this story may be specific in terms of its action, it is universal in terms of its emotional resonance.

Ben Adams, my editor at PublicAffairs, has seen that resonance all along. I appreciate him for believing in me and this project. When I was so deep into my own head I wasn't sure if I was even still writing the same book I had set out to, Ben listened patiently, and he helpfully nudged me forward. He has helped me find the one true story at the heart of the many small stories that make up this text and allowed me to write (and then cut) my way into the best possible version of it.

This book would not have existed without the friendship of Ted Walker, Craig Robinson, and Pete Beatty. Ted was the first person I met who shared my spaced-out, cosmic version of baseball fandom, and he, more than anybody else, encouraged me to write about it. Craig taught me to see the game in brand-new ways and was there alongside me as the Mexico portions of this book took shape in my subconscious. Pete has simply always been there: to encourage me to plow, to remind me to trust my instincts. I couldn't ask for a better friend.

When I moved back home to Los Angeles in 2014, I had two magnificent strokes of luck. The first one was getting hired to work at VICE Sports. I learned more from my friends and colleagues in that small, underappreciated corner of the internet than I had any right to. Thank you to Jorge, Caitlin, Sean, Patrick, Aaron, Karisa, Dave, Mike P, Michael P, Brian, and Liam.

The second stroke of luck was signing up for a fiction-writing workshop at UCLA Extension taught by Lou Mathews. Lou and Alison—thank you for bringing my family into yours. I'll ascribe your decision to do so to the mystery of personality.

Thank you to the experts, scholars, journalists, and librarians who shared their time: Jerald Podair, Cindy Hayostek, Lawrence

Bouett, Adam Goodman, Rodolfo Acuña, Matt Garcia, Gabriel Thomson, Max Baumgarten, Simon Judkins, Christopher Hawthorne, Jon Weisman, Bill McCawley, Jesús Alberto Rubio, Brent Shyer, Robert Schweppe, and Michele Welsing. Thank you to the Society for American Baseball Research, the Oviatt Library at Cal State Northridge, the John F. Kennedy Library at Cal State Los Angeles, the Charles Young Research Library at UCLA, the Getty Research Institute, and the Southern California Library.

Thank you to John Schulian for your wisdom on the page and off.

Thank you to Will Camponovo, Reeves Wiedeman, Patrick Dubuque, Chris Crawford, Nathaniel Friedman, and the Westshire Drive home group. Thank you to the poets and writers at the University of Washington—in Seattle and in Rome.

Thank you to Notable Illustrator Adam Villacin.

Thank you to Peter O'Malley for opening a piece of his father's life to me.

The story of Palo Verde, La Loma, and Bishop does not belong to me. When I first set out to write this book, I thought I would write a comprehensive history of the communities before their destruction. But the deeper I dug, the more clear it became that this story is too big for one volume, and it is theirs to tell. I hope they continue to tell it.

Thank you to everybody who sat with me for an interview or allowed me to bug them over the phone. Chief among them are Jeannie Aréchiga, Beto Elias, Camilo Arevalo, Feliz Arevalo, Al Zepeda, Mario Zepeda, Carmen Acosta, Gene Cabral, Pete Urrutia, Helen Lamp, Johnny Lamp, Dolores Klimenko, Donna Wilkinson, Jeffry Wilkinson, Tony Wilkinson, and especially Jo Wilkinson.

Thank you to the Wilkinson family for your radical honesty.

Thank you to Buried Under the Blue. Thank you to Melissa Aréchiga, Irving Aréchiga, and Vincent Montalvo for helping me understand the social and emotional depth of this story, for not compromising, and for challenging my thinking every step of the way.

Thank you to all the friends who checked up on me, distracted me, and encouraged me.

Thank you to my grandparents, Murray, Rosita, Henry, and Rose. You taught me to be inquisitive. You showed me what it was to persevere. You taught me the meaning of history.

Thank you to Clay and Marco. You were always there to shut my laptop when it was time to stop working and always there to remind me what was most important.

Thank you to Janelle, my best friend, my editor, and my everything else.

# NOTES ON SOURCES

The early drafts of this book were heavy with in-text citations, references, and explanations of my own research practices. But the more I wrote and edited, the more I realized that these explanations bogged down the story. I have organized these notes in a way that befits the structure of this book, which comprises short chapters that jump between settings and story lines; the notes for some chapters are long and individuated. The notes for others are bunched together.

## Two Notes/Preface

The best resource on the early history of the communities is the independent researcher Lawrence Bouett, whose work got me looking at maps and other primary sources from nineteenth-century LA. His website is chavezravine.org. The original Julian Chavez land grant can be found in the Huntington Library's online collection. For information on the Tongva people (also known as the Gabrielino tribe), see *The First Angelinos* by William McCawley.

## Chapters 1, 3, 6, 8

I pieced together the Aréchiga/Cabral family history from a combination of oral interviews and primary-source documents, including census forms, immigration forms, draft cards, and church registers. For information on emigration from Zacatecas to Arizona, I relied on Rodolfo Acuña's *Corridors of Migration, Borderline Americans* by Katherine Benton-Cohen, and *Beyond Smoke and Mirrors* by Douglas Massey, Jorge Durand, and Nolan J. Malone. I want to thank Dr. Acuña and Dr. Adam Goodman for taking time to walk me through this history over the phone.

In the course of research, I visited Clifton/Morenci as well as a variety of other mining towns in Southwest Arizona. The scenic picture of the towns is the product of firsthand reporting, as well as browsing old issues of *The Copper Era and Morenci Leader*, accessed via the invaluable Arizona Memory Project. I heavily consulted *Arizona: A History* by Thomas Sheridan and *Race and Labor in Western Copper: The Fight for Equality 1896–1918* by Philip J. Mellinger. For a good explanation of the Immigration Act of 1917, see Barbara Driscoll's *The Tracks North: The Railroad Bracero Program of World War II*. The wage information came from James R. Kluger's master's thesis, "The Clifton Morenci Strike of 1915–16."

The best description of the Mexican cemetery in Morenci that I have seen was in a remarkable spiral-bound volume titled *The Writings of Al Fernandez*. Fernandez, a former newspaper columnist and historian, was around in those hard mining days. For a quick rundown on the transition from tunnels to an open-pit mine in Morenci, check out David F. Briggs's *History of the Copper Mountain (Morenci) Mining District, Greenlee County, Arizona*. The Greenlee County Historical Society in Clifton was a great source for firsthand knowledge about the district and the hard work of copper mining in general. I also appreciated the vivid portrait of early-twentieth-century copper mining in the short documentary *Los Mineros*.

## Chapters 2, 4, 9

Amy K. Polk's *A Wicked War* was a guiding star for me as I learned about the Mexican-American War. This chapter was also informed by the early pages of James McPherson's *Battle Cry of Freedom* and Will Fowler's *Santa Anna of Mexico*. Grant really did call Scott "the finest specimen of manhood my eyes have ever beheld" in his memoirs (unless the rumors are true, and it really was ghostwritten by Mark Twain).

The myth of Santa Anna and his leg has been told and retold in books, articles, and pamphlets for almost as long as baseball has been the national pastime. The earliest credulous retelling of the story I could find is in *Terry's Guide to Mexico: The New Standard Guidebook to the Mexican Republic*, published in 1909. (*Terry's Guide* is home to some of the most antiquated, racist writing on Mexico you can find, but the prose is so over the top as to be almost psychedelic, and Terry definitely did his research.)

The sections on this book on Abner Doubleday and the invention of baseball are deeply indebted to John Thorn, the dean of baseball historians. His book *Baseball in the Garden of Eden* lives up to its title as both a vivid history and a nearly biblical exploration of just how weird and spirit-laden the early game was. It was Thorn who dug up the letter from Doubleday to Emerson. To get a good sense of Theosophy and Madame Blavatsky, I recommend reading some of *Isis Unveiled*, then of William Emmette Coleman's (contemporaneous) investigations into her plagiarism. In addition to Thorn, I turned to Mark Lamster's book *Spalding's World Tour* for a good perspective on Spalding the man and Spalding the salesman. Spalding and Thorn made it easy to tell Spalding and Lizzie's unlikely love story. The Point Loma compound where they lived is now Point Loma Nazarene University. Spalding's "American Dad" letter was reproduced by George Vescey in *Baseball: A History of America's Game.*

## Chapters 5, 7

Every chapter about Frank Wilkinson in this book owes a debt to his massive oral history interview, conducted by Dale Treleven and housed at UCLA. However, memory is fallible. Where I could, I always cross-checked Frank's memories against newspaper reports and other interviews. The chapter about life in Douglas was put together with the benefit of contemporaneous newspaper accounts from the *Bisbee Daily Review.* When I visited Douglas and wandered into the Historical Society, I was lucky to run into Cindy Hayostek, a great historian with endless energy for research. Cindy taught me a ton about Douglas, and she managed to dig up primary-source documents from the Wilkinsons' time in Arizona, such as photos and pages from old church yearbooks, even an obituary for Dr. A. M. Wilkinson published in the local paper long after he had already left for California. This chapter also relied on the accounts written by Frank's sister Betty in her self-published book, *Life and Times of Betty Evans.* I was able to confirm details of bootlegging raids around Douglas in newspaper clippings in the *Bisbee Daily Review.* One such headline, from March 3, 1922: "Officers Make Many Raids in Pursuit of Elusive 'White Elephant.'"

## Chapters 10, 12

The population growth of LA in the 1920s is right there in the census results, but because immigrants from Mexico were classified as white, the demographics were skewed. The classic read on the subject is *Becoming Mexican American* by George Sanchez. In *East Los Angeles: History of a Barrio*, Richard Romo does good work on population growth as well. Marshall Stimson appears all over the place in early-twentieth-century histories of Los Angeles. His papers are held at the Huntington Library in San Marino.

For more on the ethnic demography of Palo Verde, see Lawrence Bouett's 2015 blog post "Were the Chavez Ravine Evictions Racist?" at chavezravine.org.

The Los Angeles Department of Building and Safety has a handy tool that allows you to look up old building records, including those in Palo Verde and other communities that no longer exist. The war over the brickyards in Los Angeles was omnipresent in the city's newspapers in the 1920s, especially the *Los Angeles Times.* I highly recommend William Deverell's *Whitewashed Adobe* for a rich portrait of the working life of Mexican immigrants and a deep exploration of how Los Angeles was physically built in the early twentieth century.

The stories of life in Palo Verde were compiled from interviews with residents, family members, and descendants. The sections on anti-Mexican activism are informed primarily by the well-researched and insightful book *Decade of Betrayal* by Francisco E. Balderrama and Raymond Rodriguez. Fittingly, Balderrama is also a leading scholar of Mexican American baseball history.

## Chapters 11, 14, 17, 20, 22, 25

I pieced together the early days of Frank's life in LA from his oral history and interviews with his children. There was also a wealth of correspondence in his personal archive at the Southern California Library. The letter from Frank to his mother came courtesy of Jo Wilkinson, who patiently (and generously) dug through boxes of old family treasures with me. The David Graham Fischer story came up in Frank's oral history. At first it seemed like something he made up, but there it was in the *Los Angeles Times* archives: not just the stories about Fischer but also ads he took out for the Inter-Oceanic University. Copies of *The Hooded Asp* are available on specialty-books websites but are prohibitively expensive. Frank told of his time in Maxwell Street in his oral history. There is ample correspondence from his journey in the Wilkinson papers at the Southern California Library. His sister Betty wrote about Frank's travels in her memoir as well. (The changes he went through were quite shocking to the family.) Gilbert Harrison's statement about Frank's sincerity appeared in his own oral history through the JFK Library. (Harrison went on to be the owner and editor of *The New Republic*.) The hearing-aid receipts remain scattered about Frank's personal papers. (Frank kept everything.) Frank also told these stories repeatedly over the years, so his return from Europe and the ensuing events took on a kind of fable quality in his life, like a superhero origin story. A side note: Frank's traveling companion, Del Harter, did not become a minister either. He became a schoolteacher in San Diego, where he died tragically attempting to swim the length of Mission Bay on a dare.

The A. M. Wilkinson-Guy McAfee kerfuffle played out in the pages of the local papers, as did the ensuing CIVIC-related violence. In addition to *L.A. Noir* by Buntin, I found Tom Sitton's *Los Angeles Transformed: Fletcher Bowron's Urban Reform Revival* to be a great resource and a great read. The Robert Browning poem was included in the A. M. Wilkinson funeral program, a copy of which I dug up with Jo Wilkinson from a box in her home.

## Chapters 13, 41

The history of Chutes Park and Jim Morley is told exceptionally in Dennis Snelling's history of the Pacific Coast League, *The Greatest Minor League*. I turned to Snelling repeatedly as a guide in writing about the early history of baseball in Los Angeles; he is also responsible for writing brilliantly on Rube Waddell. The best write-up of Chutes Park itself is probably Jeffrey Stanton's article on it at Westland.net. Stanton is an independent historian of Venice, California. Jim Morley was also a regular in the *Los Angeles Times* during his run as owner of the Angels. He was one of many minor characters in this book who probably deserve their own biographies. The other great piece on Chutes Park is an article titled "The Short Life of a Downtown Amusement Park" in *L.A. Downtown News*, published in 2006 by Jay Berman and Sesar Carreño.

The early history of the Pacific Coast League was so insane it was nearly impossible to keep up with. For the story of Hal Chase, I turned to contemporaneous newspaper stories, as well as Al Figone's article "The Pacific Coast League Scandal of 1919: Hal Chase Had Nothing on Babe Borton" and Robert C. Hoie's "The Hal Chase Case." For more on the early Pacific Coast League, I recommend Amy Sissington's *The Integration of the Pacific Coast League: Race and Baseball on the West Coast* and Chris Goode's *California Baseball: From the Pioneers to the Glory Years*.

The Farmer John slaughterhouse is located at 3049 East Vernon Avenue. Twice a week, animal-rights activists visit to offer water to pigs in trucks who are on their way to their ends. John Schulian's *Twilight of the Longball Gods* offers the atmospherics and the little touches of detail. I also turned to the work of the pre-eminent Pacific Coast League historian Dick Beverage, including his piece "When the Angels and Stars Ruled Los Angeles" for SABR.

## Chapter 15

No subject in this book presented more conflicting information than the tragic death of Manuel Jr. I struggled with how best to present this story. Ultimately, I decided that it was important to present all the evidence but to make clear that I believed the family's version of events. Three relatives—Gene Cabral, Helen Lamp, and Dolores Klimenko—all confirmed some version of it independently of one another. In the 1920s and 1930s, racists used false claims about tuberculosis rates as a way to argue that Mexicans did not belong in LA. The work of Emily K. Abel on this subject is sensational. Her article "From Exclusion to Expulsion: Mexicans and Tuberculosis Control in Los Angeles, 1914–1940" does its subject justice and is an insightful work of historical writing as well. Abel points out that before death, and even in autopsies, white health officials were likely to misdiagnose Mexicans as having suffered from tuberculosis.

## Chapter 16

Jennifer Mathews's *Chicle* remains the gold standard on the subject of chicle and gum. Santa Anna's late travels and career machinations are chronicled expertly by the aforementioned Will Fowler in *Santa Anna of Mexico*. Thomas Adams's patent for chewing gum (US 111798A) was filed in 1871: "My invention consists in a method of preparing the natural product known as chickly to produce a chewing-gum." Another good resource for chewing-gum history is Michael Redclift's *Chewing Gum: The Fortunes of Taste*. For more on early baseball cards, see Marshall Fogel's thorough article "The History of the Goudey Gum Company" at psacard.com.

## Chapters 18, 21

I learned of the trips up to the *piscas* in interviews with various members of the Palo Verde, La Loma, and Bishop communities. It was not just the Aréchigas but also nearly every family who traveled to work the fields. Beto Elias, who passed away in the course of my writing this book, told me the story of going up with his family and not returning with any kind of savings. Nobody I interviewed spun better yarns than Beto; his stories are a book unto themselves. The legend of Two Guns Brooks was passed down by Beto, Pete Urrutia, Helen Lamp, Gene Cabral, and other community and family members.

## Chapter 19

Clifford Clinton's life is captured in full color by his grandson Edmond Clinton III in the book *Clifton's and Clifford Clinton: A Cafeteria and a Crusader*. The origins of CIVIC—including A. M. Wilkinson's place in it—have been written about in many histories of crime in Los Angeles, but rarely as a subject unto themselves. I thank Simon Judkins of USC for taking the time to correspond with me, for teaching me all about domestic surveillance in Los Angeles, for forwarding me materials, and for writing the article "Citizen Surveillance: CIVIC and the Investigation of Vice in the City of Los Angeles, 1935–1938." I also turned to Jon Buntin's excellent book *L.A. Noir* and the online writings of the crime author J. H. Graham at her personal website, jhgraham.com.

## Chapter 23

Duke Snider's autobiography, *The Duke of Flatbush*, is a fun and relatively frank read. More on the Duke can be found in Peter Golenbock's oral history *Bums*. The racist Compton Chamber of Commerce language was unearthed by the historian Josh Sides and featured in his article "Straight into Compton: American Dreams, Urban Nightmares, and the Metamorphosis of a Black Suburb." Sides (a great writer on LA) was instrumental for me in developing an understanding of racist real-estate policies and practices.

## Chapter 24

Thanks to Lola's daughter Dolores for telling me the story of Lola's romance with Porfidio Vargas and for showing me pictures of Lola and Pio as young people. Thanks to Al Zepeda for setting a vivid scene of what it was like to be a young man in Palo Verde with the trash-can fires burning at night. Lawrence Bouett's chavezravine.org set me on the path to tracking down all the historical information about the Vargas family in the first place. Lawrence was also a great resource by e-mail and over the phone. The jalopy duel was chronicled extensively in the *Los Angeles Times* in August 1941. (For instance, the article on gangs threatening witnesses appeared on page A2 on August 28, 1941, under the headline "Youthful Gang Threats Aired.")

## Chapters 26, 30

Jorge Pasquel may not be well-known to casual baseball fans, but quite a few researchers have (justifiably) found him to be worthy of their attention. My favorite piece of writing on Pasquel is Gerald F. Vaughn's article "Jorge Pasquel and the Evolution of the Mexican League" from volume 12 of SABR's magazine

*The National Pastime.* I also reached out to the Mexican baseball historian Jesús Alberto Rubio, who provided me with great material on Pasquel. Finally, there is John Virtue's *South of the Color Barrier: How Jorge Pasquel and the Mexican League Pushed Baseball Toward Racial Integration.* Even the foreword to Virtue's book, written by Monte Irvin, is a tremendous resource. Roy Campanella wrote about Pasquel in his autobiography, *It's Good to Be Alive.* César González Gómez wrote about Pasquel's wooing of Jackie Robinson in the Mexican baseball publication *Cuartobat* ("Jorge Pasquel y la oferta a Jackie Robinson para que viniera a la Liga Mexicana"). Bernardo Pasquel's statement about destroying the US monopoly on baseball appeared in an Associated Press report on March 12, 1946. Lou Hernandez's *The Rise of the Latin American Baseball Leagues, 1947–1961* features great details on Pasquel's efforts to woo American stars such as Ted Williams.

## Chapters 27, 29, 34

The brochure for the Pacific Mercado was reprinted in the *Congressional Record* during a hearing of the Foreign Affairs Committee ahead of a joint resolution in favor of federal participation in the Mercado (August 4, 1937). The most in-depth history of the Naval Armory is the article "Naval and Marine Corps Reserve Center Los Angeles" by Bruce R. Lively, from the Fall 1987 issue of *Southern California Quarterly.* (Lively's article provides a nifty history of the pre-armory days and great details on the armory itself but also skips over the Zoot Suit Riots.)

Camilo Arévalo and Gene Cabral walked me through life during wartime in Palo Verde. I didn't touch on Gene's own service—he enlisted toward the end of the war and was stationed in Guam. The article about the goat injury appeared in the *Los Angeles Times* on September 28, 1943. For a fascinating look at the military career of Armand Muñoz and the 100th Bomb Group, complete with primary sources like journals and photos, check out 100thbg.com.

## Chapter 28

For an easily accessible and very-well-put-together resource on the rise of the Communist Party in the United States, check out the University of Washington's *Mapping American Social Movements* project (www.depts.washington.edu/moves). Richard Neutra's Channel Heights project in San Pedro was an architectural wonder, but it was sold to private developers and by the 1990s was demolished beyond recognition. Otherwise, this chapter, like the previous Wilkinson sections, relies on oral history, family interviews, correspondence, and contemporaneous newspaper reporting.

## Chapter 31

I thank Juan and Nellie's daughter Jeannie and granddaughter Melissa, and their daughter Helen and grandson Johnny, for helping me bring Juan and Nellie to life. Both families warmly welcomed me into their homes to share memories. Both were very generous with their time. The definitive book on the Zoot Suit Riots is Eduardo Obregón Pagán's *Murder at the Sleepy Lagoon: Zoot Suits, Race, and Riot in Wartime L.A.* (The Eleanor Roosevelt story is from this one.) I also turned to the article "The Los Angeles Zoot Suit Riots Revisited: Mexican and Latin American Perspectives" by Richard Griswold Del Castillo. Mario Zepeda, Al Zepeda, Gene Cabral, Beto Elias, Pete Urrutia, Feliz Arevalo, and Camilo Arevalo all shared memories of the Zoot Suit Riots. I also recommend the historical podcast L.A. Meekly on this subject.

## Chapter 32

I could not have put together the story of Mel Almada without the benefit of his SABR biography by Bill Nowlin. Nor could I have written about his experience without the benefit of Adrian Burgos's work on the Latino history of baseball, especially his book *Playing America's Game: Baseball, Latinos, and the Color Line*. The vivid tales of Mel and Lou Almada were shared by Carlos Bauer on his website Minor League Researcher (www.minorleagueresearcher.blogspot.com). I also consulted Baseball-Reference for stats and newspaper archives to get a sense of LA's booming semipro baseball community. To learn more about Los Chorizeros, read Francisco E. Balderrama and Richard A. Santillan's article "Los Chorizeros: The New York Yankees of East Los Angeles and the Reclaiming of Mexican American Baseball History." The same authors are also responsible for the books *Mexican-American Baseball in Los Angeles* and *Mexican-American Baseball in East Los Angeles*. Their material forms the basis of the fantastic baseball archives at Cal State Los Angeles.

## Chapters 33, 36, 40

The great scholar on public housing in Los Angeles was Don Parson, who passed away in the course of my writing this book. His *Making a Better World: Public Housing, the Red Scare, and the Direction of Modern Los Angeles* is as clear and well-researched a book as you could hope to find on any topic. Frank Wilkinson discussed his short-lived decision to enlist in the army in his oral history. James T. Keane does a great job explaining the housing fight as well in *Fritz B. Burns and the Development of Los Angeles*. The first landmark article on public housing as it relates to the future of Dodger Stadium was Thomas Hines's "Housing, Baseball, and Creeping Socialism: The Battle of Chavez Ravine" in *The Journal of Urban History* in 1982.

Thanks to the Wilkinson family for scrounging up some pages of Frank's massive (and still missing) FBI file, including some that reference his membership in the Altgeld Club. Frank tells of his thwarted congressional campaign and of HICCASP in his oral history. For more on HICCASP and its primary role in Reagan's conversion from Hollywood progressive to conservative icon, see Stephen Vaughan's *Ronald Reagan in Hollywood*.

The phrase *urban renewal* gets thrown around a lot, to varying purposes and with varying definitions. In this case I use the term as Frank Wilkinson understood it. The slum tours were a huge part of Frank's sense of self. He spoke of them often, and his children recalled them vividly. They were also featured on occasion in the newspapers. The film *And 10,000 More* is in the digital archives of the Getty Research Library in Los Angeles and can be viewed there. In the Rodolfo Acuña Papers at Cal State University Northridge, I found a pamphlet titled "What Is Urban Renewal" released by the LA city government in the 1950s. It features an anthropomorphic cartoon version of the City Hall building named Mr. Los Angeles.

The Getty has a treasure trove of material on housing, mostly thanks to the work of Thomas Hines. Among the treasures are recordings of firsthand interviews that Hines conducted with major players like Simon Eisner. The Getty was also where I found *Rebuilding the City*, Bryant and Alexander's plan for housing in Los Angeles.

The development of the Elysian Park Heights project has been chronicled by Hines, by Parson, and by a number of other writers. Frank spends a great deal of time on it in his oral history as well. I found Hines's interview with Eisner in the Getty archives to be especially insightful. Eisner understood the social cost of the housing project and spoke in detail about the specific problems with the site, and the great lengths that Neutra went to to obtain buy-in from the community. In his own oral history and writings, Robert Alexander, who had authored that foreboding message in *Rebuilding the City*, was quick to talk with regret and wisdom about the mistakes made in site selection.

## Chapter 35

I highly recommend Jackie's late-in-life autobiography *I Never Had It Made*. The best book on Jackie and social movements is David Falkner's *Great Time Coming*. The definitive book on breaking the color line is Jules Tygiel's *Baseball's Great Experiment*. For more on Disney and Communism, check out Karl F. Cohen's *Forbidden Animation*. The Disney anti-Communist ad was in the July 2, 1941, issue of *Variety*. In 2012 the *Hollywood Reporter* acknowledged and apologized for its leading role in creating the Hollywood blacklist.

## Chapters 37, 39

The story of Ramón Ríos was reported on in the *San Bernardino Sun* over the course of July 1949. There are two great books that tell the story of Ignacio López, but he deserves his own biography. One is Matt Garcia's *A World of Its Own*, and the other is Mario Garcia's *Mexican Americans*. Mario Garcia also authored Bert Corona's memoir *Memories of Chicano History*. Old issues of *El Espectador* can be found at Stanford University; López's FBI papers and other files recently became available at the Claremont Colleges in the Honnold/Mudd Library. The story of Ramón Ríos was featured in Matt Garcia's *A World of Its Own*.

## Chapter 38

This chapter is built out of newspaper stories and firsthand interviews. The *Los Angeles Times* published a comprehensive obituary of Gonzales when he passed away ("Julio Gonzales, 86; Helped LAPD Reach Out to Latinos," December 14, 2003). Former residents recalled Gonzales, Matin, and Salvin fondly. Matin's memory has been kept alive by the church in Los Angeles. Salvin was portrayed in detail in the Hoelzel Gumbinger thesis, which can be accessed through the USC Digital Library.

## Chapter 42

So much great writing on LA begins with Carey McWilliams. He saw the city and its people with an empathetic eye and a sweeping historical perspective. The statement in this chapter is from his book *North from Mexico: The Spanish-Speaking People of the United States*. I am also fond of his *Southern California: An Island on Land*. As progressive as McWilliams was, it took scholars like Ronald López to issue the corrective to McWilliams's backward view of the communities. López's *Community Resistance and Conditional Patriotism in Cold War Los Angeles: The Battle for Chavez Ravine* is a fascinating look at how the communities organized, in particular behind women leaders such as Agnes Cerda.

## Chapter 43

As I mentioned in the text, my writing on Burns owes a great deal to James T. Keene's *Fritz B. Burns and the Development of Los Angeles*. For a relatively unknown figure, it's hard to overstate how fascinating Burns was or how important he was to the city's development. Keene's book is deeply researched, well written, as colorful as it needs to be to do its subject justice, and as measured as it needs to be to put him in perspective. For a more panoramic view of Burns full of great insight about development in Los Angeles, see Dana Cuff's *The Provisional City*.

## Chapter 44

Frank's activities in the 1950s are all carefully noted in his calendars and planners, which remain in great shape at the Southern California Library. From those, and from his correspondence, it was easy to build a sense of his (very busy) day-to-day life. Once again, I was struck by the consistency of his memory. His activities three and four decades prior are recalled vividly in his oral history. But this chapter is not really about Frank; it's largely a reflection on the complicated politics of Ignacio L. López, which I could not have written without the insight of Matt Garcia (López's writing on housing appears in Garcia's *A World of Its Own*) and Mario Garcia. I also learned a great deal about López and political organizing from Gabriel Thompson's *America's Social Arsonist: A Biography of Fred Ross*.

## Chapter 45

Branch Rickey's fawning over the Duke appears in the June 27, 1955, issue of *Sports Illustrated*. Tales of Walter O'Malley's card playing appear in Golenbock's *Bums*. The Snider-authored article "I Play Baseball for Money—Not Fun" appeared in *Collier's Weekly* on May 25, 1956.

## Chapter 46

Simon Eisner expounded on the effort to recruit Matin and Salvin in his interview with Hines, which is at the Getty. Hines also wrote about this in "Housing, Baseball, and Creeping Socialism." Camilo Arevalo spoke with longing and sadness about the process of clearing out the neighborhood. So did Beto Elias. The resistance led by the Cerda family and others is covered at length by Ron López in both "Community Resistance and Conditional Patriotism" and in his excellent Ph.D. dissertation, "The Battle for Chavez Ravine: Chicano Community Resistance in Post War Los Angeles, 1945–1962." To get a good sense of hearings and council meetings, I reviewed minutes from Los Angeles City Council and Planning Commission meetings.

## Chapter 47

Don Parson's "'The Darling of the Town's Neo-Fascists': The Bombastic Political Career of Councilman Ed J. Davenport" is a marvel of an article. Although it is not part of Parson's *Making a Better World*, it is a perfect accompaniment. Parson is also responsible for the anecdote about Frank Wilkinson writing Davenport's speeches. Thankfully, Davenport was a self-promoter and easy to find all over every newspaper in the city during his career. Dana Cuff's *The Provisional City* was especially helpful in helping me understand the scope and consequences of the housing debate.

## Chapter 48

These pages drew upon the work in Martin Duberman's *Paul Robeson: A Biography*. (Duberman tracked down the original transcripts of Robeson's speech in Paris.) For a great accounting of that episode, check out Gilbert King's *Smithsonian Magazine* article "What Paul Robeson Said." The transcript of Robeson's speech to Major League Baseball owners on December 3, 1943, is in the Baseball Hall of Fame archives. Paul Robeson Jr. was featured in the documentary *The Brooklyn Dodgers: The Original America's Team*. Robeson's open letter to Jackie Robinson appeared in the April 1953 issue of *Freedom*, a monthly newspaper that he published in Harlem between 1951 and 1955.

## Chapter 49

For a thorough history of the Chandlers and the *Los Angeles Times*, turn to Robert Gottlieb and Irene Wolt's *Thinking Big*. Bonelli's *Billion Dollar Blackjack* is a great read and a useful frame of reference—it gives a sense of the atmosphere of the politics of the era—but I would not read it as a work of careful history. Bill Boyarsky's *Inventing L.A.* is a beautiful recap of the history of the Chandlers and the paper, with spectacular photos. Baus and Ross both completed oral history interviews, which are easily available online through the California Secretary of State's Oral History Program. The *Los Angeles Times* clippings of the era speak for themselves in terms of the paper's bias and agenda. The McCarthy history is everywhere, but my favorite read on it is Geoffrey R. Stone's article "Free Speech in the Age of McCarthy: A Cautionary Tale" in the *California Law Review*. Hoover's *U.S. News & World Report* interview was published in August 1950. The Davenport memo remains in the Ruth & Ed Lybeck Papers at UCLA Special Collections. (The Lybecks, who more famously worked with Helen Gahagan Douglas, were briefly Davenport's campaign managers.)

## Chapter 50

Thanks especially to Al Zepeda for the story of the death-sensing dog on Paducah Street.

## Chapter 51

The Wilkinson children, Jeffry, Tony, and Jo, all were very helpful in painting a picture of Frank as he went about his days and prepared for hearings like the one that changed his life. The transcripts of the hearing are all in Frank's papers at the Southern California Library. The events of that week were all over the newspapers, and Frank reflected on them at length in his oral history. For a powerful read on the Red Scare, pick up Griffin Fariello's *Red Scare: Memories of an American Inquisition*, which features insightful interviews with both Frank and Jean. (Jean's story, and that of her fellow fired public schoolteachers, deserves its own book-length treatment.) Copies of Frank's public statement were found in his papers. I wish this book had more room for material on Frank's home life and the Wilkinson family.

## Chapter 52

The emptying of the communities was both slow and sudden. Even as people moved out, they had a hard time actually leaving their neighborhoods behind. Normark's *Chavez Ravine 1949* is a beautiful book of photos and features powerful remembrances from residents. The *L.A. Times* article featuring Abrana ran on August 20, 1951, on the front page.

## Chapter 53

Frank's oral history and his children's remembrances were the basis for the domestic details in this chapter. Frank recounted the story of Ignacio López helping him escape the Clare Hoffman hearings. Parson recounts the madness of that mayoral race in great detail, as does Tom Sitton in *Los Angeles Transformed: Fletcher Bowron's Urban Reform Revival.* Parson and Sitton both dug up Bowron's anti-Chandler speeches. The Bowron-Hogya melee was, unsurprisingly, featured heavily in the papers. Robert Gottlieb wrote about Chandler's "Dear Norrie" letter in the March 15, 2000, issue of *L.A. Weekly* in an article titled "Fits and Starts." The Hoffman-Roosevelt impeachment tidbit is from *Life,* April 13, 1942. Parker's testimony can be found in full at the end of Parson's *Making a Better World.*

## Chapter 54

Unfortunately, Roz Wyman declined multiple interview requests for this book, but fortunately she has spoken at length about her role in bringing baseball to Los Angeles. I pieced together her biography from contemporaneous news reports, from her own oral history through UC Berkeley, and through interviews she has granted over the years. (Her interviews for walteromalley.com are very frank and go into great detail.) It's hard to overstate how groundbreaking Wyman's election was in 1953; no other woman was elected to the council until 1969. One of the many great qualities of Andy McCue's Walter O'Malley biography *Mover and Shaker* is its extensive history of early LA baseball boosterism. Michael D'Antonio's O'Malley volume, *Forever Blue,* is similarly compelling. Both were instrumental. Kenneth Hahn's op-ed in the Flaherty column space appeared in October 8, 1954, edition of the *Examiner.*

## Chapter 55

The story of the trip to Mexico City was told by both Camilo and Féliz Arévalo and Helen Lamp, who accompanied her parents and the Arevalos on the trip. Tlatelolco is an endlessly fascinating historical subject, and Mario Paní, who also designed UNAM, Mexico's national university, was an endlessly fascinating architect. His statement about regenerating Mexico City comes from Graciela de Garay's *Mario Paní: Vida y Obra.*

## Chapter 56

The most detailed, well-researched, and well-told account of the final stretch of the Dodgers' move west is Jerald Podair's in *City of Dreams.* Podair's work was a guide star for me as I wrote this book. Neil Sullivan's *The Dodgers Move West* and the aforementioned O'Malley biographies by McCue and D'Antonio were also crucial. The Abbott and Costello council meeting was on October 6, 1953. I would not have been able to write in detail about O'Malley's plans without access to some of his old papers and archives. For this, and for their excellent work in curating his legacy and presenting it online in great depth, I thank the people at O'Malley Seidler Partners, namely, Brent Shire, Robert Schweppe, and Peter O'Malley. The Bob Cobb article in the *Los Angeles Times* ("Bob Cobb Favors 2 Major League Franchises in L.A.") was published on June 7, 1957. Stiles O. Clements designed the Wiltern and El Capitan theaters among other LA landmarks; his ballpark design was even more modernistic than anything Walter O'Malley would come up with for Dodger Stadium. O'Malley's helicopter ride is often misrepresented as having included Hahn himself. This was not the case. The political machinations and implications of the Dodgers move have been told and told well by Podair, Sullivan, and others. For more on that subject, I suggest you turn their way.

## Chapter 57

This chapter is constructed almost entirely from interviews. The newspaper item was titled "Family's Suit Delays Housing Condemnation" from the October 5, 1953, edition of the *Los Angeles Times*.

## Chapter 58

The name "Popsiedoodle" appeared all over Frank's correspondence—he even used it signing letters. Carl and Anne Braden became close friends of the Wilkinson family as they got involved in the fight against HUAC. William K. Sherwood's tragic suicide note was reported in the June 17, 1957, edition of the *Madeira Tribune*. Frank's jail-for-speech line was one he kept in his pocket. I put together his thinking from his oral history and from interviews with his children and his second wife, Donna.

## Chapter 59

I was able to stitch together the arrival scene using various newspaper reports, including Paul Zimmerman's Sputnik-citing *Los Angeles Times* article from October 24, 1957. Parson and Podair offer great detail on the stadium campaign, but I found the John Holland papers at Cal State Los Angeles to be especially helpful: Holland's correspondence was littered with letters to major figures in the anti-Dodgers movement, especially the Citizens Committee to Save Chavez Ravine. For more on the O'Malley-Stoneham relationship, see Lincoln A. Mitchell's *Baseball Goes West*.

The story of the Dodgers' Spanish-language broadcast history was surprisingly complex. Jaime Jarrín remains a treasure to the city. His audio interview for the Cal State Los Angeles Mexican American Baseball archive is fascinating and was a great resource for this chapter (it included the Ortega anecdote and the details of how early broadcasts were conducted). The definitive article on this subject is "Dodgers Béisbol Is on the Air: The Development and Impact of the Dodgers Spanish-Language Broadcasts, 1958–1994" by Samuel O. Regalado. The Snider injury at the Coliseum was discussed in Golenbock's *Bums* and written about in the newspapers. I was able to sift through the stadium campaign material in the Holland papers, as well as in Walter O'Malley's. The letter from Blackjack Smith to Clarence Detoy was in the Holland papers (May 6, 1958). The feature on O'Malley in *Sports Illustrated* was in the June 16, 1958, issue. The telethon was captured in detail by Podair, D'Antonio, McCue, and others. Sullivan's *The Dodgers Move West* has the most extensive write-up on Praeger's ruling.

## Chapter 60

Thanks to Dolores Klimenko for her beautiful remembrances of her parents and her childhood home. The story of the disappearing homes of Palo Verde turning up on the Universal lot has appeared in a few articles over the years. I could not confirm the legends about *To Kill a Mockingbird* even after contacting the studio.

## Chapter 61

Although this book focuses more on Carl Braden, it was Anne Braden who was the more interesting and enduring civil rights figure. She wrote about their experience with the Wades in her 1958 book *The Wall Between*. She also recorded an oral history project through the University of Kentucky. In 2014 Rick Howlett wrote a great article on them for WPFL titled "Remembering the Wades, the Bradens, and the Struggle for Racial Integration in Louisville." Frank's papers at the Southern California library were full of correspondence and pamphlets related to his stand against HUAC. I also highly recommend Richard Criley's short book *The FBI vs. the First Amendment*. Criley was a good friend of Frank's and a close ally. He wrote with expertise and intimacy on the struggle. Frank's statement to the subcommittee can be found in the text of *Wilkinson v. United States*.

## Chapter 62

I would not have been able to write so vividly about Willie Davis if not for finding the film *Biography of a Rookie: The Willie Davis Story*. Willie generously sat down for tons of video interviews later in his life. The two interviews that aided me most in assembling this chapter were his conversation with Roy Firestone for *ESPN Sports Look* and another interview celebrating his induction into the Roosevelt High School Hall of Fame. Rick Obrand's article for SABR, "The Sandlot Mentors of Los Angeles," features a great passage on Kenny Myers.

## Chapter 63

The Glen Walters–dominated scene at City Hall appeared in Ridgely Cummings's syndicated column of April 16, 1959, a column that appeared in the *Wilshire Press*, among other places.

## Chapter 64

Attendance figures come via Baseball-Reference. The Campanella game was heavily featured in the various newspapers and in the O'Malley biographies by McCue and D'Antonio. Campanella himself wrote vividly about his own experience in *It's Good to Be Alive*.

## Chapter 65

The stories of the Aréchigas' resistance to earlier attempts at eviction come from a combination of interviews (Carmen Acosta recalled the hose; Dolores recalled the tussle between Lola and the deputy, Gabrielle Johnston) and newspaper stories. The story of the family moving out, then back in again appeared in the *Mirror-News*, August 21, 1957. (This story inaccurately ascribes the tussle with Johnston to Tolina, not Lola.) Podair and Parson offer the most detailed blow-by-blow of the legal events preceding the eviction. The Roybal papers at UCLA were a great help in assembling this scene, as were the O'Malley papers.

## Chapter 66

The O'Malley index cards are remarkable: bound by a rubber band inside a plain manila folder. The O'Malley legacy is beautifully presented on walteromalley.com. The Bavasi letter was in the O'Malley papers, as were O'Malley's memos in reference to Walt Disney. The Didion line was published in *The White Album*. All of O'Malley's ambitions for the park are there in his files.

## Chapter 67

The Normark and Ry Cooder references are self-explanatory. The Hawthorne line about Dodger Stadium came in the April 3, 2017, edition of the *Los Angeles Times*.

## Chapters 68–72

These chapters were built from a combination of interviews, newspaper reports, city council minutes, and newsreel footage, which can be found at UCLA's Film and Television Archive. There are a lot of versions of how the evictions went down. I tried to consider all perspectives and address all questions in this write-up. It was helpful to compare the ultra-sympathetic Ridgely Cummings reports from the Civic Center News Agency with less friendly reports from the *Times*, *Mirror*, and *Examiner*. It was also helpful to compare my personal interviews with community members with those of politicians of the day, such as Roz Wyman. I also closely read *La Opinión's* Spanish-language coverage of the evictions. (At the time, *La Opinión* was a pretty conservative paper.) Manuel's old shotgun is still in the family, in the possession of his great-granddaughter Melissa.

## Chapter 73

I thank the Wilkinson family once again for helping me put together this chapter. They were able to share Jean Wilkinson's planners for the years of 1952–1959; flipping through them I was instantly transported back into their lives and instantly aware of how much time Frank spent apart from the family. Jo Wilkinson was generous sharing her experience of the bombing. Frank's essay with the Pontius Pilate accusation appeared in *It Did Happen Here: Recollections of Political Repression in America*, compiled by Bud and Ruth Schultz. Frank's prison correspondence, held at the Southern California Library, is extensive and deeply emotional. So are old copies of the petitions for clemency featuring famous signatures.

## Chapter 74

Lola's breakdown was covered in the *Los Angeles Times* (May 11, 1959). Poulson's statement was published all over the place. Wyman has told the story of the anonymous tip in her oral history and elsewhere. Juan's letter is tucked away among other citizen correspondence in the Roybal papers at UCLA. Lola's comment about wishing she could own more houses was printed in *La Opinión* on May 15, 1959. Manuel's "I won't go" statement appeared in the *San Bernardino Sun* on May 16, 1959. Abrana's cemetery statement appeared in *La Opinión* on May 19, 1959. Manuel's arrest appeared on a clipping in the O'Malley files, but it is undated and impossible to even say which paper it appeared in.

## Chapters 75–76

The *Times* reported the Fritz Burns purchase on June 22, 1959, and the Palo Verde school shuttering on June 23, 1960. The proposal to turn the old school into office space was found in a pamphlet in the Holland papers at Cal State Los Angeles. For more on Vinnell, see William Hartung's article "Bombings Bring U.S. 'Executive Mercenaries' into the Light" from the May 16, 2003, *Los Angeles Times*. Everything I wrote about the financing of Dodger Stadium, I cross-checked against Podair's *City of Dreams*, which contains a detailed account (and accounting). McCue's *Mover and Shaker* features a great look at the buildup to Opening Day, with lots of detail on the gala held the night before at Dodger Stadium. The April 11, 1962, edition of the *Los Angeles Times* featured an article on the Dodgers' landscaping ("O'Malley's Garden"), in addition to its coverage of the logistics of Opening Day and the game itself.

The "run, hit, throw, and field" statement about Willie Davis was from former Dodgers general manager Buzzie Bavasi. It can be found in Wayne Stewart's *Gigantic Book of Baseball Quotations*. Bill James wrote about Davis in his *New Historical Baseball Abstract* before we had the benefit of new statistics to evaluate him by. Those statistics, like Wins Above Replacement, which take into account his defense and base running, are very kind to Davis. The story about Davis and Sandy Koufax appears in Jane Leavy's excellent book *A Lefty's Legacy*.

Thanks to Melissa Aréchiga for sharing her grandfather Juan's sentencing documents (and his elementary school report cards). Thanks to all the Aréchigas, Cabrals, and other members of the communities who welcomed me into their lives and shared their stories. Thank you to Father Leandro Fossa of St. Peter's Italian Church on Broadway, who graciously allowed me to peruse the old registries and trace the generations of life and death in Palo Verde, La Loma, and Bishop on their pages.

# INDEX

JENNIFER MAHARRY

**ERIC NUSBAUM** is a writer and former editor at VICE. His work has appeared in *Sports Illustrated*, *ESPN the Magazine*, the *Daily Beast*, *Deadspin*, and the *Best American Sports Writing* anthology. Born and raised in Los Angeles, he has also lived and worked in Mexico City, New York, and Seattle. He now lives in Tacoma, Washington, with his family.

PublicAffairs is a publishing house founded in 1997. It is a tribute to the standards, values, and flair of three persons who have served as mentors to countless reporters, writers, editors, and book people of all kinds, including me.

I. F. STONE, proprietor of *I. F. Stone's Weekly*, combined a commitment to the First Amendment with entrepreneurial zeal and reporting skill and became one of the great independent journalists in American history. At the age of eighty, Izzy published *The Trial of Socrates*, which was a national bestseller. He wrote the book after he taught himself ancient Greek.

BENJAMIN C. BRADLEE was for nearly thirty years the charismatic editorial leader of *The Washington Post*. It was Ben who gave the *Post* the range and courage to pursue such historic issues as Watergate. He supported his reporters with a tenacity that made them fearless and it is no accident that so many became authors of influential, best-selling books.

ROBERT L. BERNSTEIN, the chief executive of Random House for more than a quarter century, guided one of the nation's premier publishing houses. Bob was personally responsible for many books of political dissent and argument that challenged tyranny around the globe. He is also the founder and longtime chair of Human Rights Watch, one of the most respected human rights organizations in the world.

•　　•　　•

For fifty years, the banner of Public Affairs Press was carried by its owner Morris B. Schnapper, who published Gandhi, Nasser, Toynbee, Truman, and about 1,500 other authors. In 1983, Schnapper was described by *The Washington Post* as "a redoubtable gadfly." His legacy will endure in the books to come.

Peter Osnos, *Founder*